Rhodesia/
Zimbabwe
1971-77

WITHDRAWN

Rhodesia/ Zimbabwe 1971-77

Edited by Lester A. Sobel

Contributing editors: Melinda Maidens,
John Miner, Maurie Sommer,
Barry Youngerman

Indexer: Grace M. Ferrara

Facts On File
119 West 57th Street, New York, N.Y. 10019

Rhodesia/ Zimbabwe 1971-77

Library of Congress Cataloging in Publication Data
Main entry under title:
Rhodesia/Zimbabwe, 1971–77.
  (Checkmark books)
  "Based principally on the account presented by Facts on file in its weekly reports."
  Includes index.
  1. Rhodesia, Southern—Politics and government—
1965–   2. Rhodesia, Southern—Race relations.
I. Sobel, Lester A.   II. Facts on File, Inc., New York.
DT962.75.R525   320.9′689′104   77-87240
ISBN 0-87196-194-6

9 8 7 6 5 4 3 2 1
PRINTED IN THE UNITED STATES OF AMERICA

Contents

ILLUSTRATIONS

Introduction

R HODESIA, ZIMBABWE—OR SOUTHERN Rhodesia. The very name one chooses to identify this troubled African area can reveal a viewpoint that may be supported with passionate zeal.

The term *Rhodesia* is used by white inhabitants and the white *de facto* but minority regime that was still in control of this former British colony during the closing months of the year 1977. To many people, the term Rhodesia, however, is a convenient and fairly neutral name.

The designation *Zimbabwe* was chosen by the territory's black nationalist activists and their supporters who have been battling to win control of the government in the name of the country's black majority. (Zimbabwe was the name of an ancient city in the area thought to have been built by a Bantu people in the Fifth Century.)

Southern Rhodesia is a designation used by Great Britain and some other nations that refuse to recognize the white-ruled Rhodesian government yet may have reasons for not calling the area Zimbabwe. The name Southern Rhodesia had been used to differentiate two British Rhodesian dependencies—the former protectorate of Northern Rhodesia, which now is the independent nation Zambia, and the Southern colonial area under contention. The term is used by the British and others to signify their rejection of the white regime's "illegal seizure" of independence.

This book refers to the troubled land as *Rhodesia* because that is the name by which the country is generally known.

1

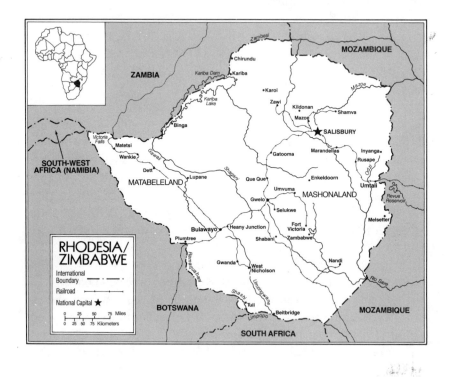

The Land & the People

Rhodesia is a landlocked country of some 150,333 square miles in southcentral Africa. It is bordered by South Africa to the south, Botswana to the west, Zambia and the Zambesi River to the north and Mozambique to the north and east. Most of the country consists of high plateau varying in altitude from 3,000 feet to more than 5,000. The climate is generally mild and has been described as similar to that of Southern California.

The population of Rhodesia totals 6,420,000, according to the official estimate of December 1975. This total includes about 6,111,000 black Africans, 278,000 whites (Europeans) and 30,900 Coloreds (people of mixed African and European parentage), Asians and "others."

The white population had grown steadily but slowly until after World War II. There had been fewer than 70,000 whites in Southern Rhodesia at the beginning of the war. After the war, however, a surge of immigration, largely from Britain and South Africa, was principally responsible for tripling the white population in three decades.

The black population also expanded at a great rate—by perhaps three million in the past two decades. The African natives spring from the Bantu stock that has peopled the rest of southern and central Africa. The two predominating tribes in Rhodesia are the Mashona, the older and larger of the tribes, and the Matabele, which is related to South Africa's warrior Zulu tribe.

English is the official language and is spoken by virtually all whites in Rhodesia, but members of the black majority of the people overwhelmingly speak Bantu languages, principally Sindebele and Chishona.

The Rhodesian economy is based on the country's farmlands and mineral deposits, which support strong manufacturing, commercial and financial sectors. Despite United Nations sanctions requiring U.N. members to sever commercial relations with Rhodesia, the country still exports such items as tobacco and other farm products, asbestos, chrome, copper, iron, coal and chemical products.

Cecil John Rhodes

Historical Background

Bantu-speaking people had first started migrating to what is now called Rhodesia sometime after the Fifth Century, supplanting an earlier Iron Age people.

The first modern Europeans known to have reached the area were the Portuguese, in the early Sixteenth Century. The Portuguese built up a trade in gold and other commodities with Shona-speaking people there. Ndebele invaders subjugated the Shona inhabitants during the 1830s. British and Boer traders, hunters and missionaries operated in the area during the following half-century.

Cecil John Rhodes, the British empire-builder for whom the territory was later named, negotiated in 1888 with Lobengula, the Matabele ruler, and won an agreement giving him mining concessions in Matabeleland and Mashonaland. Rhodes' British South Africa Co. in 1889 secured a British charter to colonize and promote commerce there. The following year a Rhodes associate, Leander Starr Jameson, led a British and white South African expedition into the area's heartland and founded Fort Salisbury. The British South Africa Co. fought and defeated the Ndebele in 1893 and became the *de facto* government of the territory. The Shona and Ndebele revolted against the company during 1896-97 but were d_feated.

Most of the white settlers were lured to the land by fantasies of mineral rights and quick fortunes. After these dreams proved false, many of them found it possible to earn comfortable livings by farming. Conditions were so good that the population grew to an estimated 10,000 whites and 400,000 blacks before the end of the Nineteenth Century.

Agitation for political rights, however, accompanied prosperity. In 1914, when the time came to renew the British South Africa Co.'s charter, the British government did so on the condition that the settlers be given self-government by 1924. Britain's Privy Council ruled in 1918 that Southern Rhodesia belonged not to the company but to the Crown. In 1922, Britain gave the white settlers

Wide World Photos

Ian Douglas Smith

a choice between union with South Africa and the status of a self-governing colony of Britain. The choice, by 8,744-to-5,989 vote, was colonial status, and self-government was put into effect under these terms Sept. 12, 1923.

A constitution approved in 1923 gave Southern Rhodesia its own legislature, civil service, armed forces and police. Britain retained the right to approve any constitutional amendments and any laws affecting the black African population. Control, however, rested solidly in the hands of the white settlers. The voting franchise was "color-blind," but it had qualifications for income, property and education that served to keep the vast majority of black Africans from voting.

Thirty years after the 1923 constitution went into effect, there were only 380 black Africans on a voter roll of almost 50,000. During these 30 years the European minority set the pattern of privileged position for whites. A Land-Apportionment Act passed in 1930 divided the country into black and white areas, with the white area much larger and more desirable than the black one. The whites were given about half of Southern Rhodesia's 96 million acres, including all urban areas, and the black Africans received 33%. Black Africans were forbidden to buy land in cities or even to occupy premises in urban areas. The Land Apportionment Act established a clear division by race and was a formidable barrier to Britain's later attempts to achieve a multiracial society.

In 1953, Southern Rhodesia entered a federation with two British protectorates, Northern Rhodesia (now Zambia) and Nyasaland (now Malawi). The Federation of Rhodesia & Nyasaland was created by the British in what was seen as a hope for the eventual development of a multiracial society in southcentral Africa. Federation was accepted by Southern Rhodesia because its leaders saw economic advantages in joining the two British protectorates, both of which had much smaller white populations. Black Africans however, objected to the white domination of the federation.

The federation lasted only ten years. It was a victim largely of rising African nationalism in Northern Rhodesia and Nyasaland. Both seceded and became independent states under majority rule in 1964.

When it became clear in 1961 that the federation was going to disintegrate, a constitutional convention was held in Salisbury (capital of both the federation and Southern Rhodesia) to decide the future of the self-governing colony. The resulting constitution gave middle-class black Africans a minor voice in the Rhodesian Legislative Assembly (Parliament). It contained a Declaration of Rights and provided for a Constitutional Council, both aimed at preventing discriminatory legislation. The Declaration of Rights and Constitutional Council, however, had no effect on the Land Apportionment Act or other discriminatory laws previously passed. The 1961 constitution, therefore, did not alter the socio-economic foundations of Rhodesia.

The 1961 constitution was believed to have been passed, by 42,004-21,846 vote of the largely white electorate, chiefly because the voters hoped that it was a step in the direction of independence.

Any illusions that the 1961 constitution signaled a more liberal policy for Rhodesia were shattered in the December 1962 elections. Sir Edgar Whitehead, Southern Rhodesia's prime minister, and his United Federal Party (UFP) promised to abolish racial discrimination, repeal the Land Apportionment Act and appoint a few black Africans as junior ministers. The chief opposition was the eight-month-old Rhodesian Front, made up of various dissidents against the "establishment" UFP. The Front's platform was "Southern Rhodesia first," no repeal of the Land Apportionment Act, no lowering of voter qualifications, and independence for Rhodesia. In an election boycotted by most eligible black Africans, the Rhodesian Front won an overwhelming victory, taking 35 of the 50 "white" seats in Parliament and control of the government.

Winston Field became prime minister and Ian D. Smith finance minister. But Field did not move quickly enough toward gaining Rhodesia's independence to satisfy most members of the Rhodesian Front, and in April 1964 the party removed him from office.

The new prime minister chosen was Ian Smith. Smith made it clear in a series of speeches that he did not expect to see black African majority rule in Rhodesia during his lifetime, and this stand helped him consolidate most white Rhodesians behind his party. In August 1964, open African nationalist activities within Rhodesia ended with the banning of the *African Daily News*, the only newspaper that gave the black African point of view, and the outlawing of the African nationalist political parties.

The Rhodesian Front's hard-line policy was quickly shown to be popular among whites. In a by-election Oct. 1, 1964, Sir Roy Welensky, a United Federal Party leader and former federal prime minister, was defeated overwhelmingly by Clifford Dupont of the Rhodesian Front. Meanwhile, Smith had been in London trying to negotiate independence on the basis of the 1961 constitution. The British government, however, insisted on guarantees that the black African majority would be able to move toward political dominance. In a referendum November 5, 1964, the white-dominated electorate was asked to express its feelings about the independence issue. The result: a vote of 9 to 1 for independence (58,076 to 6,101).

The United Nations Security Council voted May 6, 1965, one day before a bitterly fought general election in Rhodesia, to adopt a resolution urging Great Britain to firmly oppose any Rhodesian effort at a unilateral declaration of independence (a term already familiarly referred to an UDI). The following day Smith's Rhodesian Front won an overwhelming election victory.

Smith's triumph apparently convinced many African nationalists that black majority rule could be obtained only by forcibly overthrowing the white regime. As rumors of nationalist activity spread, the Smith government replied with emergency regulations, restrictions on nationalist leaders and arrests of alleged violators and suspected dissenters.

Negotiations between the Smith regime and the British government proved futile, and a unilateral declaration of independence was issued by Smith Nov. 11, 1965. He broadcast a declaration proclaiming Rhodesia to be an independent nation.

Britain replied immediately with an announcement that it had suspended Smith and his ministers from office. British Prime Minister Harold Wilson "condemn[ed] the purported declaration of independence by the former government of Rhodesia as an illegal act and one which is ineffective in law.'' He described Smith's government as a ''rebel regime'' whose actions to remain in power as leaders of an independent Rhodesia ''will be treasonable.''

The United Nations Security Council Nov. 12 also condemned the Rhodesian declaration of independence and called on all states to deny recognition or aid to ''this illegal racist minority regime.'' The Security Council Nov. 20 approved a resolution calling for voluntary sanctions under which all states were to end economic relations with Rhodesia and were to embargo oil and petroleum products to the new pariah nation.

Thirteen months later the Security Council Dec. 16, 1966 voted for mandatory, selective sanctions against Rhodesia. The resolution banned the sale or shipment of oil, petroleum products and arms to Rhodesia and the importation of Rhodesian asbestos, iron ore, pig iron, chrome, sugar, tobacco, copper, meat, meat products hides and skins. But the Security Council rejected amendments of a group of African countries that, *inter alia*, called for British use of force to prevent oil from reaching Rhodesia and for deploring Britain's refusal to use military force to unseat the Rhodesian regime.

The years that followed produced a hardening of attitudes on both sides. A growing black guerilla movement mounted attacks on Rhodesian targets. The Rhodesian regime resorted to frequent repressive acts. In a national referendum June 20, 1969, the predominantly white electorate approved a new constitution designed to keep the government ''in the hands of the civilized Rhodesians for all time'' and voted to establish a republic under which all remaining organic ties with Britain would be cut.

Rhodesia then became a republic and severed its last ties with Britain at midnight March 1, 1970.

The events outlined above, from the controversy that resulted in Rhodesia's declaration of independence in 1965 to its transformation into a republic in 1970, are detailed in the FACTS ON FILE book *Rhodesian Independence* (1971).

These events were greatly influenced by the character of Rhodesian Prime Minister Smith. His sincere dedication to his beliefs about Rhodesia made him a determined and, some thought, inflexible negotiator. Although some Rhodesian Front members thought him too liberal, he had, throughout this period, the backing of the large majority of white Rhodesians. Ian Douglas Smith was the first Rhodesian-born prime minister of Rhodesia. He was born in Selukwe April 8, 1919, the son of a farmer who had migrated from Scotland. Smith was educated at Rhodes University in South Africa and served as a fighter pilot in the Royal Air Force during World War II. Smith entered Rhodesian politics in 1948 when he was elected to Parliament as a Liberal Party member. In 1953 he shifted to the ruling United Federal Party and was chief government whip for Sir Roy Welensky in the Federation Parliament in 1958. But when the UFP approved the 1961 constitution, which gave black Africans some representation in the Rhodesian Parliament, Smith resigned and began to put together the Rhodesian Front.

The present volume, *Rhodesia/Zimbabwe 1971-77*, picks up the Rhodesian narrative from the point where the book *Rhodesian Independence* ended. It continues it on into the closing months of 1977, when Rhodesia's experiment with white-ruled independence and defiance of the overwhelming majority of the world's nations were becoming increasingly hard to continue. The material that follows is based principally on the account presented by FACTS ON FILE in its weekly reports on world affairs. A conscientious effort was made to record all events without bias and to make this book a balanced and accurate reference tool.

LESTER A. SOBEL

New York, N.Y.
November, 1977

White Regime Retains Power

Republic in Control

Great Britain's efforts to persuade Rhodesia's white minority government to yield power to the country's black majority met with continued failure during the closing half of the 1960s decade and the opening years of the 1970s. As further evidence of its determination to go its own way on this matter, the minority Rhodesian government of Ian Smith proclaimed the country a republic in March 1970 and cut its final organic ties with the Crown.

Republic proclaimed. Rhodesia proclaimed itself a republic March 2, severing its last ties with the British crown. The proclamation, signed in Salisbury by Clifford W. Dupont, the officer administering the government, dissolved parliament and set April 10 as the date for general elections to be held under the new constitution. Dupont automatically became interim president.

Addressing a group of American journalists March 2, Prime Minister Ian D. Smith said Rhodesia had not wanted to sever all ties with Britain, "but when we asked our queen if she would continue to be our queen and the British politicians made her decision for her and said she wouldn't, what have we been since but a de facto republic? We have now turned ourselves into a de jure republic."

When informed of Rhodesia's impending action Feb. 26, the British Foreign and Commonwealth Office had said that the move was an illegal act by an illegal government.

U.K. calls republic 'illegal'—Following Rhodesia's announcement of its shift to the status of a republic, British Commonwealth Secretary Michael Stewart March 2 explained his government's position to the British House of Commons:

"The purported assumption of a republican status by the regime in Southern Rhodesia is, like the 1969 declaration of independence itself, illegal.

"This latest event does not in any way affect the [British] government's determination to maintain economic sanctions and to increase their efficiency whenever possible. The international isolation of the [Rhodesian] regime remains a fact. No government has granted formal recognition to the regime, and the great majority of governments including the 13 who maintain consular or other offices in Southern Rhodesia, share our view that real progress can be made and long-term harmony established in Southern Rhodesia only as the result of a return to legality.

"But this further act of illegality and disloyalty does have certain legal consequences for those who perpetrate it or are associated with it. It can no longer be disputed that the members and supporters of the regime are seeking to deprive the queen of her authority in a part of her dominions. . . .

". . . [T]he policy of sanctions has the full support of countries throughout the world, with one or two notorious exceptions; . . . it has had grave results on the gross national product in Rhodesia; . . . it has created a situation in which those who purport to be the Rhodesian government have had to make it what they call a 'criminal offence' to tell the truth about the economic situation in Rhodesia; and . . . in any case, it is of vital importance for good relations between the different races of mankind that this policy should be maintained and that the illegality of the Rhodesian rebellion should be formally asserted."

Consulates closed. The U.S. March 9, 1970 ordered the closing of its consulate general in Salisbury in protest against the Smith government's proclamation that Rhodesia was a republic. By March 16, eight other Western nations followed suit and severed diplomatic relations with Rhodesia.

The U.S. announcement was made by Secretary of State William P. Rogers. He said the Smith regime's action "constitutes the final and formal break" with Britain, while the U.S. "has regarded and continues to regard the United Kingdom as the lawful sovereign" of Rhodesia.

State Department officials said the closing of the American consulate reflected Washington's desire to deny formal recognition to the Rhodesian republic. "We strongly disapprove of minority-based governments" because they "exclude for all time the possibility of majority rule," the officials said. The interests of the 1,000 Americans in Rhodesia, mainly missionaries, would be handled by U.S. consulates in Johannesburg, South Africa and in Blantyre, Malawi, the department said.

The U.S. had reduced its consulate general staff in Salisbury from 27 to six

officials after Rhodesia's unilateral declaration of "independence" from Britain in November 1965. The U.S. subsequently cut off all trade with Rhodesia except for shipments of educational material and medicine.

A statement issued by the Rhodesian cabinet March 10 expressed regret that the U.S. had "allowed itself to be forced into this decision by the British government." The statement assured Rhodesians that the American action "will make no difference to Rhodesia or to themselves."

The other nations that had decided to sever relations with Rhodesia were Switzerland, France, Belgium, Denmark, West Germany, the Netherlands, Italy and Norway. The only countries with diplomatic missions in Rhodesia were South Africa, Portugal and Greece.

U.S. backs Britain in U.N. The U.S. exercised its U.N. Security Council veto for the first time March 17, 1970 in rejecting a resolution that would have condemned Britain for failure to use force to overthrow the white-ruled regime of Rhodesia.

Sponsors of the resolution were Burundi, Nepal, Sierra Leone, Syria, and Zambia. The vote was nine in favor, two opposed (Britian and the U.S.), four abstaining. A single veto was enough to kill the measure.

The Council debate on Rhodesia had begun March 6 when Britain proposed a resolution directing U.N. members not to recognize the "racist minority regime in Southern Rhodesia." Zambian representative Lishomwa Sheba Muuka, speaking for the African members of the Council, derided the proposal as inadequate for the situation. At the request of the African members, the Council adjourned the debate to March 10.

The African members March 11 asked for a resolution requiring U.N. members to sever all ties with the Rhodesian regime. A spokesman for the council of the Organization of African Unity said this should include postal links, economic ties, and all communications systems.

In the voting March 17, the milder British resolution was defeated by abstentions. There were five votes in favor and 10 abstentions.

Two paragraphs in the 14-paragraph African-Asian draft proposal that would have called for sanctions against Portugal and South Africa were defeated in a separate vote.

The remaining 12 paragraphs declared that any government "not based on the principle of majority rule" should be declared "null and void." The draft condemned "the persistent refusal [of Britain] . . . to use force to bring an end to the rebellion in Southern Rhodesia and enable the people of Zimbabwe to exercise their right to self-determination and independence."

Other provisions called for the "immediate" severing of all ties and communications links. Britain and the U.S. were reluctant to give up the possibility of any contact with Rhodesia.

U.S. Ambassador Charles A. Yost March 18 explained the reason for the exercising of the first U.S. veto: "If you believe strongly in something, it is right and proper to stand up for what you believe rather than to hide behind someone else's skirts." The veto was cast "reluctantly" but "it was obvious that a situation was coming where we had gone as far as we could in seeking a consensus and concessions," he said.

U.N. condemns regime—The U.N. Security Council March 18, 1970, by 14-0 vote (one abstention: Spain) approved a compromise resolution condemning the white minority government of Rhodesia.

The new resolution, drafted by Finland, deleted these two key points that had led to the March 17 veto: that force be used against Rhodesia and that postal, telegraph and radio communications with Rhodesia be severed.

Principal points of the compromise document:

■All U.N. member nations "immediately sever all diplomatic, consular, trade, military and other relations" with Rhodesia, "terminate any representation that they may maintain" and "imme-diately interrupt any means of transportation to and from" Rhodesia.

■"Immediate withdrawal of South African police and armed personnel from" Rhodesia, which were there at the request of the Rhodesian government.

■All U.N. members were "to increase moral and material assistance to the people of Southern Rhodesia in their legitimate struggle to achieve freedom and independence."

The Athens press agency reported March 19 that Greece, in compliance with the council resolution, had decided to close the office of its honorary consul in Salisbury, Rhodesia March 22.

U.N. demands racial equality—The U.N. Security Council unanimously approved a resolution Nov. 17 urging an end to Rhodesia's defiance of previous U.N. calls for granting racial equality to its black African citizens.

The resolution called on Britain, "as the administering power," to "take urgent and effective measures to bring to an end the illegal rebellion in Southern Rhodesia and enable the people to exercise their right to self-determination in accordance with the charter of the United Nations" and in conformity with the U.N. General Assembly's Dec. 14, 1960 resolution calling for an end to all colonialism.

The resolution affirmed previous ones that had placed a mandatory embargo on all trade with Rhodesia. It expressed concern that some nations had defied resolutions of the previous five years and continued to trade with Rhodesia.

The Security Council Nov. 10 had voted 12 1 with two abstentions on an African-Asian resolution calling on Britain not to grant independence to Rhodesia before black majority rule. But the resolution was defeated by a veto cast by Britain, its fifth in council history. The abstainers were the U.S. and France. British Ambassador Sir Colin Crowe had said in advance that his government opposed the resolution because it encroached upon the prerogatives of the British Parliament. He argued that the resolution's remaining clauses calling for continued sanctions and nonrecognition of Rhodesia were redundant.

U.S. policy statements. Secretary of State William P. Rogers said in an African policy statement March 28 that the U.S. sought a "relationship of constructive cooperation" with African countries. "We want no military allies," he said, "no spheres of influence, no big-power competition in Africa. Our policy is a policy related to African countries and not a policy based upon our relations with non-African countries."

The statement was submitted to President Nixon, who told Rogers in a return message, that he "wholeheartedly approved" of the policy statement.

Rogers' statement declared that the U.S. would "work to bring about a change of direction in parts of Africa where racial oppression and residual colonialism still prevail." While there were "no easy solutions" in sight for "the problem of southern Africa," it said, "we take our stand on the side of those forces of fundamental human rights in southern Africa as we do at home and elsewhere."

Regarding Rhodesia, the statement said the Administration was determined not to recognize the white minority regime and would continue to support United Nations economic sanctions against that government.

U.S. policy in Africa was further detailed by Assistant State Secretary (for African Affairs) David D. Newsom Sept. 17, 1970 in an address before the Chicago Committee of the Chicago Council on Foreign Relations. In regard to Rhodesia, Newsom said:

"The present situation [in Rhodesia] is not accepted as wholly satisfactory by anyone—this includes many Rhodesians as well as Rhodesia's immediate neighbors. We will continue to support fully the U.N. economic sanctions against Rhodesia and will seek ways to insure more uniform compliance with the sanctions.

"In our enforcement of Rhodesian sanctions during the last three years, we have become aware of ... special difficulties encountered by American firms. We believe some relief can be given by permitting U.S. firms to sell their assets in Rhodesia. This is consistent with our commitments and with the U.N. sanctions. ... Because of controls imposed by the Smith

regime, most American firms no longer have effective control over their Rhodesian assets.... The total book value of U.S. investments was estimated to be about $56 million shortly after sanctions were imposed. Of this total some $50 million is invested in chrome mining enterprises.

"A special difficulty concerns firms which legally paid for goods in Rhodesia *before* the U.S. government prohibited such imports. At the time our implementing regulations were published, the Treasury Department announced that such transactions would be licensed.... If any American firm can demonstrate that it did legally pay for the goods prior to the Executive order ... , we consider that it may complete the transaction, thus denying to Rhodesia the benefit of keeping both the foreign exchange and the goods. ...

"The real solution to the Rhodesian problem lies in an agreement which will gain for Rhodesia international acceptance through a formula reopening the door to eventual majority rule in that territory. The United States sincerely hopes that further exploration of this problem by the government of the United Kingdom, and perhaps a recognition of common interest in such an exploration by Rhodesia's neighbors, will lead in this direction. ..."

Smith party wins election. Prime Minister Smith's ruling Rhodesian Front party won all 50 white seats in parliamentary elections April 10, 1970. The defeated white opposition parties were the moderate Center Party and the right-wing Republican Alliance, which campaigned for stricter racial policies than those pursued by Smith.

In the voting for the eight seats reserved for blacks, seven of the eight candidates supported by the Center Party were elected.

Rhodesia's first cabinet under its new republican status was sworn in April 13. The cabinet was similar to the outgoing one with the exception of Roger Hawkins, who was appointed minister of transport and power. He replaced Brig. Andrew Dunlop, who had decided not to run for re-election because of ill health.

Clifford Dupont was appointed first president of the Rhodesian Republic April 14. Dupont, who had been acting president since announcement of the formation of the republic March 2, was sworn in April 16.

Smith retains Front control—Prime Minister Smith was elected president of the ruling Rhodesian Front at the party's 1972 annual congress, held Sept. 21–23.

Smith appeared to emerge from the congress in a stronger leadership position after defeating several right-wing challenges. Opponents withdrew a motion asking that black townships be located in rural sectors rather than on the fringes of white residential areas, leaving the Cabinet with power to decide each case individually.

Internal Affairs Minister Lance Smith told delegates Sept. 22 that the government planned to go ahead in January 1973 with its policy of "provincialization." Under the plan, black regional authorities would be formed which would exercise a measure of direct responsibility for "enlisting African financial support for the social services needed by Africans."

Party chairman Desmond Frost declared Sept. 21 that the press, which had been barred from the congress, ought to be nationalized "because, in my opinion, at this moment of time few people believe them when they refer to internal politics—knowing their intention is the downfall of our present government."

Prime Minister Smith told the congress Sept. 23 that he had new ideas for settlement of the independence dispute with Britain but that it would not be "tactically advantageous" to reveal them.

In a related development, the formation of a Rhodesian political party which aimed to oppose racial discrimination was reported Nov. 1. An introductory manifesto said the new group, known as the Rhodesia party, supported a common electoral roll with high franchise qualifications.

Political control, however, was to remain with persons having the "educa-

tion, income and possessions to give them an interest in stability and . . . qualify them for this responsibility." The party was headed by an interim committee which included Roy Ashburner, a former Rhodesian cricket player, and two former members of Parliament, Allan Savory and Dr. Morris Hirsch.

U.K.-Rhodesian Negotiations

No lasting progress was made during the early 1970s in efforts to end the dispute between Britain and Rhodesia's white minority government over the latter's refusal to permit majority (and therefore black) rule in Rhodesia. Attempts to negotiate the differences had been made throughout the 1960s, and such efforts continued even after the Rhodesian regime had proclaimed Rhodesia a republic and had cut all organic links with the United Kingdom.

Fresh British efforts promised. At the 1970 annual conference of Britain's ruling Conservative Party, held in Blackpool Oct. 7–10, government spokesmen promised new efforts to persuade the Rhodesian regime to agree to majority rule.

At the conference Oct. 8, Foreign Minister Sir Alec Douglas-Home announced that Britain would approach Rhodesia in a new attempt to settle their longstanding dispute. Any future talks, he said, would have to be based on the principle that the all-white Rhodesian government must provide for eventual rule by the country's black majority.

Douglas-Home told the British House of Commons Nov. 10 that he had undertaken new moves to see whether Britain and the Rhodesian regime could come to terms.

Douglas-Home said he had contacted the British and Rhodesian ambassadors to South Africa in Pretoria and asked them to explore the possibility of further negotiations. The message had been transmitted to Rhodesian Premier Ian D. Smith. The foreign secretary said the effort to reach an agreement should be made "even though the evidence suggests chances of success are remote."

Smith also had expressed the same view Oct. 28 that there was "little chance of a settlement." But he said he was prepared to go anywhere for talks with the British.

In further comments on the possibility of negotiations, Smith said Nov. 10 that Rhodesia's new apartheid-type constitution "has been framed in such a way that it can be changed to meet changing circumtances." He stressed, however, that "the crux of the matter" remained whether the constitutional alterations Britain might demand would be in the interest of Rhodesia.

In an April 15, 1971 interview with the Rhodesia Herald, a Salisbury newspaper, Smith dismissed as "no longer of any consequence" the list of principles established by successive British governments for negotiating a solution to the Rhodesian issue. The Smith interview followed months of speculation that British and Rhodesian representatives were meeting in Capetown.

Britain's six principles, as reiterated March 2, 1970 after the Rhodesian regime had proclaimed Rhodesia's republican status: "(1) Unimpeded progress towards majority rule. (2) No retrogressive amendment of the [1961 amended] constitution. (3) Immediate improvement in the political status of the African population. (4) Progress toward ending racial discrimination. (5) Proof of acceptability to the people of Rhodesia as a whole of any proposed basis for independence. (6) No oppression of majority by minority, or of minority by majority."

British-Rhodesian talks. British and Rhodesian officials held exploratory discussions in Salisbury, Rhodesia June 30, July 1 and July 5–7, 1971.

The British representatives were Lord Goodman, Sir Philip Adams and Philip Mansfield. Rhodesia was represented by M. F. Gaylard, secretary to the Cabinet, and E. A. T. Smith, the attorney general.

A communique issued July 7 said only that the talks had reached the stage "where it is necessary for the two sides to report back to their respective governments. It has been mutually agreed that details of the discussions will continue to remain confidential."

About 230 students, mostly blacks, were arrested in Salisbury July 1 when they attempted to express their views on the talks. Some 150 university students were rounded up by police as they demonstrated outside Milton Buildings, where the officials were meeting. They carried signs criticizing Prime Minister Ian Smith and asking for an end to "white imperialism." All were freed on bail after being seized under the Law and Order Maintenance Act and charged with unlawful assembly.

A group of 80 students from a local high school were found guilty of the same offense after police ended their protest march into the city. Those under 19 years of age were punished by six strokes of the cane, and the older students were fined approximately $35 each.

Lord Goodman held six more meetings with Rhodesian representatives in Salisbury between his arrival there Sept. 17 and his departure for London Sept. 21. A meeting of junior representatives of each side was held Sept. 22.

Goodman declared Sept. 21 that although "I have accomplished the task I was assigned" to do, "it would be foolish to believe that sensational changes are imminent." He reported the results of his visit to British Foreign Secretary Sir Alec Douglas-Home in London Sept. 24.

Prime Minister Smith told reporters during the junior-level talks Sept. 22 that his government would never allow a one-man, one-vote situation in Rhodesia. "We disapprove of that sort of thing—at any time," Smith emphasized. The unimpeded progress by Rhodesia's black inhabitants toward majority rule had been one of the principles advocated by the British government for settling the dispute.

Smith told an Oct. 8 congress of the ruling Rhodesian Front that there were still "basic and major differences" between the British and Rhodesian positions; he added: "If we have made progress since I last mentioned the subject in public seven months ago it has been insignificant and of little consequence." However, Smith said he felt that prospects for a settlement were greater than previously because Britain's negotiating stance had become more conciliatory since 1968, when Smith met former British Prime Minister Harold Wilson.

Prospect of black rule accepted. An agreement to end Britain's constitutional dispute with Rhodesia's white supremacist government was signed Nov. 24, 1971 in Salisbury by Foreign Secretary Sir Alec Douglas-Home and Rhodesian Prime Minister Ian Smith after 10 days of negotiations. The settlement's terms would enlarge the political rights of black Africans and could open the way to their eventual assumption of political power.

Disclosing the terms of the agreement Nov. 25, Sir Alec told the House of Commons that the proposals in the document signed the previous day were "fully within the five principles to which the government have constantly adhered" in efforts to reach a settlement.

Sir Alec told Commons that unimpeded progress toward majority rule would be effected by abolishing a provision of the 1969 constitution stipulating that blacks would become eligible for more seats in the Rhodesian House of Assembly (lower house) when they paid more than 24% of Rhodesia's income taxes.* (The Rhodesian Senate, similar in powers to Britain's House of Lords, was not affected by the agreement. The Senate was composed of 23 members—10 whites selected by whites in the House of Assembly, 10 black chiefs elected by the Council of Chiefs and three members of any race appointed by the Rhodesian president.)

The House of Assembly currently had 50 white and 16 black members. Eight of the blacks had been directly elected and eight had been chosen by electoral colleges of government-appointed chiefs.

With the amended constitution, the 16 directly and indirectly elected black seats would be retained but new black voters would be registered on an African Higher Roll, subject to the same qualifications as the European Roll. Persons with a high school education would be admitted to these rolls if their yearly income was $1,200 or if they owned property worth $2,400. Those lacking a high school education were required to earn $1,800 yearly or to own property worth $3,600.†

When the number of voters on the African Higher Roll reached 6% of those on the European Roll, two additional black seats would be created and filled by direct election by black voters. When the proportion reached 12%, two more seats would be created and filled by indirect election by the tribal colleges. The sequence of alternate direct and indirect elections for black seats was to continue until parity of black and white seats had been attained. Sir Alec remarked that the new voting arrangements would bring about an immediate improvement in the political status of blacks, as "on present estimates it seems likely that four new African seats will be due to be created when the procedures for registration are completed."

Within one year after the election in which parity was achieved, a referendum of all black voters (including those on the African Lower Roll, whose membership standards would be eased by the agreement) would be held to determine whether the indirectly elected seats should be replaced by directly elected seats. According to the text of the agreement published by the London Times Nov. 26 and 27, "The new seats will all be African Higher Roll seats unless the legislature has before the referendum provided for up to one-quarter of the new seats to be African Lower Roll seats. The legislature may also provide that a specific number of the extra seats should be rural constituencies."

Following the referendum and any subsequent elections, a three-man commis-

---

*Blacks currently paid less than one percent of Rhodesia's income taxes.

†Rhodesia had a population (1970 estimate) of 5,-050,000 blacks, 239,000 whites and 25,000 others. There were 24,201 black African students in Rhodesian high schools in 1970.

sion (one black member) would be appointed by the government after consultation with all parties represented in the House to determine if the creation of 10 Common Roll seats would be "acceptable to the people of Rhodesia" or "whether any alternate arrangements would command general support." The Common Roll seats would be filled by vote of all members of the European Roll and all members of the African Higher Roll considered as a single constituency. Each voter would have 10 votes to cast as he chose among the candidates. Afterward the separate rolls would be retained to fill the existing directly elected seats.

From the time of the enactment of the settlement until the filling of Common Roll seats, the chief guarantee against retroactive amendment of "specially entrenched" clauses of the constitution would be a mechanism that required such amendments to obtain the approval of two-thirds of the Senate and House voting separately and two-thirds of the black and white members of the House, again voting separately. After the Common Roll seats had been filled, a two-thirds majority of the House would be required for amendment. Among the specially entrenched clauses, as defined by the agreement, were all the provisions detailing aspects of the new voting arrangements and an amended Declaration of Rights which forbade new discriminatory laws or the extension of existing discriminatory laws.

According to the Times text, the Rhodesian government had "given an assurance" that it would not try to amend the specially entrenched clauses until the first two African Higher Roll seats had been filled or three years had elapsed, whichever was sooner. A three-man commission to include one black member was to examine the question of racial discrimination, particularly the Land Tenure Act, which divided the land in equal portions between blacks and whites. While the Rhodesian government recognized that the commission's findings would "carry special authority," it could ignore the commission's legislative recommendations if it felt there were "considerations that any

government would be obliged to regard as of an overriding character." Nor did the agreement depend on British government approval of the commission's findings. Until the commission had reported, there were to be no evictions of blacks from white areas such as Epworth and Chishawasha Missions, described in the text as "the only two cases in which the Rhodesian government are considering the eviction of Africans from land in the European area . . ."

The agreement said that 54 black detainees had been or would be released shortly and that a further 93 detainees and two restrictees were to have a special review at which a British observer would be present.

Britain was to provide Rhodesia with $120 million over the next 10 years in economic and educational development aid for black areas, with that sum being matched by the Rhodesian government in addition to its "annual expenditure currently planned." The agreement contained no procedures for verifying that the money actually would be spent on blacks.

Sir Alec announced that his government's fifth principle—that the agreement be found acceptable to the people of Rhodesia as a whole—would be implemented by a commission headed by Lord Pearce, chairman of the Press Council, which would travel to Rhodesia and conduct its inquiries there. Lord Harlech, former ambassador to Washington, and Sir Maurice Dorman, former governor general of Malta, were to be among its other members. When the commission had returned a favorable report, economic sanctions would be lifted and the state of emergency in Rhodesia revoked "unless unforeseen circumstances intervene." (Britain Dec. 15 appointed Sir Glyn Jones and Sir Frederick Pedler as additional deputy chairmen to the Pearce Commission, but Pedler was reported Jan. 8, 1972 to have resigned because of questions raised about his business interests in Rhodesia.)

An organization opposed to the settlement and known as the African National Council was formed in Salisbury Dec. 16 under the leadership of Bishop

Abel Muzorewa, head of the United Methodist Church in Rhodesia. The council's first meeting Dec. 18 was attended by approximately 700 blacks.

Sir Roy Welensky, prime minister of the country when Rhodesia was a member of the Central African Federation, said Dec. 18 that Lord Pearce should "make the terms of reference of his commission of inquiry crystal clear as soon as possible."

The British foreign secretary described the accord as "fair and honorable" and asked members of the House to examine it "considering past history and the present realities of power."

In his report to the Rhodesian parliament Nov. 25, Prime Minister Smith gave an account of the document which did not differ in any substantive way from Douglas-Home's. He emphasized that the "sole task" of Lord Pearce's commission would be to "assess the acceptability of these proposals and they will have no mandate to consider other proposals." It would, he said, be a "fruitless exercise" to try to determine how long it would take "under this system" for blacks and whites to reach a parity of representation in parliament but "no European need harbor any anxiety about the security of his future in Rhodesia."

The accord would better allow Rhodesia to oppose "the vanguard of Communist infiltration into southern Africa," which was "at our borders."

Smith added: "We all know the frustrating position in which we have found ourselves in recent years, when we have been forced to devote more of our time, more of our efforts to combating our traditional friends in the free world at the expense of being able to concentrate on our real enemies."

Smith warned against "over-optimistic expectations in the short term, for the return to normality will be a gradual business" and "sanctions will continue until such time as legislation is passed through the British House of Commons." Although the agreement was a "fair and practical instrument," some people would "interpret certain sections in different ways, in some cases deliberately, in order to mislead." The agreement would "enable us to comply with our

most important principle, the retention of government in civilized hands."

The Salisbury negotiations—Sir Alec's trip to Rhodesia had been preceded by the arrival of a preliminary British delegation Oct. 21. After his arrival Nov. 15, Douglas-Home had a brief meeting with Smith but spent a number of the following days in conversation with black groups. During an interview Nov. 17 with three former detainees, Douglas-Home was handed a memorandum smuggled from the prison cell of the Rev. Ndabaningi Sithole, leader of the Zimbabwe African National Union (ZANU), who denounced Sir Alec's five negotiating principles as being "devoid of any political meaning for the African people. They are based on fundamentally wrong assumptions that a white minority will hand over power to an African majority of which it is so fearful." Sithole declared that blacks would be satisfied with nothing less than majority rule.

The full British delegation of 40 persons met their Rhodesian opposite numbers for the first time Nov. 19 but canceled a session scheduled for the following day. Douglas-Home met for an hour Nov. 20 with Joshua Nkomo, leader of the Zimbabwe African Peoples Union (ZAPU), who had been brought to Salisbury from detention in Gonakudzingwa, an area near the Mozambique border.

Smith met twice with his Cabinet Nov. 22 and once with Douglas-Home. After another meeting Nov. 23, the two men announced they had reached a tentative accord.

International reaction—In London Nov. 24, Former Commonwealth Secretary Arthur Bottomley declared that the agreement would fail "because Africans will realize they cannot get what they want by democratic and peaceful development, and they will be turning more and more to violence." The Labor party announced that a delegation headed by Denis Healey, a party spokesman on foreign affairs, would visit Rhodesia to help assess the settlement's acceptability.

South African Prime Minister John Vorster said Nov. 24 that he was glad of the agreement "for the sake of Rhodesia, states in southern Africa and the free world."

The Soviet Union, in a dispatch from the official press agency Tass, termed the accord Nov. 24 a "betrayal of the interests of the African majority" which would "go down in history as an undisguised and shameful collusion between the imperialists and their racist henchmen in Africa."

Sir Colin Crowe, the chief British delegate to the U.N., told the Security Council Nov. 25 that the agreement would improve the status of Rhodesian blacks, which was "bad and getting steadily worse." (The U.N. General Assembly Nov. 22 had voted 102-3 with nine abstentions to demand that Rhodesia not be given independence before majority rule became effective. The negative votes were Britain, South Africa and Portugal. The abstentions were Australia, Belgium, Canada, France, Italy, Luxembourg, the Netherlands, New Zealand and the U.S.)

The Organization of African Unity (OAU) called the settlement Nov. 26 an "outright sellout" and advised blacks to "take matters into their own hands." Newspapers in Zambia denounced the accord Nov. 26.

Joseph Godber, an official of the British Foreign Office, explained the agreement to Undersecretary of State John N. Irwin 2d in Washington Nov. 26, but the State Department had no comment.

The U.N. Security Council Dec. 2 invited two Rhodesian black nationalist leaders to present their views on the Rhodesian settlement proposals to the council. Joshua Nkomo of the Zimbabwe African People's Union (ZAPU) was in preventive detention and Ndabaningi Sithole of the Zimbabwe African National Union (ZANU) was in jail. The measure, passed without objection or formal vote, required Britain to "take the appropriate steps to insure compliance with this decision."

Zambian President Kenneth Kaunda Dec. 3 called the Anglo-Rhodesian accord a "despicable sellout" of Rhodesia's black population. Kaunda added: "The British government has given moral ammunition to oppression, to unending violation of human rights."

Gen. Idi Amin, president of Uganda, and Gen. Joseph Mobutu of Zaire (formerly Congo-Kinshasa), declared in a joint communique Dec. 19 that the settlement "deprives the African majority population of their legitimate right to self-determination and excludes them from running their country."

The U.N. General Assembly voted Dec. 21 to condemn the settlement as "a flagrant violation of the inalienable rights of the African people of Zimbabwe [Rhodesia] to self-determination and independence." Voting on the proposal was 94-8 with 22 abstentions.

British Parliament accepts settlement— Both houses of the British Parliament approved the U.K.-Rhodesian settlement.

The vote in the House of Commons Dec. 1 was 297-269, with Douglas-Home remarking that he did not believe "in conscience" that "better terms could have been negotiated." He said that during his talks with Smith he had been aware that "Britain's influence [in Rhodesia] was running out." Denis Healey, the Labor party's foreign affairs spokesman, called the agreement "the greatest obstacle race of all time."

The House of Lords passed the measure Dec. 3 after an amendment declining approval had been defeated 201-76.

Pearce Commission Finds 1971 Plan Unacceptable

The British commission headed by Lord Pearce went to Rhodesia in January 1972 to see whether the 1971 agreement between Rhodesian Prime Minister Smith and British Foreign Secretary Sir Alec Douglas-Home would serve as a satisfactory basis for settling the controversy over the future of Rhodesia. It reported back to the British government four months later that the settlement could not succeed because the people of Rhodesia considered it unacceptable.

Pearce team in Rhodesia. The Pearce Commission, whose task was to determine on behalf of the British government whether the proposals for a settlement with Rhodesia were acceptable to the people of that country as a whole, arrived in Salisbury Jan. 11, 1972. The members were met at the airport by a silent demonstration organized by the African National Council (ANC), a group formed to oppose the settlement.

Bishop Abel T. Muzorewa, chairman of the ANC, had assailed Smith Jan. 1 for a New Year's broadcast charging that "international communism" was behind his council.

Muzorewa added: "It is this tragic ignorance of his about African aspirations which possibly makes him believe that when Africans reject or oppose a government measure they are being intimidated and agitated by what he calls mischief-makers or Communists. The ANC has instructed its supporters, young and old, to be disciplined, non-violent and to respect all men, black and white, and all views."

Expressing a different opinion on the proposed settlement, the government-appointed Council of Chiefs issued a statement after a meeting in Salisbury Jan. 4 in which it "voiced its pleasure that the quarrel between Britain and Rhodesia had been settled in such an amicable manner and looked forward to the progress and prosperity which should benefit all Rhodesians." The council asked that information given the Pearce Commission be treated as confidential because of "intimidatory tactics seen in the past."

Garfield Todd, a former prime minister of Rhodesia, had urged caution Jan. 2. He said: "It is better to keep our options open than to commit ourselves to a course of action which keeps the nation divided. A great many of the country's white population are unaware of the Africans, nor do they know of their mounting discontent. If Africans stopped work, Rhodesia would stop also."

Former Prime Minister Sir Roy Welensky spoke in favor of the settlement plan Jan. 4 and asked: "Are we about to see a repeat performance of those tragic years of 1961–62 when African nationalist leaders, by their folly, misled their people and in no small way are responsible for the last eight sterile years this country had endured?"

The London Times said Jan. 7 that six blacks had been arrested at a meeting called two days earlier to discuss the settlement terms. The incident took place at Humbany rest camp on the Belingwe tribal trust land in Matabeleland.

The Rhodesian Information Department said Jan. 13 that one black had been killed and nine wounded the previous day when police opened fire at an unspecified disturbance in Shabani, 300 miles southwest of Salisbury. The report also said that since December 1971 there had been "a number of incidents involving intimidation and riotous behavior which have necessitated police intervention."

Rhodesian blacks riot. Rioting and other disturbances rocked three Rhodesian cities Jan. 16–20 as blacks expressed opposition to the proposed Anglo-Rhodesian agreement.

The trouble began Jan. 16 in Gwelo, where blacks in outlying townships smashed windows and burned cars and buildings. The following day an estimated 8,000 persons were turned back by police tear gas as they attempted to march into the predominantly white center of the city. One black youth died Jan. 18 after he fell while running from police; two other blacks were injured, one by police bayonet, and 55 persons were arrested.

Ex-Prime Minister Garfield Todd and his daughter, Judith, were arrested Jan. 18 at their home in Shabani. The detention papers, signed by Minister of Justice, Law and Order Desmond W. Lardner-Burke, declared the Todds were being imprisoned because "you are likely to commit or to incite the commission of acts in Rhodesia which would endanger the public safety or disturb or interfere with the maintenance of public order."

The document said the detention would remain in effect until the nationwide state of emergency, imposed shortly before Rhodesia declared its independence, was removed or until the detention order itself was revoked or amended.

Lardner-Burke and P. K. van der Byl, the information minister, toured Gwelo by armored car Jan. 18 and were greeted by crowds of blacks screaming "No! No!" to the British proposals.

A two-man team of Pearce commissioners, attempting to test public opinion regarding the settlement proposals, had to cancel a meeting Jan. 18 in Gwelo at the request of the Rhodesian government, but six other teams held sessions throughout the country that day. At Goromonzi, some 25 miles east of Salisbury, tribal chiefs listened to a public explanation of the settlement terms from the commissioners but reportedly expressed opposition in a private conversation afterwards.

Eleven black youths were shot and killed by Rhodesian police Jan. 19–20 and another died from wounds received several days earlier.

Violence broke out near Salisbury, the Rhodesian capital, Jan. 19 as black youths looted shops and stoned cars, injuring at least 10 persons.

Police in the black suburbs of Fort Victoria, 200 miles to the south, shot and wounded two black youths who were attempting to ransack a liquor store Jan. 19.

In a sparsely worded dispatch Jan. 19, the government said three blacks had been killed by police that day in violence in Harari, a township on the outskirts of Salisbury. Another 44 blacks were arrested there, 24 of them with gunshot wounds. Police killed eight blacks Jan. 20 in Sakubva township in Umtali, near the Mozambique border, as they opened fire on a crowd of some 1,000 blacks who had smashed windows and stoned a police vehicle. Authorities in Fort Victoria arrested 200 blacks for similar disturbances.

The government Jan. 21 arrested Josia Chinamano, a leader of the African National Council and former political detainee, and his wife in Salisbury. Another ANC member, unofficially identified as Zacharia Kanyasa, was detained at Mrewa, 55 miles northeast of the capital.

Pearce withdrawal discussed—The violence and death that accompanied efforts to test acceptability of the Anglo-Rhodesian settlement provoked speculation about the continued usefulness of the Pearce Commission's stay in Rhodesia.

(The appointment of two more commissioners was reported Jan. 18—John Strong, who had served in the British Foreign Service in East Africa, and Ian Butler, an official of the Housing Corporation.)

A statement issued by the commission Jan. 20 and made public the following day revealed a difference of opinion with the Rhodesian government as to whether "normal political activities" were being allowed in the country during the Pearce team's visit. The text of the Anglo-Rhodesian agreement specified they should be.

The commissioners said they had known there would be difficulties over the text's limiting normal political activities to those "conducted in a peaceful and democratic manner." They declared: "The contention of the Rhodesian government is that they have a problem of law and order on their hands which, to cite the instances of Gwelo and Harari, cannot be denied. They hold that, as they promised us at the beginning, they have permitted meetings wherever considerations of law and order allowed. This is disputed. . . . A general point of difficulty has arisen with regard to the refusal for political meetings in the tribal trust lands. On our provisional construction of the agreement, the phrase 'normal political activities' must to some extent be read in the context of Rhodesian conditions. But we cannot accept that a total denial of any political activities can be read into an agreement which does not specifically exclude them."

The commissioners added: "If people are detained simply to silence them, then even in existing conditions it is not allowing normal political activity."

(A spokesman for the Pearce team said Jan. 23 that the previous week's violence had not disrupted the group's work and that Lord Pearce "has no intention of pulling out." He also remarked that when "everything is placed in its true perspective, less than 10% of the commission's meetings have been postponed. Elsewhere there has been a very useful evaluation exercise.)

Smith's warnings—Prime Minister Smith Jan. 21 delivered a radio broadcast in which he discussed the recent violence and its possible affect on the Pearce Commission's work.

"As we believe that this will be the last time that such a visit will take place, whichever way the decision goes, we have gone out of our way to meet the British request to release the maximum number of detainees for the purpose of the test of acceptability," Smith said. His government had "warned the British of our concern" about trouble and "our predictions were correct."

He declared that "Rhodesians understand this kind of thing. In fact it proves how right we are in our determination to maintain high standards in Rhodesia. Those responsible for all this barbaric destruction have ironically played right into our hands. What greater proof can anyone have of the lack of maturity, lack of civilization, the inability to make any constructive contribution?" Smith said the rioting had been carried out by "teenagers" led by a "hard core of experienced campaigners who are using these youngsters as a tool to implement their policy of upsetting the commission."

He said that if "the present generation of Africans are so stupid as to reject this offer of advancement for their people, they will bear the curse of their children forever." But if blacks did reject the proposals "I and my party will be perfectly happy for the present [1969] constitution to remain." It would be "a most pleasant surprise, indeed a great day in our history."

Smith, however, appeared to rule out a spontaneous rejection of the settlement terms by blacks: "When a person who is otherwise normal rejects an offer of something which is for his betterment, for his advancement, then he has

either been misled or he has been intimidated."

He had heard suggestions that the Pearce Commission be withdrawn or that its work be postponed "until the troubles cease. I believe this would smack of weakness and appeasement and therefore cannot support the idea. In any case, if you tried to carry out the same exercise next year or the year after, it would be no different."

Council asks nonviolence—The African National Council released a statement Jan. 22 in which it sought to join Smith "in telling our people to be nonviolent, disciplined and decent and let the Pearce Commission carry on its work in a free atmosphere." The council, however, said that the 1969 constitution had been imposed by the Smith government following its illegal seizure of independence from Britain and was the "number one reason why the majority of Africans are not accepting these proposals." But if "our rejection of the proposals means that the 1969 constitution will remain, then the African would rather live with an imposed oppressive position than go down in history as having accepted an oppressive constitution for himself." Another problem, the council said, was not the settlement terms themselves but trusting the Rhodesian government to carry them out, which was "impossible for anyone, particularly the African."

Newspaper says commission should leave—The Sunday Mail, Rhodesia's biggest-circulation newspaper, recommended Jan. 23 that the Pearce team return to Britain. "They should go home," the paper said, "not because their mission has failed but because it is impossible. Their brief presence has confirmed what many here and in Britain already knew—that even this modest excursion into a democratic procedure in which all and sundry, qualified or not, are invited to have their say has failed. The Pearce Commission should go home because the longer they stay the greater the danger to life and property and the more lasting the unsettling effects of the disorder staged for the Commission's benefit."

Opposition to plan continues. Eight black members of the Rhodesian parliament met with Lord Pearce Jan. 24 and urged his group to leave the country because "this exercise is costing many lives." The eight, who constituted the Rhodesia Electoral Union and had been chosen by tribal chiefs, also rejected the settlement proposals.

The commission met with about 1,000 blacks Jan. 24 at Mrewa. The crowd listened to an explanation of the Anglo-Rhodesian proposals and dispersed after chanting "No! No!" Denis Blain, one of the commissioners, disputed the suggestion by a Rhodesian newsman that the meeting had been "broken up," saying the blacks had "expressed their views and then left." According to the New York Times Jan. 25, Blain and his colleague at the meeting, Dennis F. H. Frost, had doubts about this type of gathering as a means of determining black opinion.

Gerry Raftopolous, head of the National Association of Colored People, a group representing those of mixed black and white ancestry, had talks Jan. 24 with members of the Pearce group in Salisbury. Raftopolous said afterwards it looked as though "we are not going to gain anything at all from these proposals. If there is going to be no change, it is difficult to imagine the Colored people saying yes."

He also revealed: "The commissioners were under the impression that we Coloreds had the same rights in Rhodesia as Europeans. We had to put them right on this. We had to tell them we were discriminated against. It was quite an eye-opener for them." (Colored persons in Rhodesia were recognized as whites for electoral purposes but lived in segregated areas.)

The Council of Chiefs, on record as favoring the settlement plan, met with Pearce Commission members in Salisbury Jan. 25, but no statement was issued afterwards.

The multiracial Center party, which held seven of the eight elected black Parliament seats, told commission members Jan. 26 that it favored the proposals "under duress."

Pat Bashford, the party's leader, explained: "We support the settlement proposals, with reservations, because we believe that they are a small step" towards "racial peace." He believed "the alternative, a period of uncertainty, the duration of which no one can foresee, a period of tension, a period of violent conflict even, cannot be justified on the completely speculative grounds that the end result would be better than the proposed settlement terms." Bashford said his party "fully realizes the dubious value of solemn assurances uttered by men to whom oaths of allegiance are but scraps of paper to be torn up at will."

The party holding the remaining elected black seat, the National People's Union, rejected the settlement Jan. 26 because its terms "do not provide for immediate majority rule, and because they are to be implemented by a government which is racialist in character and outlook."

ANC meets with Pearce team. Members of the African National Council told Pearce Commission members in Salisbury Jan. 28 that it "unhesitatingly rejects" the U.K.-Rhodesian settlement proposals.

The six members of the council attending the meeting included Bishop Abel Muzorewa, its chairman, and Eddison J. Zvobgo, Edison Sithole and Arthur Chadzingwa. The Pearce commissioners taking part in the discussions were Lord Pearce, Lord Harlech and Sir Glyn Jones.

Reading a prepared statement to the council, Muzorewa declared that "this is the first and last chance for the African people to pass a verdict on white minority rule." He also said his group's basic demand was "that no settlement of the Rhodesian problem can be achieved without the active participation by the African people, through the leaders of their choice."

It was his opinion that "no sane and fair-minded person could accept" the Anglo-Rhodesian settlement's new voter qualifications, "taking into account the legal disabilities" that blacks were "subjected to in this country." Individual property qualifications of the kind envisioned in the settlement were "nonsensical" in a country where most of the land set aside for blacks was held communally by tribes. Muzorewa characterized the proposals as a "seedbed of bloody revolution" and said the recent killings of blacks had been "murders of unarmed people."

Zvobgo remarked that if blacks approved the proposals "we would be the only species of human being who ever went down on record as saying, yes, it's nice to be ruled by a minority in your own land." Referring to plans for a joint Anglo-Rhodesian development program to aid black welfare, Sithole said it was "political idiocy on the part of whites to think that in 1972 Africans can be bought with a few more jobs, houses and schools."

(The London Times Jan. 28 reported Sithole claimed the previous day that about 100 of the council's supporters had been detained since the Pearce team's arrival. Sithole said that at Que Que and in other areas council officials had been held for the duration of the Pearce commissioners' visit with local tribesmen and then released afterwards.)

A spokesman for the Pearce Commission disclosed Jan. 27 that two of the group's members Jan. 20 had visited Garfield Todd, the former Rhodesian premier arrested with his daughter, Judith. Commissioners visited Miss Todd Jan. 22 and saw Josiah Chinamano, an African National Council official detained the previous week, Jan. 26 at Connemare prison near Que Que.

In other contacts with elements of the Rhodesian population, members of the Pearce team met Feb. 2 with Sir Humphrey Gibbs, who had served as a governor of Rhodesia, at a farm he owned near Bulawayo. A group of white officials from the Rhodesia Railway Workers Union declared themselves in favor of the proposals. Representatives from Bulawayo's African Chamber of Commerce said they opposed the settlement. Some 300 Matabele tribesmen vetoed the proposals Feb. 8 at a meeting in the Sabi tribal trust land.

The New York Times reported Feb. 16 that a new group had been formed in the country to fight racism. The organization, called People Against Racial Discrimination, was headed by Kenneth Mew, principal of the multiracial Ranche House College in Salisbury. The Times said the group's principal aim would be to persuade blacks to accept the Anglo-Rhodesian proposals.

Rekayi Tangwena, chief of the Tangwena tribe, Feb. 20 told Colin Rawlins, a Pearce commissioner, that his people rejected the proposed settlement with Britain. Tangwena told Rawlins: "The children of the queen are doing very much wrong here. Let them be put in jail and then we'll know there is a law of the land." Tangwena also said that some 300 families, most of his tribe, had returned to their homes at Gaeresi Ranch, thereby thwarting government efforts to relocate them.

British legislators barred—A four-man delegation of British opposition parliamentarians was refused permission to enter the country Jan. 29 by the Rhodesian government.

The announcement said that some members of the delegation, composed of two representatives from the Labor party and two from the Liberal party, were on record as supporting black guerrilla movements in Rhodesia. David Steel, the Liberal parliamentary whip, was specifically mentioned.

(Jeremy Thorpe, the Liberal leader, said Jan. 30 that the Rhodesian action was "outrageous." Thorpe added: "MPs at Westminister are not in the habit of being told this kind of thing. To condemn my chief whip in the terms he [Rhodesian Premier Ian D. Smith] has may perhaps go some way to explain why he has refused to give Sir Alec [Douglas-Home] any information on the reasons for the imprisonment of the Todds.")

Pearce hints at intimidation. Lord Pearce hinted again Feb. 7 that Smith's regime might be breaking its pledge to allow normal political activity during the commission's visit.

Pearce declared that, in addition to Garfield Todd and his daughter Judith, and Josiah Chinamano and his wife,

Ruth, a number of persons had been taken into custody by police and that this "seems to have had the result in some cases, whether intended or not, of preventing them from appearing before the commissioners visiting their particular area." He added: "We fully recognize the responsibility of the Rhodesian government to maintain law and order throughout the country. Nevertheless, in the absence of any satisfactory explanation about those detained . . . the commission must infer that the purpose of their detention is to inhibit the free expression of opinion." (Judith Todd, detained at Marandellas, 40 miles east of Salisbury, said Feb. 5 that she had begun a hunger strike that would last "until I am released from prison.")

Bishop Abel Muzorewa, chairman of the ANC, had made his own charges of "explosive intimidation" by the Rhodesian government Feb. 3. Muzorewa said his group had evidence that five blacks had been dismissed from their jobs and evicted from their homes for refusing to approve the settlement, that 250 had been arrested and that 31 blacks had been killed in the January rioting.

(Muzorewa later denounced the Anglo-Rhodesian accord Feb. 7 in London. "The constitutonal provisions are so full of reservations and escape clauses, the declaration of rights so open to abuse, as to render the document meaningless. For every right there is a restriction which renders it void. The road to majority rule is booby-trapped every inch of the way," he said. Muzorewa told a press conference that he had been "sent by the people of Rhodesia to try to convince the British government that if they continue to pursue their unreasonable and short-sighted policies, and continue to ignore the Africans in their constitutional ventures, then the responsibility of a future holocaust in Rhodesia will lie heavily upon them."

(Muzorewa told the U.N. Security Council in New York Feb. 16 that most Rhodesian blacks opposed the settlement pact and that the country would see massive civil disobedience if the Smith government were maintained. At a news conference in Washington the following

day, Muzorewa said blacks would accept hardships brought about by U.N. sanctions as "the price of their struggle for freedom." He said he had been "grieved and hurt" by the recent lifting of a ban on the import of Rhodesian chrome and other metals to the U.S.)

Two additional members of the Pearce Commission were named to investigate the question of intimidation in Rhodesia. Aldhelm Sugg arrived in Salisbury Feb. 11 and was to be joined within a few days by Anthony Whitfield.

Smith blames ANC—Prime Minister Smith charged Feb. 10 that ANC members were responsible for violence in Rhodesia, and he promised to present a "formidable dossier" of evidence to the Pearce group.

Speaking at a news conference in Salisbury, Smith declared that "many of the leading personalities" of the African National Council had been officers in the banned Zimbabwe African People's Union (ZAPU) and the Zimbabwe African National Union (ZANU), both of which now had their headquarters in Zambia. Smith said that ZAPU and ZANU had claimed, over Zambian radio, "responsibility for the trouble in Shabani, for example, and the recent troubles at a mine near Salisbury."

The Republican Alliance and the Rhodesian National party, neither of which had seats in the House of Assembly, formed a right-wing united front against the Smith government at a mass rally in Salisbury Feb. 10.

The Rhodesian House of Assembly met Feb. 29 but adjourned until June 2 without debating the Anglo-Rhodesian proposals. A request for debate, made by the leader of the Center party's caucus of six black members, was rejected by Desmond Lardner-Burke, leader of the House and minister of justice, law and order.

Settlement rejection attacked—The rejections of the settlement proposals were assailed by some white leaders.

The chairman of the ruling Rhodesian Front party, Desmond Frost, told members of the Pearce commission Feb. 4 that black rejection of the settlement was "tantamount to a slap in the face for the European, resulting in a hardening of European opposition to the proposals." Frost warned that unless "the African shows some willingness to reciprocal cooperation with the European, I cannot in all honesty guarantee that the Rhodesian Front party will continue to support wholeheartedly the proposals as a package deal." He charged that "agitators and self-seekers" were "intimidating the African." Frost informed Lord Pearce: "The sooner your commission completes its task and returns to England, the sooner we shall be able to return to the peace and tranquillity that Rhodesia has enjoyed for the last decade."

Ex-Prime Minister Roy Welensky expressed alarm at a defeat of the settlement. He said Feb. 18: "I believe that in many respects a mortal blow will have been struck at the efforts of many Rhodesians who have tried to encourage the Africans to believe that the vote was something of importance and value which could eventually lead to political power. If the illiterate mass, that element of the community least able to understand the intricacies of a complicated constitutional proposition, are allowed to veto it on the advice of people who are, to say the least, suspect, then what is the value of the vote?"

Pearce team leaves Rhodesia. Lord Pearce, who had spent two months in Rhodesia testing the public's reaction to the Anglo-Rhodesian settlement proposals, ended his commission's work in Africa and flew back with other commission members to London, where they arrived March 12.

In a farewell radio broadcast in Salisbury March 10, Pearce thanked those who presented evidence to his commission, noting that the public's response was "most impressive." He added: "Not only the politically-minded whose views we expected to hear, but all sections of Rhodesian society have willingly presented their views. We are particularly grateful to the so-called silent majority who have not let their views go by default." (More than 75,000 letters re-

ceived by the Pearce commission had been sent to London March 6 for analysis.)

A Soviet view of the Pearce Commission and its activities was presented in the March 16 issue of the Soviet journal Krasnaya Zvezda (Red Star):

"The trip, made ... by a group of former British colonial officials, was a flagrant farce. The point is that it was clear from the very beginning that the African majority ... rejected the collusion between the Smith racialist clique and the Heath Tory cabinet. Yet those in London apparently hoped that the Pearce Commission, with pressure being brought to bear on the black population by the Rhodesian authorities, would manage to make the people of Zimbabwe approve the dirty deal aimed at perpetuating the rule of the racialist clique over the black population.

"Pressure was indeed brought to bear. The blood of many Africans ... was shed, and dozens of people were killed. Yet, this did not scare the Africans, who clearly expressed their condemnation of the collusion. ... It is noteworthy that according to Western correspondents, 'black demostrators shouting their last No' gathered at the Salisbury airport when the Pearce Commission was flying away.

"The desire of the Tory government to perpetuate the racialist rule in Rhodesia is prompted by the interests of British imperalism. ... And these interests are in preserving Rhodesia as a springboard for the struggle against the national-liberation movements in Africa. It is for this purpose that London is betraying the people of Zimbabwe...."

Members of the Pearce commission began several days of hearings in London March 20 to gather the opinions of Rhodesians living in Britain. Among those interviewed was Guy Clutton-Brock, deported by the Rhodesian government in 1971.

Smith vs. Pearce unit. Prime Minister Smith, at a May 8 news conference, criticized the Pearce Commission, which had several days earlier delivered to British Foreign Secretary Sir Alec Douglas-Home its verdict on the acceptability of proposals for a Rhodesian settlement to the people of that country as a whole.

Smith said the investigation conducted by members of the Pearce team was "one of the most ridiculous things I have ever seen in my life. It was a complete and utter farce. . . . We advised them against carrying out this test, but they knew more about Rhodesia than we did evidently and decided that they were going to go on with it."

He said that at one point "it was even intimated to us that in some ways it might be desirable if the Rhodesian government remained aloof from this exercise, because by taking part in the exercise certain people might have got hold of the wrong end of the stick. . . . It was only after a few weeks when they [the Pearce commissioners] saw things going wrong that they came round and said: Well, perhaps we should have accepted your right advice and listened to you, and they were then more ready to do so, but unfortunately it was a bit too late then."

A questioner asked Smith whether voting or saying "No" on the part of blacks, as was advised "by Garfield Todd and others," had influenced the Pearce Commission's verdict. Smith replied: "I think it may have had some effect, but quite frankly the main problem was that over 90% of the Africans did not know what it was all in aid of. Ninety per cent of them don't even know what a constitution means. So how you can explain to them what is commonly termed one of the most complicated constitutions in the world is just beyond my reckoning." Smith said he thought the Pearce team had met with "less than 10%" of the black population.

The Rhodesian leader explained his concept of majority rule: "What I believe I have said on many, many occasions was that I have no objection to majority rule as long as this is responsible majority rule. I was opposed to irresponsible majority rule based on one man, one vote. We have always had majority rule in Rhodesia, and after all, today I represent the majority of the electorate in Rhodesia—the Rhodesian Front does. This has always been my qualification—if it's irresponsible majority rule,

if it's the counting of heads, if it's black majority rule just because they are black, I am opposed to this. Now, I believe that even under the new constitution we had negotiated conditions which would have ensured responsible majority rule the same as we have under the present constitution."

·**Pearce Commission finds pact unaccepted.** The Pearce Commission, reporting on Rhodesians' reactions to the constitutional and racial proposals negotiated by British and white Rhodesian leaders in 1971, declared that the "people of Rhodesia as a whole do not regard the proposals as acceptable as a basis for independence."

British Foreign Secretary Sir Alec Douglas-Home presented the Pearce findings to the House of Commons May 23 and said that as a result of the Pearce report Britain's economic sanctions against the rebel colony would remain in force. Douglas-Home implied that Britain would continue its efforts to reach a settlement with the Salisbury government.

In his remarks May 23, Douglas-Home asserted that "anyone who tries to re-establish in Rhodesia the basis for a multiracial society" faced a choice between "a compromise settlement which by definition will not wholly satisfy anyone, but which will gain for the Africans substantial new opportunities for advancement, and a rapid and complete polarization of the races and the prospect of conflict. . . . It may be that on further reflection the majority of Rhodesians, African and European, will decide to choose the way of compromise and to work together for orderly political change. . . . Although the proposals have failed to gain acceptance, they still represent a genuine attempt to find a sensible and in all the circumstances a just solution of Rhodesia's special social and political problems."

He said Britain was interested in seeing that "plenty of time should be given in which the position can be clarified and that meanwhile no door should be closed. . . . We feel that the best atmosphere for constructive discussions and advance will be provided if we maintain the situation as it is today, including sanctions, until we can judge whether or not an opportunity for a satisfactory settlement will occur."

In the question period following his speech, Douglas-Home was asked if the five principles evolved by successive British governments for settling the crisis would continue to apply and if blacks in Rhodesia would be brought into future consultations on the issue. He replied: "Any new proposals must be within the five principles. I would not like at this stage to commit myself exactly as to the method that will be used with the fifth principle [acceptability to Rhodesians as a whole] in future when we are looking at the matter entirely new and completely blind."

Black rejection seen genuine—In their 50,000-word report, the members of the Pearce commission explained their methods of canvassing opinion and of insuring that the proposals were "fully and properly explained to the population of Rhodesia."

The document said the commissioners had met Rhodesians both publicly and privately because "as much as we would have preferred to deal only with information which we could reveal publicly, we knew that in many cases truth would not be revealed except under the seal of confidence."

Most of the whites met by the commissioners accepted the proposals for economic reasons, declaring that the country needed some 40,000 new jobs a year in order to employ blacks. The report said this opinion "impressed us by its cogency and sincerity; and had we been considering what ought to be done as opposed to what people wanted we should have rated it highly indeed." The Colored (estimated 15,000) and Asian (estimated 9,000) communities accepted the proposals "reluctantly" and "in default of anything else."

The commissioners said they had interviewed some 6% of the black population over the age of 18, and the overwhelming majority rejected the settlement's terms. Although the Council of Chiefs had earlier registered its approval, a majority of the chiefs declared their opposition when interviewed in their villages and tribal areas. The report described the chiefs as persons who "cannot be said to be political leaders. In fact the evidence is that some of them and the majority of their people regard their embroilment in modern national politics as a serious embarrassment. They are unsuited for such a role, not only because they are mainly interested in their administrative and traditional duties but also because many of them are insufficiently educated to cope with the intelligent and sophisticated people who are accepted—we feel certain—by a great majority of Africans, particularly in the towns, as the political leaders of the country."

Giving the reasons for black rejection of the settlement, the commissioners declared: "Mistrust of the intentions and motives of the [Rhodesian] government transcended all other considerations. Apprehension for the future stemmed from resentment at what they felt to be the humiliations of the past and at the limitations of policies on land, education and personal advancement." Many blacks objected to their not having been consulted prior to the agreement. "Most refused to accept statements by the British government that there would be no further negotiations."

The commission dealt at length with charges on all sides that intimidation had been used to influence reaction to the proposals. It said there was "no evidence at all of any action by the Rhodesian government" to compel blacks to accept the agreement. However, in the case of four persons detained by the Salisbury regime the commissioners expressed reservations: former Prime Minister Garfield Todd, detained along with his daughter, Judith, and Joseph Chinamano and his wife, Ruth.

There was likewise "no real evidence" that the executive of the African National Council, the organization formed by blacks opposed to the settlement, had ordered violence "but the upsurge of political activity—so long banned—coinciding with the arrival of the commission led to situations in which agitators urged people to take part in violent demonstrations against authority.... We accept the allegation that during the disorders and rioting of the first fortnight there were a limited number of cases of serious intimidation against some who were likely to support the proposals." "It was our considered view that, had there been no intimidation, there would still have been a substantial majority against the proposals," the commission said.

Smith vs. report—Prime Minister Smith, in a nationwide address May 23, said the Pearce report was characterized by "naivete and ineptness" and "many misrepresentations and misconstructions of true positions."

Nonetheless, Smith said, he wished to inform the British government that "we are fully prepared to implement the [Anglo-Rhodesian] agreement if they will do so," although "there will be no negotiations with a view to changing any of the terms of the settlement." If the agreement could not be implemented, "we shall govern firmly and . . . not tolerate any attempt to disturb the peace and harmony to which, in very large measure, the country has returned since the departure of the Pearce Commission."

Smith declared he was not worried about a white backlash because "white Rhodesians are too mature and too sensible to allow their emotions to get the better of them." They would not "blame the ordinary decent African," who was "the biggest loser."

Smith said it was "difficult to see how the British government could in honor be party to the continuation of sanctions" against Rhodesia since their "declared purpose" was to "bring us to the negotiating table" with a view to reaching the kind of agreement the Pearce report negated.

(Smith's copy of the report had been handed to him May 17 by Sir Denis Greenhill, who, as permanent undersecretary at the Foreign Office, was head of the British diplomatic service.

(South African Prime Minister John Vorster described the Pearce report May 23 as a "tragic shock" but said that relations between Rhodesia and South Africa would not be influenced by it.)

Attitudes Harden

Smith denies U.K. talks. In a June 28, 1972 interview with the Rhodesian Broadcasting Corp., Prime Minister Ian Smith denied rumors that secret negotiations had been going on with a view to solving the independence dispute with Britain.

Smith said that after the British government's Pearce Commission had rejected the recent Anglo-Rhodesian proposals, he had offered to implement the proposals if Britain would do so. Since Britain refused to implement them, however, "that is the end of that particular offer." He said the next move toward a settlement would have to come from London.

U.N. action. The U.N. Security Council had held a special session Jan. 28–Feb. 4, 1972 in Addis Ababa, Ethiopia. It was the council's first session outside New York in 20 years and the first in Africa. Among proposals the council considered was a resolution, vetoed by Britain Feb. 4, that would have condemned the proposed British-Rhodesian settlement of 1971.

The resolution on Rhodesia, sponsored by Guinea, Sudan and Somalia, asked Britain, "as a matter of urgency, to desist from implementing" the agreement with the white-ruled Salisbury government and to convene "a constitutional conference in which the African people, through their genuine representatives, would be able to participate in the formulation of new proposals for the political and constitutional advancement of their country."

In announcing the veto, Sir Colin Crowe, Britain's delegate, remarked, "My government cannot accept a directive to change their policy while it is in the process of being worked out." The U.S., Japan, Belgium, Italy and France abstained. Nine countries, including China and the Soviet Union, supported the resolution. In debating the text Feb. 3, both China and the Soviet Union had accused Britain and the U.S. of being "allies of the white racist regimes" in Southern Africa. George Bush, the U.S. delegate, had replied: "I am going to resist turning this meeting into a name-calling contest. There's too much to be done."

The Security Council heard Feb. 1 from representatives of most of the African liberation movements in Southern Africa, including a spokesman for the Zimbabwe African National Union (ZANU), who read a letter smuggled from the Rhodesian prison where Ndabaningi Sithole, the group's leader, was being held. Sithole characterized the Anglo-Rhodesian agreement as "naive and unrealistic, but also basically dishonest in its conception and tragic in its consequences."

Two British parliamentarians told the council Jan. 30 that there had been a "massive and overwhelming rejection" of the settlement proposals by blacks in Rhodesia, although "whites, for different reasons, but almost universally, accept the terms." The men, Conservative Nigel Fisher and Laborite Maurice Foley, had just returned from six days in Rhodesia, where they claimed 133 members of the African National Council had been detained by the authorities. (The Rhodesian Ministry of Information asserted Jan. 31, "Only four people have been detained. Others have been arrested in connection with criminal offenses and their cases are being investigated. Some have already been tried and convicted, and some have been released.)

Rhodesian delegation visits Britain —Sir Alec Douglas-Home, British foreign secretary, received in London May 1 a delegation from the Rhodesian Center party led by Pat Bashford, its chairman.

Two Rhodesian government officials had met earlier with Douglas-Home, according to the London Times April 21. They were Attorney General E. A. T. Smith and J. G. Gaylard, secretary to the Cabinet.

Neither group was in contact with members of the Pearce Commission or its staff.

African Council to continue—The African National Council, which had worked for the rejection of the British-Rhodesian settlement, announced at a news conference in Salisbury March 10 its intention of continuing under the same name as an "organization," rather than a "political party," whose "main aim" would be the calling of a multiracial constitutional conference to negotiate a "just settlement" of Rhodesia's problems.

Bishop Abel T. Muzorewa, the group's leader, announced the names of 55 members of its national executive council, many of whom were former political detainees. There was also to be a central committee of 23 members. In a manifesto, which Muzorewa read, the group invited comparison with the banned African nationalist parties when it described itself as the heir to "the people's struggle which has ceaselessly been waged since the imposition of alien rule in 1890." The document explained: "We believe in a nonviolent, peaceful, orderly but permanent and continuing struggle to be waged within the law.... We challenge the people of this country to come out of the current political dream world by realizing that what has been called 'peace' and 'happiness' and 'good race relations' are, in fact, repressed fear, restless silence, forced tolerance and hidden hatred of one another."

Muzorewa repeated at an out-of-doors press conference in Salisbury May 24 his group's call for a national convention of all Rhodesians to work out constitutional reforms.

He said the gathering would be open to delegates from the ruling Rhodesian Front and from all other parties, labor, church and racial organizations. Observers from Britain, the United Nations and the Organization of African Unity (OAU) would be welcome.

Premier Smith said May 25 he would have "no truck" with the Council. He said "they present to me a picture of a bunch of unscrupulous politicians who have hoodwinked the poor African."

Pat Bashford, leader of the Center party, said he was in favor of a convention but "could not agree to outside participation or even the presence of outside observers in . . . a purely domestic affair."

Rhodesian Minister of Justice, Law and Order Desmond Lardner-Burke ruled June 6 that the African National Council was a "designated political party" and effectively barred from receiving money from foreign sources. The regulation said the Council could not take the money if, in the view of the Rhodesian government, "it appears likely that the receipt of such external funds will result in activities likely to cause an interference with public safety, the maintenance of public order and the preservation of peace."

The London Times reported Oct. 5 that the Rev. Ganaan Banana, ANC vice president, had said Oct. 4 that his group was "deeply disappointed" by the cancellation of talks that had been scheduled for Oct. 3 with Internal Affairs Minister Lance Smith.

Banana declared: "We suspect this must be the result of pressures from anti-settlement elements in the Rhodesian Front." He emphasized that his organization's negotiators would participate in future talks only as leaders of the African National Council and not as "African individuals who have problems."

U.K. stiffens terms. British Foreign Secretary Alec Douglas-Home stiffened the terms of a Rhodesian pact April 17, 1973. He said that an agreement to replace the one tentatively negotiated by Britain and the Rhodesian government in 1971 would have to be reached in direct talks between "responsible Africans and the Rhodesian administration" before Britain would consider proposals for further talks.

Britain had reportedly been under pressure to stiffen its stand from oil- and gas-rich Nigeria and from new labor governments in Australia and New Zealand.

Smith bars accord. Ian Smith said June 29, 1973 that no political settlement between Rhodesia's blacks and whites was likely "as long as Britain maintains the fiction that she can influence events here."

Smith's warning, in a speech to Parliament, came four days after a team of British diplomats led by Foreign Office Under Secretary Denis Greenhill completed an unannounced mission to Salisbury to ascertain the views of the Smith regime and of the black opposition, including the African National Council (ANC). British Prime Minister Alec Douglas-Home said in London June 27 that the views of the two parties had not changed, but that the Smith regime now realized the necessity of a settlement.

Smith said in the June 29 speech that a settlement would come when the "arrogant and obstinate" ANC and its sympathizers stopped counting on "their fairy godmother, the British government, and realize where the realities of power lie in Rhodesia." He said he did not intend to renew talks with Britain.

■ The National Association of Colored People, representing 16,000 persons of mixed racial descent, withdrew its support from the 1971 British-Rhodesia independence proposal, which had been opposed by most black groups, it was reported June 9.

(The formation in Rhodesia by black businessmen of a group called the African Settlement Convention was reported Feb. 12. The new organization, headed by George Charambarara, was seeking an end to the Anglo-Rhodesian constitutional dispute.)

Commonwealth leaders for majority rule. Leaders of 32 British Commonwealth nations, meeting in Ottawa, Canada in August 1973, called for action to end minority rule in Rhodesia.

The conference ended Aug. 10 with a final communique that supported majority rule in Rhodesia and expressed "intense concern" about the situation there. It also endorsed Britain's wish that discussions with Rhodesia be broadened to include "all representatives of Rhodesian opinion." A Rhodesian settlement plan proposed by some Caribbean and African leaders had been rejected because of opposition by Britain, which regarded it as an internal matter.

Black Guerrillas Attack

As the decade of the 1970s opened, nationalist guerrillas based in neighboring Zambia renewed attacks in Rhodesia.

Guerrillas resume raids. African guerrillas in January 1970 carried out their first infiltration attacks in Rhodesia since mid-1968.

One guerrilla force crossed the Zambezi River from Zambia Jan. 3 and attacked a Rhodesian patrol launch, wounding a policeman.

Rhodesian officials reported that another nationalist band Jan. 16 raided the Victoria Falls airport and a detachment of South African police there. One infiltrator was killed and four South Africans were wounded. The Zimbabwe African People's Union claimed in a statement issued in Lusaka, Zambia Jan. 18 that its forces had killed eight South Africans and five Rhodesian soldiers in the raid.

The government announced Jan. 26 that an African member of the Rhodesian security forces and three nationalists were killed in another battle in the Zambezi Valley. The insurgents were said to include members of a banned South African party, the African National Congress.

Rhodesian forces Feb. 2 reported killing another guerrilla in operations in the Zambezi Valley, bringing to 12 the number slain since Jan. 1. The Rhodesian forces were said to have lost two men during that period.

Prime Minister Smith had warned Feb. 1 that Rhodesia would take economic retaliation against Zambia if it continued to harbor and assist the guerrillas. A reply issued by Home Affairs Minister Lewis Changufu disavowed any Zambian responsibility for the clashes.

Smith warned the Zambians again Feb. 10, saying "we know that they are aware of the presence" of the anti-Rhodesian forces in Zambia.

Clash in 1971. In the first reports of clashes with guerrillas since early 1970, Rhodesian security police killed seven and wounded one member of FRELIMO, the Mozambique Liberation Front, according to a communique released in Salisbury Sept. 7, 1971.

The dispatch said the fighting had taken place Aug. 29 near Mukumbura on the Rhodesian side of the Mozambique-Rhodesian border when "terrorists" apparently looking for food had threatened the occupants of an African kraal. Security police responded to the "blatant transgression" of the border by firing on the intruders.

The London Times said Sept. 9 that a FRELIMO spokesman in Dar es Salaam had dismissed the Salisbury report as "utter nonsense." He said: "Our war is conducted inside Mozambique for the liberation of Mozambique."

(Twenty black Rhodesians were reported July 3 to have been taken into police custody that week when authorities discovered a cache of military equipment in a Salisbury warehouse.)

Rhodesia-Zambia border violence. Rhodesia closed its border with Zambia to all road and rail traffic Jan. 9, 1973 in apparent retaliation for the killing of two South African policemen near the border Jan. 8.

The policemen, who were aiding Rhodesian security forces in patrols against black nationalist guerrillas, were killed near Victoria Falls when their vehicle struck a land mine. Five other persons, including two more South Africans, were injured. A government spokesman explained that pamphlets "emanating from a terrorist organization operating from within Zambia were found at the scene of the incident."

Closure of the frontier was to be maintained, according to the spokesman, until Zambia gave "satisfactory assurances" it would take action against the guerrillas. The only exceptions to the ban would be international travelers and freight cars bearing Zambia's copper exports.

The South African Transport Ministry announced Jan. 10 that the nation's railroads would honor a Rhodesian request not to ship freight bound for Zambia.

Zambian President Kenneth D. Kaunda said Jan. 10 that his country would maintain "solidarity with those gallant people struggling for their freedom" in southern Africa. He added: "We cannot be passive observers to a situation that daily affects our people, particularly on our long borders. We have already suffered the consequences of our geographical proximity to the den of iniquity and mass exploitation." (The Zambian government had confirmed July 10, 1971 that it had been required by domestic food shortages to order 1.5 million bags of maize from Rhodesia in direct breach of U.N. sanctions against Rhodesia.)

Political organizations in Rhodesia opposed the government's move Jan. 10. The right-wing United Front said the regime of Premier Ian Smith had taken half-measures in exempting Zambian copper from the ban. The newly-formed Rhodesia party said the move amounted to "focusing attention on another country when much is wrong internally." A similar condemnation was expressed by the African National Council.

A Zambian government spokesman said Jan. 11 that Zambia would no longer export copper by rail through Rhodesia.

A Central Bank of Zambia directive Jan. 11 suspended all foreign currency dealings with both Rhodesia and South Africa, which had announced it would hold up rail freight destined for Zambia.

In revealing that copper would be exported by other means, primarily the 1,000-mile truck route to Tanzania, the spokesman called on the Organization of African Unity and the United Nations to "take appropriate measures to deal with Rhodesia's provocative act." He said "the right of landlocked countries to have access to the sea must be observed by all civilized countries."

Kenyan Foreign Minister Njoroge Mungai said Jan. 12 his country would make available the port of Mombasa for the handling of Zambian goods. He denounced Rhodesia's closure of the border, saying it would have no effect on the activities of black guerrillas there, which was purportedly the reason for the move.

Ghana's head of state, Col. Ignatius K. Acheampong, urged black nations Jan. 13 to take "concerted action" on Zambia's behalf, adding: "Let our brothers in Zimbabwe [Rhodesia] and Zambia take one white Rhodesian each and they will be liquidated in a matter of days."

South African Prime Minister John Vorster, in a radio address Jan. 19, criticized Rhodesia's closure of the border.

Although Vorster condemned Zambia's support of terrorists, he said South Africans "do not initiate boycotts, and we do not reply to sanctions with counter-boycotts."

The U.N. Security Council Feb. 2 voted, 13–0 (the U.S. and U.K. abstaining) to ask Britain to act to end Rhodesia's "economic blockade, blackmail and military threats" against Zambia. The resolution called on Britain to take "effective measures" to halt repression in Rhodesia by the "illegal and racist regime." It also authorized dispatch of a four-man team to assess the Zambian situation.

Three Zambians were killed in two separate landmine explosions Jan. 12. Both blasts occurred in Zambian territory—one near Kazungula on the border with the Caprivi Strip area of Namibia (South-West Africa), the other near Chirundu, close to the main bridge crossing the border into Rhodesia. Andre Kapuman, a Rhodesian citizen, was charged in a Lusaka court Jan. 20 with helping Rhodesian soldiers plant the land mines that exploded at Chirundu.

A Zambian spokesman said Jan. 19 that he was "absolutely certain" that 4,000 white South African troops had arrived in Rhodesia to help the government in its effort to round up guerrillas. The spokesman was replying to a denial of the charge the previous day by Adm. Hugo Biermann, commandant-general of the South African defense force.

Rhodesian security forces announced Jan. 24 that three South African policemen had been slightly injured in the recent explosion of a land mine at an undesignated place.

In a Jan. 28 interview in Salisbury, Rhodesian Premier Ian Smith dismissed as "a blatant lie" charges that his troops had crossed the Zambian border in an effort to deal with guerrillas. Smith called the accusations "something they have sucked out of the end of their thumbs" which was "in keeping with the behavior we have grown to expect from these people."

Smith defended his failure to inform South Africa and Portugal before closing the Zambian border. To have done so, he said, would have been a "diplomatic blunder" making it hard for South Africa to avoid the charge of having initiated the closure and creating a precedent obliging South Africa and Portugal to consult with Rhodesia on future decisions.

Radio Uganda Jan. 29 said President Idi Amin had placed the country's armed forces on alert to defend Zambia against an attack from Rhodesia.

U.N. censure sought—Zambia asked the U.N. Security Council Jan. 29, 1973 to condemn Rhodesia for its "grave acts of aggression" and for threats that could lead to a "Vietnam situation" in southern Africa.

Paul Lusaka, the Zambian delegate, repeated his country's charge that South Africa had dispatched 4,000 troops to help the Rhodesian government, saying the "real reason" for the move was to "stem nationalist feeling, which is sweeping through all of southern Africa."

Christopher H. Phillips, a U.S. representative, criticized Rhodesia's closure of its border with Zambia in a Security Council speech Jan. 31. Phillips also declared the U.S. believed economic sanctions against Rhodesia "should be maintained and tightened."

Zambia border 'reopened'—Rhodesian authorities announced Feb. 3, 1973 that the Zambian border would be reopened Feb. 4. Rhodesia had awaited "satisfactory assurances" that Zambia would withdraw its support from black guerrillas.

In announcing the border opening, a Rhodesian government dispatch said only that as "a result of messages which have been received" officials were "satisfied that their objectives in closing the Zambian border have been achieved."

Kenneth Kaunda, the Zambian president, strongly denied Feb. 4 the implication that his government had sent messages to Rhodesian Premier Ian Smith. Kaunda said he had "given no undertaking to Smith," whom he described as "not a reliable man." The Zambian leader added that his country's border with Rhodesia would remain closed and that recent arrangements to reroute copper exports would be permanent. (Zambia

cut telephone, telegraph and telex links with Rhodesia Feb. 6.)

Zambian President Kaunda flew home from Tanzania Feb. 5 after less than a day of a scheduled three-day conference with Zaire President Mobutu Sese Seko and Tanzanian President Julius K. Nyerere. The men had met at Arusha to discuss the Zambian-Rhodesian problem but no details of the talks were released.

Smith said Feb. 8 that before making the decision to reopen the border, he had been given assurances by an "honest broker" that Zambia would do all it could to prevent terrorist raids into Rhodesia. (The British Foreign Office refused to say Feb. 9 whether Britain was the intermediary but it denied the function had been performed by Richard Wood, minister of overseas development and a recent visitor to Zambia.)

Kaunda accused Smith Feb. 8 of using "Nazi tactics" by "creating lies—and sticking to them." Kaunda repeated earlier declarations that he had maintained no contact with Smith over the border issue.

The 20th ministerial conference of the Organization of African Unity (OAU) ended five days of work Feb. 9 in Addis Ababa, Ethiopia. Emperor Haile Selassie of Ethiopia had told the opening session Feb. 5 that Rhodesia's closure of its border with Zambia, "aimed at the economic strangulation of that country," was "yet another testimony of the conspiracy of colonial regimes to subvert independent African states."

Zambia-Rhodesia incidents continue—A Rhodesian civilian on a fishing trip in the Zambezi River with two other persons was killed by machine-gun fire Feb. 9 from the river's north shore, the Rhodesian Information Ministry said. The man, whose companions were wounded in the incident, was identified as Winston Austin from Que Que. Zambia denied responsibility for the incident Feb. 11.

A Rhodesian Railways engineer was arrested by Zambia at Victoria Falls Feb. 25 when he crossed the bridge separating the two countries. Rhodesia announced Feb. 26 it was suspending mail services with Zambia until the man was returned.

According to an account of the incident in the London Times Feb. 27, the employe, identified as John Smith, had connected his locomotive to a train of Rhodesian freight cars that had been moved to the center of the dividing bridge by Zambian railway officials. Smith was arrested, the Times said, when he left the locomotive and walked toward the Zambian side to inspect what he thought was a malfunction in the braking system.

Smith was released by Zambia March 4. He was freed after a March 2 statement by Gibson Chigaga, Zambian director of public prosecutions, that there was insufficient evidence to bring a case against Smith. Trevor Wright, general manager of Rhodesian Railways, said March 4 that the movement of rail traffic to and from Zambia would be resumed immediately.

A farm worked by white Rhodesians in the Mangula area, near the scene of earlier terrorist attacks, was partly destroyed Feb. 28 by raiders who set fire to the sleeping quarters.

2 Canadians killed near Zambia—Two Canadian women tourists were killed and an American tourist was wounded by gunfire from Zambia May 15 while visiting the Rhodesian side of Victoria Falls.

Zambia said May 18 that the three had been shot by a single Zambian sentry in the belief that they were on their way to attack a nearby power station. Zambia President Kenneth Kaunda said June 5 that the tourists had been "victims of a racist conspiracy to involve Zambia in a nasty incident." He charged that if they had been unmolested "then the next visitors to the gorge would have been commandos." Zambia noted in a statement at the U.N. May 30 that the Zambezi River frontier had been tense since Rhodesia closed the border.

Carol Crothers, the wife of the American victim, who was with him at the time, said May 17 that the tourist party had come under heavy fire from various angles for two and a half hours.

The parents of the dead women were offered compensation by Kaunda, according to reports June 13.

Smith on situation. In a radio broadcast Jan. 18, 1973, Rhodesian Prime Minister Smith admitted that Rhodesian blacks were supporting nationalist guerrillas who had entered the country recently from Mozambique.

Smith declared that for months terrorists had been "quietly and methodcially undermining the local population" by "intimidation at the point of a gun" and by bribing "a few witchdoctors of doubtful character."

As far as Zambia's connection with the guerrillas was concerned, Smith said Lusaka had "openly admitted" supporting the "international gangsters." In view of this, he said, the "pathetic wailing of the Zambian government" at Rhodesia's closing of the border "rings a particularly hollow note."

Smith claimed the Kaunda government was afraid to take action against the guerrillas, although "President Kaunda has already had occasion to arrest a large number of Rhodesian terrorists because they were siding with Zambians opposed to his government. For over a year now they have been incarcerated in a Zambian prison. Moreover, a batch of these prisoners were handed over to the Rhodesian authorities through mutual agreement at about the same time."

(The London Times reported Jan. 23 that the Zambian president, interviewed by BBC that weekend, had told of the arrest of 36 Zambians allegedly recruited by "a Zambian political party to help Smith's men." Kaunda reportedly called them "treasonable fellows who are able to sell our own country to our enemies.")

Attacks from Mozambique. The March 1973 issue of Africa Report, published in New York by the African-American Institute, carried a dispatch in which journalist Peter Niesewand outlined the situation facing Rhodesian security forces along the country's northeastern border with Mozambique.

Niesewand contended the recent guerrilla incursions were carried out by ZANU (Zimbabwe African National Union) terrorists operating "in an extremely sophisticated manner" from Mozambique Liberation Front (FRELIMO) bases "so well equipped and entrenched that they even have cinema shows." The ZANU guerrillas had not entered Rhodesia from Zambia, Niesewand maintained, although ZAPU (Zimbabwe African People's Union) operatives regularly crossed from Zambia to plant land mines in Rhodesia.

Prime Minister Smith's decision to reopen the border with Zambia, closed to protest the Lusaka government's support for Rhodesian terrorists, therefore had "no bearing on the situation in the northeast, as the guerrillas there crossed from Mozambique." Niesewand continued:

"Had Mr. Smith felt able to disclose that the Portuguese territory had become self-sufficient as a rebel base, and that the insurgents operating in the northeast had never touched Zambia at all, he would not have lost as much political credibility internally. But on the other hand, he would have angered the Portuguese authorities, who are extremely touchy about their conduct of the Mozambique war, and who vehemently deny that FRELIMO is in control of any territory at all. Yet this is the position—and Mr. Smith chose to protect the Portuguese sensibilities, rather than his own political back."

In an anti-guerrilla move, Rhodesia was reported Jan. 6 to have moved additional army units to Centenary, in the northeast part of the country about 40 miles from the Mozambique border, following the killing in December 1972 of two members of a black guerrilla group that had fired on a local farmhouse and wounded a young girl.

Defense Minister Jack Howman, who had extended the period of national service in December from nine months to one year, said Jan. 6 that Rhodesia was also policing its border with Botswana because of "undoubted evidence of terrorists" operating from that country.

Another raid in the Mozambique border area, this one east of Centenary at Mt. Darwin Village, took place Jan. 8. A security force dispatch said only that a bridge had been "slightly damaged" and that an attack on the village had been "unsuccessful."

Two Rhodesian government land inspectors were machine-gunned to death and a third was kidnapped Jan. 12 near Mt. Darwin, scene of a guerrilla raid earlier in the week. An official statement said only that terrorist action "could not be discounted" as an explanation for the incident.

Guerrillas operating in the area near the Mozambique border, where previous attacks had taken place, killed a farmer's wife and wounded her husband Jan. 24.

The guerrilla attack took place 10 miles northeast of Centenery. The London Times Jan. 27 said more than 100 white farmers had asked the government to take "immediate action" against a local mission run by German Jesuit priests after the reported discovery nearby of a guerrilla base camp.

Guerrillas operating Feb. 4 in northeastern Rhodesia near the scene of earlier fighting conducted a grenade attack against a local farm, killing Leslie Jellicoe, who had been in the country from Britain visiting his son. Police were reported Feb. 7 to have closed black schools, shops and businesses in tribal lands adjoining the farm.

The New York Times Feb. 28 published what it described as unconfirmed reports that Rhodesian Air Force jets had strafed suspected guerrilla bases the previous weekend in the Centenary area bordering Mozambique.

Guerrillas entering Rhodesia from Mozambique killed two more white farmers:

Andries Hendrick Joubert was shot March 30 on his farm at Wedza, 65 miles southeast of Salisbury. Four armed blacks later held up a farm store several miles away. An April 2 communique from Security Force headquarters said one terrorist had been killed and another captured as a result of government operations in the Wedza area.

Delville Joseph Vincent was killed April 4 on his farm between Umvukwes and Centenary near the scene of earlier terrorist activity.

In the same area, four Rhodesian soldiers were killed in an ambush by guerrillas near the Mozambique border, it was announced April 24. Three guerrillas were killed and several captured in the engagement, but, for the first time, surviving guerrillas managed to escape over the Mozambique or Zambia borders.

Children kidnapped. Several incidents were reported during 1973 of guerrillas kidnapping African children with the intention of training them to be guerrillas.

Guerrillas kidnapped 282 children, teachers and nurses in two raids on a Roman Catholic mission in northern Rhodesia July 6, avowedly to train the children as guerrillas outside Rhodesia. Rhodesian security forces rescued all but 20 of those kidnapped by the next day.

Guerrillas raiding from Mozambique kidnapped 93 more children and young villagers in September, but 62 were reported freed by security forces by Sept. 18.

Other 1973 developments. Among other 1973 developments involving the increasing violence in Rhodesia:

Rhodesia was reported Feb. 12 to have imposed its first collective fines against blacks suspected of helping guerrillas. Fines of $100, paid in cattle, were collected from a village in the Chiweshe tribal trust land, adjacent to Centenary, where schools and shops had been closed "for security reasons." A tribal leader, Chief Makope, was arrested.

An organizer for the African National Council, Sonny Hlangwane, was sentenced March 27 to five months in prison on charges of making a subversive statement at a meeting in Gwelo in December 1972.

After their trial and conviction, three guerrillas were sentenced to death March 30 in Salisbury for possessing "arms of war." The men said they had been told "we were going to fight for the redemption of the people. We were not told to select isolated farmsteads. We were sent to fight armed soldiers." They were hanged in Salisbury prison June 22. Three other blacks had been hanged in Salisbury May 21 after being convicted of murder for a guerrilla attack in December 1972.

After another trial, a Salisbury court sentenced George John Murtagh to six years in jail April 4 for harboring two guerrillas, one of them his brother. All three men were Colored.

Rhodesia confirmed July 11 that South African military helicopters were being used in Rhodesia security operations, as "normal back-up aircraft for South African police in this country."

Zambia charged Aug. 9 that Rhodesian troops had driven "several score" African villagers into Zambia by indiscriminate shootings in retaliation for support to rebels.

The London Observer charged Sept. 2 that Rhodesian troops, helicopters and bombers had systematically killed Mozambique civilians in an attempt to cut off supplies for the guerrillas. Lisbon had denied that any Rhodesian or South African troops were involved in the war, it was reported Aug. 24.

Rhodesia had called up reserve units July 25, while continuing to give military training to civilians, including white women in the Northeast.

Terrorists shot an African headman and hijacked four buses at the northeastern border, it was reported Aug. 20. It was thought to be the first time terrorists had hijacked buses.

Five blacks were executed Oct. 21 and Dec. 14 for killings connected with the rebellion.

Parliament approved a bill Nov. 8 providing the death penalty or life imprisonment for anyone who harbored rebels, failed to report their presence, or recruited or trained them. The law had been opposed by opposition black members of Parliament.

1974 guerrilla-related events. A security forces aircraft used for insurgency reconnaissance was shot down by guerrillas Jan. 7, 1974.

A paper published by the London based Institute for Strategic Studies claimed that Moscow and Peking had been providing training, armaments and financial assistance to the rebels, the London Observer reported Jan. 26. In attacks since 1972, guerrillas had used land mines, machine guns, automatic rifles, and 122 mm. rockets, demonstrating a growing technical and strategic sophistication.

A new military recruitment program announced Feb. 6 doubled the size of the army draft and instituted other measures to insure a bigger security force.

Guerrilla operations had changed the role of the army from a defensive to offensive unit, a government statement said.

Minister of Internal Affairs Lance Smith said a special militia, armed with shotguns, "the most effective anti-terrorist weapon for a civilian," would be formed on the Tribal Trust land reserved for Africans, it was reported Feb. 23.

Meanwhile, rebel casualties mounted. Sixteen guerrillas were killed during the last week of February as security forces increased offensive sorties after three white farmers in the northeast Centerary region were killed by rebels Feb. 18. Two more rebels were hung in Salisbury March 1.

Four members of special South African police force groups were killed and a fifth was missing in a clash with Zambia-based guerrillas in Rhodesia March 1. The South African government acknowledged in a March 8 report that its police forces had been assisting Rhodesian counter-insurgent operations, but denied that its army was involved. Two South African policemen and two members of the Rhodesian security forces were killed in a skirmish with Rhodesian guerrillas in the northeast Oct. 1.

A scale of cash rewards—up to more than $8,000—was announced April 17 for information leading to the death or capture of rebel insurgents. Such rewards had long been government policy, Deputy Minister J. L. de Kock said, but this was the first time the scale had been made public.

A U.S. mission school in the northeast closed following an April 11 guerrilla raid, it was reported April 19. Two African staff members were killed in the attack.

Twenty guerrillas were killed in a clash near Mount Darwin May 19. Army and police units were supported by air force planes in the confrontation which claimed the lives of several leaders of the Zimbabwe African National Union (ZANU). Seven children and four civilians "believed to be terrorists" were also killed during the incident, the government acknowledged May 31.

Security forces killed two civilians in the area June 4 and 12 rebels June 21. The government reported June 21 that 78 guerrillas had been killed since March. Fourteen rebels were killed in the Mount Darwin area in mid-August, it was reported Aug. 15, by Rhodesian security forces reinforced by aircraft strafing.

The government announced June 7 that five black guerrillas had been hanged in Salisbury.

The Lusaka, Zambia headquarters of the Zimbabwe African National Union (ZANU), one of Rhodesia's two major liberation movements, was blown up Oct. 1. A ZANU spokesman charged that the Rhodesian government was responsible for the bombing.

A police spokesman said Oct. 26 that 10,000 white police reservists were being recruited to patrol their own residential areas at night. Aimed at preventing urban guerrilla actions, the forces would be concentrated in Salisbury and Bulawayo.

Security forces killed 13 guerrillas in the northeast, Salisbury announced Oct. 30, bringing to 438 the number reported killed since the current campaign began in December 1972.

A United Nations special commission reported Dec. 9 that Rhodesian soldiers had joined Portuguese troops in massacres of black Africans in western Mozambique over the past three years. The report, issued in New York, said that some villages had been totally destroyed, among them Wiriyamu, where 200 persons were reported killed. The Rhodesians were said to have entered Mozambique with Portuguese permission to pursue and kill rebel groups.

Guerrillas Supported

Church grants to guerrilla groups. The World Council of Churches announced Sept. 3, 1970 the grant of $200,000 to groups fighting racism, including African liberation movements. The decision was made by the council's executive committee at a meeting near Frankfurt, Germany.

A "Special Fund to Combat Racism" would issue grants of $2,500 to $20,000 to each of 19 organizations. They included two Rhodesian groups—the Zimbabwe African National Union and the Zimbabwe African People's Union.

Reaction in South Africa and Rhodesia by churchmen and political figures was uniformly against the decision.

OAU to aid guerrillas. The liberation committee of the Organization of African Unity (OAU) met in Kampala, Uganda May 15–22, 1972 and agreed on ways to help the Rhodesian guerrillas. George Magombe, the committee's executive secretary, revealed May 21 that, in its first such action, the OAU would give military and financial aid to "all military cadres" active in Rhodesia. This was to include both the ZAPU-ZANU joint military command (recently formed) and the separate Front for the Liberation of Zimbabwe (FROLIZI), which had been established earlier.

U.N. support. In an action seen as supporting the Rhodesian and similar guerrilla groups, the U.N. General Assembly voted Nov. 2, 1972 in favor of recognizing the "legitimacy" of anticolonial armed struggles. The resolution, passed 99–5, also called on the U.N., its world agencies and all countries to withhold all assistance from Rhodesia, Portugal and South Africa, and urged colonial powers to withdraw military installations from colonial territories.

The resolution was opposed by the U.S., Portugal, South Africa, Great Britain and France. George Bush, the chief U.S. delegate, said after the vote that while the U.S. supported independence for colonial peoples, it felt support for "liberation armies" was contrary to the U.N. Charter.

The General Assembly also approved Nov. 2 three resolutions seeking support against colonialism outside the U.N., opposed only by Portugal and South Africa. One called for expanded dissemination by the U.N. of information on colonialism; another, for U.N. co-sponsorship, with the Organization of African Unity, of a 1973 conference to speed the end of colonialism and of official policies of racial separation; and a third, for an annual "week of solidarity" with African colonies in their fight "for freedom, independence and equal rights."

Iraqi financial aid. Financial aid to the Rhodesian guerrillas was promised by Iraq in 1974.

Baghdad Radio announced March 28 that Iraq had contributed $60,000 to the insurgency movement in Rhodesia.

Rebel Problems & Progress

ZAPU members kidnaped. Two senior officials and 19 other members of the Zimbabwe African Peoples Union (ZAPU) were reported kidnapped March 11, 1971 from the guerrilla organization's headquarters in Lusaka, Zambia.

Edward Ndhlovu, ZAPU's deputy national secretary, said the kidnapings had been carried out by a "group of ZAPU dissidents who have always refused to go to the front and have been masquerading [as guerrillas] in Lusaka for some time." Ndhlovu said the dissidents "have recently been holding a series of secret meetings in and near Lusaka aimed at frustrating the desire of the majority of ZAPU members in Zambia to hold a conference at which differences in the ZAPU leadership would be ironed out once and for all for the benefit of the armed struggle."

(It was reported Feb. 22 that the Liberation Committee of the Organization of African Unity [the OAU] had threatened to cut off aid to ZAPU unless the organization settled its leadership disputes.)

Rival groups merge. The two major Rhodesian rebel groups with offices in

Lusaka, Zambia agreed to join forces under a single leadership Oct. 1, 1971. The merger was between the Zimbabwe African People's Union (ZAPU) and the Zimbabwe African National Union (ZANU) to form the Front for the Liberation of Zimbabwe (FROLIZI). Shelton Siwela, 29, a former guerrilla commander with ZAPU, was elected chairman of the new group's Revolutionary Command Council, which included former Vice President James Chikerema and former National Secretary George Nyandoro (from ZAPU) and former Foreign Affairs Secretary Nathan Shamuyarira (from ZANU).

Edward Ndhlovu, who had served as ZAPU's deputy national secretary, denounced the new group Oct. 1 because it "does not have either the blessings of the peoples of Zimbabwe or those of their leadership" and because it was short of "the necessary military power which all true revolutionary movements cannot do without."

ZAPU and ZANU announced in Dar es Salaam, Tanzania March 23, 1972 that they had formed a "joint military command" which would plan "revolutionary war" in Rhodesia.

Zambia deports Rhodesian blacks. The Zambian government-owned Daily Mail reported Dec. 14, 1971 that 129 presumed members of the Rhodesian black liberation movement had been deported to Rhodesia because they were working for that country's security services.

The paper said Rhodesian Prime Minister Ian D. Smith was preparing the men for new intelligence work and had ordered that their court cases be held in secret.

Other sources reported that the deportations, believed to have taken place in August, had occurred partly because of rivalry among different liberation organizations and to some degree because some of the guerrillas had supported plans for forming a new Zambian opposition, the United Progressive Party (UPP).

Joint political unit. The two black Rhodesian rebel groups headquartered in Lusaka, Zambia announced the formation of a joint political council March 17, 1973 after four days of talks.

The council would be responsible for diplomatic activity and public relations. A joint military command, which had failed to promote unity between the two organizations, was to be revived.

The agreement was signed by Herbert Chitepo of the Zimbabwe African National Union (ZANU) and Jason Moyo of the Zimbabwe African People's Union (ZAPU). Each group was apparently to continue functioning on its own, while the united front made common policy.

Representatives of Ghana, Kenya, Tanzania, Cameroon and Zambia attended the talks, held under the auspices of the Organization of African Unity (OAU).

Four black nationalist groups unite— Rhodesia's four black nationalist movements signed an agreement, the Zimbabwe Declaration of Unity, in Lusaka Dec. 9, 1974 to unite into a single body and to "struggle for the total liberation of Zimbabwe." This development followed the rejection by the Rhodesian government of a preliminary set of peace proposals submitted to the government at the Lusaka talks; the groups subsequently reached agreement with the government for a cease-fire and release of detainees.

The purpose of the agreement was to bring the ANC, ZANU, ZAPU and the Front for the Liberation of Zimbabwe (Frolizi) together, with the ANC acting as an umbrella organization within which the groups would "merge their respective organs and structures." (Particular difficulty had been encountered at the Dec. 4–6 Lusaka talks in bridging the decade-long rift between ZAPU and ZANU, the latter being the more militant organization, responsible for maintaining the guerrilla warfare in northern Rhodesia.)

The seven-point document stated that the movements' four leaders—the ANC's Bishop Abel Muzorewa, ZAPU's Joshua Nkomo, ZANU's Rev. Ndabaningi Sithole and Frolizi's James Chikerema— "recognized the inevitability of continued armed struggle until the total liberation of Zimbabwe" and pledged to hold a congress within four months to adopt a constitution, establish policy and choose a leadership for "the united people of Zimbabwe."

ZANU leader killed in Zambia blast. Herbert Chitepo, a leader of the Zimbabwe African National Union (ZANU), was killed in Lusaka March 18, 1975 when his car backed over a landmine planted in his driveway. Killed along with the 52-year-old Rhodesian nationalist, who served as representative outside Rhodesia for the African National Congress (ANC), were one of his two bodyguards and a two-year-old child.

Within hours of the assassination, the ANC issued a statement declaring that Chitepo's death, together with the arrest March 4 of Ndabaningi Sithole, ZAPU leader, had "shattered irreparably the exercise of detente and a negotiated settlement for Rhodesia." ZANU leader Robert Mugabe told a press conference that the slaying was "undoubtedly the evil work" of the Rhodesian government. However, according to a Reuters report March 19, there were indications that Chitepo had been killed by rival elements within the ZANU organization.

Chitepo was buried in Lusaka March 22, Salisbury having denied permission for the burial to take place in Rhodesia. Zambian President Kenneth Kaunda attended the ceremonies.

Zambian Home Affairs Minister Aaron Milner said March 28 that several Rhodesian black nationalists had been arrested in Lusaka in connection with the Zambian investigation of Chitepo's death. More than 50 ZANU officials had been seized at Chitepo's Lusaka home on the evening of his funeral March 22, Claude Chokwenda, ZANU's representative to the Nordic countries, said in Stockholm March 27.

Milner also announced that the Zambia offices of ZANU, the Zimbabwe African People's Union (ZAPU) and the Front for the Liberation of Zimbabwe (Frolizi) would be closed. Only the African National Council (ANC), into which the other three groups had agreed to merge, would be allowed to operate.

The decision to crack down on the more militant liberation groups was believed in-

tended to enhance the possibilities of getting constitutional talks under way between the Rhodesian government and representatives of the black majority.

12 dead in ZANU, Zambian clash. Eleven members of the Zimbabwe African National Union (ZANU) and a Zambian army officer died Sept. 11, 1975 in an outbreak of factional fighting in Zambia, the Zambian government announced Sept. 16.

The government statement said Zambian soldiers had intervened to prevent fighting at a ZANU guerrilla camp near Kabwe, about 70 miles north of Lusaka, but were themselves attacked. In addition to the 12 dead, 13 persons were reported wounded in the subsequent clash.

Zambian President Kenneth Kaunda Sept. 16 denounced the fractious ZANU group for causing turmoil in its host country. Zambia had earlier moved representatives of the African National Council (ANC) from guest facilities within the capital to government quarters at Mulungushi, a village on the outskirts of Lusaka. ANC President Bishop Abel Muzorewa had been banned Sept. 11 from delivering statements to the press while on Zambian soil.

Political & Racial Curbs

Church vs. race rules. The newly enacted legislation further solidifying racial separation was assailed in a booklet published April 7, 1970 by the Roman Catholic Church in Rhodesia. The laws had taken effect on the proclamation of republican status for Rhodesia.

The document, written by five bishops, asserted that the church "will not compromise its principles or its conscience." It charged that the government had "entrenched separation and discrimination," and added, "the church refuses to be forced to behave as if it approved or acquiesced in racial discrimination."

The booklet was an amplification of a pastoral letter circulated by the five bishops March 22. It took particular issue with the Land Tenure Act, which divided Rhodesian land about equally between both races. The Rev. Richard Randolph, a Catholic spokesman, said the law would prevent the church from continuing interracial worship, schooling, medical care and other activities unless a government minister issued a permit "when it seems in his opinion desirable." This was in reference to a section of the act which forbade "occupation" of land by members of one race in the area set aside for another race. Randolph's statement recalled previous criticism of the law which said that its real purpose was to restrict or prohibit interracial worship, interracial education and black residence in white areas.

Although the government said it did not intend to use the Land Tenure Act to prevent the association of races, a government spokesman had said in parliamentary debate on the bill that in some instances "attendance" at public places might have to be defined as "occupation" if "racial friction is to be avoided."

Rhodesia's Catholic population totaled about 35,000 whites and 450,000 blacks.

The Catholic Church demanded April 29 the nullification of part of the Land Tenure Act that barred interracial worship and interracial association. Unless this were done, the church warned it would be forced to close all its schools, hospitals, orphanages and other social welfare institutions in the country.

The church warning was contained in a statement signed by the Most Rev. Francis Markall, archbishop of Salisbury, and the bishops of the four other Catholic dioceses of Rhodesia. The text was sent to each member of Prime Minister Ian D. Smith's cabinet.

The bishop's position had been supported at a meeting in Salisbury April 28 of leaders of the Catholic Church and 10 Protestant sects. A joint statement asserted that "the new constitution and the Land Tenure Act cannot be reconciled with the Christian faith, since they entrench separation and discrimination solely on the basis of race." Despite the racial restrictions of the act, the churches intend "to carry on their work in areas of either race," the statement said.

Lands Minister Philip van Heerden said April 30 that the Land Tenure Act did not prevent joint worship of blacks and whites.

The Rhodesian government Nov. 23, 1972 announced its intention of removing from the Land Tenure Act clauses which had threatened to curtail interracial religious activities. The clauses had required "voluntary associations" to apply for permission to own or lease land in racially designated areas and to declare themselves as being of one race or another.

The government statement said: "For some voluntary associations this presented no difficulty but for others, particularly the churches, it was manifestly impossible for them to say whether the majority of their members was black or white from day to day."

Asian curbs proposed. The Rhodesian government Nov. 26, 1970 made public a proposal for new legislation that would segregate the white community from the 23,000 Asians and persons of mixed race. The measure, the Property Owners' Residential bill, was patterned after the Land Tenure Act, which allocated equal areas for the five million black Africans and the country's 230,000 whites.

In announcing the measure, Local Government & Housing Minister Mark Partridge said it would authorize the Rhodesian president to set aside "exclusive" residential areas. The status of these restrictive zones would be declared if the government upheld an application of at least 15 property owners that contended their area was being infiltrated by persons of another "denomination."

A 14-man delegation representing the Asian and mixed-race communities met with Partridge after his news conference and later issued a statement denouncing the proposed legislation as a "vicious doctrine of apartheid." The multiracial Center party also assailed the bill, calling it "dangerously retrograde."

ANC membership cards seized. The Rhodesian government March 27, 1972 seized the first printing of an anticipated 250,000 membership cards belonging to the African National Council, which had recently decided to continue in existence as a black political organization.

In raiding the council's offices in Salisbury, Special Branch policemen brought with them a proclamation by President Clifford W. Dupont declaring the membership cards an "undesirable publication" under the Law and Order Maintenance Act. The proclamation further stated: "Since the date of its inception the African National Council has made extensive use of persons well known as having been associated with organizations banned for terrorism, violence, intimidation, subversion and rioting."

ANC branch office closed—A branch office of the ANC was closed June 21 and six of its officials arrested, according to Edison Sithole, the organization's publicity secretary. Sithole said the office, located about 60 miles from Salisbury at Mrewa, had been closed on the order of the local district commissioner. The London Times reported the following day that the Rhodesian government had confirmed the arrest of six men at Mrewa but denied knowing that they were officials of the council.

Outdoor meetings banned. Desmond Lardner-Burke, minister of justice, law and order, issued an order June 30, 1972 banning outdoor political meetings anywhere in the country, explaining that such gatherings had imposed an unnecessary strain on the police.

Pass law introduced. The government Nov. 17, 1972 introduced legislation requiring blacks over the age of 16 to carry identity cards similar to those used by both blacks and whites in South Africa. It was the fourth such measure put forward by the ruling Rhodesian Front since its party congress in September, when Prime Minister Ian Smith appeared to reject more apartheid-style laws for the country.

The new legislation, known as the Africans Registration and Identification (Amendment) Bill, provided for fines of $152 and six months in jail for failure to carry the proper documents at all times. It also stipulated that blacks wishing to leave the country must obtain permission from government registration officers.

The Rev. Canaan Banana, vice-chairman of the ANC, called the law "an abominable piece of legislation, designed to intimidate Africans into conniving with a corrupt system of government as perpetuated by a group of terrified little men."

Segregation—The government had ordered segregation of public swimming pools and had given notice that Salisbury's principal maternity hospital would not accept Asian or colored patients (those of mixed racial ancestry) after the end of December.

Rhodesia's High Court Nov. 16 struck down regulations that had come into force earlier in the month limiting the hours during which blacks could drink at segregated bars in white areas. Under the bar restrictions, Africans would have been prevented from entering these drinking places after 7 p.m. on weekdays, after 1 p.m. on Saturday and at all hours on Sundays and holidays.

White immigration & black resettlement. Early in the 1970s, the Rhodesian government began an intensified program aimed at inducing Europeans (whites) to come to Rhodesia and settle on farms. At the same time, it embarked on a program of removing black Africans from farm communities said to be endangered by guerrilla infiltrators and of resettling them in other parts of Rhodesia. The government justified these programs on economic and security grounds.

White immigration—According to the New York Times Jan. 2, 1971, the Smith government was offering 38 farms for occupancy by European settlers between the ages of 25 and 45. The farms, reportedly including a house, irrigation and electricity, varied in size from 300–400 acres each, with an additional 100 acres of undeveloped land to accomodate laborers.

Labor Minister Ian MacLean reported Nov. 15, 1973 that a tremendous decline in European immigration had caused a growing shortage of skilled labor. Emigration of whites had exceeded immigration by 100 in September, the first net decline since 1966. About 90,000 immigrants had arrived since independence was declared in 1965, bringing the white population to 270,000.

In an effort to reverse the trend of net white emigration, the government in late 1973 instituted a "Settler '74" program to attract a million skilled white immigrants. Rhodesia's six Roman Catholic bishops denounced the program Jan. 20, 1974 and called on the government to abandon such "racist policies." Nearly 7,000 whites had left Rhodesia in 1973; fewer than 2,500 arrived. Reasons given for the exodus included the danger from liberation forces and the uncertain political future.

Asked about the correlation between the sparse population of the northeast and the problem of security in the region, Prime Minister Ian Smith said in a March 21 interview: "We very soon realized vacant land was something which aided the terrorists . . . As a result of a definite effort on the part of the government, we have succeeded in getting good, young Rhodesians on to those vacant farms . . . The farmers do a terrific job for us in the security field simply by inhabiting the land."

Despite the "Settler '74" campaign, the Rhodesian government announced Jan. 28, 1974 that immigration in 1974 totaled only 595, the lowest annual total in the nation's eight years of unilaterally declared independence.

Black resettlement—The Rhodesian government said Jan. 14, 1971 that it had "completed its task" of resettling Tangwena tribesmen from their ancestral home at Inyanga near the Mozambique border. They had resisted government efforts, made under the Land Apportionment Act, to move them from the Gaeresi Ranch to Bende, about seven miles away, and to the nearby Holdenby Tribal Trust Land.

Rekayi Tangwena, the tribe's unofficial chief, had asked Great Britain to "rescue" his people. He made the plea in a letter to the London Times Jan. 6. Later, Tangwena was brought into a Salisbury court May 6 on charges of making abusive statements under the Law and Order Maintenance Act.

Tangwena reportedly accused the government of using brutality against members of his tribe in an effort to provoke them into retaliatory action during the resettlement action.

Desmond Lardner-Burke, minister of justice, law and order, had told the House of Assembly March 4 that Guy Clutton-Brock of the Cold Comfort Farm, a multiracial agricultural cooperative, had been "largely responsible for the [Tangwena] civil disobedience campaign."

(Clutton-Brock was ordered to leave the country Jan. 6. A government order, signed by President Clifford W. Dupont Jan. 15, declared the farm an illegal organization and charged that its members "not only sympathize with, but actively support, the terrorist cause as a means of overthrowing . . . the government." Clutton-Brock said Jan. 16 that his group had merely tried to improve race relations.)

Despite earlier government claims that the Tangwena resettlement had been "completed," Air Force helicopters flew police with dogs July 25, 1972 into an area near the Gaeresi Ranch in the Inyanga Mountains as part of the government's continuing efforts to relocate members of the Tangwena tribe. Authorities returned the following day and moved about 100 Tangwena children to Umtali, some 130 miles away, and placed them in institutions.

According to the New York Times Aug. 13, the Rhodesian High Court had once ruled that the Tangwena were occupying the land legally, since they had been there before passage of the Land Apportionment Act. The Times quoted the tribe's unofficial chief, Rekayi Tangwena, as arguing that the area had been "our land before Europeans came to this country."

The government May 17, 1973 issued new regulations to allow resettlement of the population in the northeast, to deny guerrillas civilian support.

Rhodesia's five Roman Catholic bishops said June 17 they would refuse to comply with legislation requiring persons of one race to apply for permits in order to enter the lands set aside for the other. They said the law would "further restrict the rightful freedom of the church to carry out its mission" and was "contrary to human freedom." Rev. Mark Wood, one of Rhodesia's two Anglican bishops, took the same position, it was reported June 19, as did a section of the Methodist Church.

Internal Affairs Minister Lance Smith asserted that primitive villagers were under "great pressure from terrorists and at times had to bow to their demands," according to a report released Aug. 21.

Smith said the government had resettled a large number of people from areas with terrorist activity.

More than 8,000 Africans living in the Mozambique border area were moved "with their consent" into "protected villages," the London Times reported Jan. 11, 1974. The transfer, plus a decision to strip bushes and trees that had provided cover for infiltrators, created a "no-go" 200-mile-long buffer zone as much as 10 miles wide. According to the Times, security forces would have the right to shoot anyone on sight in the area.

The security forces announced July 25 that an entire tribal community of about 60,000 was being moved from its present tribal trust land into 21 "protected villages" to deprive guerrillas of contact with the population and protect the people from terrorist harassment.

Security forces said the tribe's former homes in the Chiweshe Tribal Trust Land, about 40 miles north of Salisbury, could be seen from the fenced-in villages and that the people would not have far to walk to reach their fields.

Ivan Johnstone, district commissioner in charge of "Operation Overload," as the relocation program was called, said opposition to the resettlement had been enccuntered in only 17 of 189 kraals, the London Times reported July 28. According to an Aug. 15 report, the operation was virtually completed.

U.S. missionary ousted—An American missionary, Dr. Morgan Johnson, 45, of the United Methodist Church, was deported from Rhodesia Feb. 15, 1975 by government order. Johnson and his wife, natives of Georgia who had lived in Rhodesia for 23 years, were given no official reason for the deportation. In 1974, the government had charged Johnson with subversive activities because he drew a newspaper cartoon depicting the government removal of African tribesmen from their homes in villages where Rhodesia was fighting guerrillas. The charge was later withdrawn.

Stricter press controls set. The Rhodesian regime Sept. 21, 1975 announced new emergency powers, "in the interests of public safety or public order," under which a special advisory committee, to be established within the Ministry of Law and Order, would be vested with the power to prohibit or regulate the printing or publication of any publication within Rhodesia; prohibit the possession, sale or redistribution within Rhodesia of any publication; or prohibit the importation into Rhodesia of any publication or class of publication.

The move followed by three weeks the government's seizure of several hundred copies of the Johannesburg Sunday Times which had printed an article commenting on the constitutional situation in Rhodesia. The Gwelo newspaper Moto, a Roman Catholic weekly with a mainly black readership, had been banned for three months in 1974 under the Emergency Powers Regulations. Desmond Lardner-Burke, minister of justice, law and order, said Sept. 27 that Moto had been "strongly antagonistic against the government" and had published "inflammatory and subversive material."

Todd & Chinamano cases. The Rhodesian government Feb. 22, 1972 released from detention former Prime Minister Garfield

Todd and his daughter Judith but confined them to their family ranch near Shabani.

An official statement said the Todds, obliged to stay within an 800-yard radius of their house and forbidden to use the telephone, had been freed from prison "for health reasons and on humanitarian grounds." Only immediate members of the family would be allowed to visit them.

The dispatch said that Josiah Chinamano and his wife, Ruth, arrested at approximately the same time as the Todds, would be released when "a suitable place" had been found for their further detention.

A spokesman of the Justice, Law & Order Ministry said March 2 that a judicial review commission had unanimously recommended that the Todds and Chinamanos be held further in restricted circumstances "in the interests of public safety and public order."

Judith Todd later left Rhodesia and arrived in Great Britain July 14. She had been told that she would again be placed in detention if she returned to Rhodesia.

New law bars departures. Acting under a newly passed law, the Rhodesian regime Sept. 1, 1972 called back the passport of the Rev. Ganaan Banana, vice chairman of the African National Council, and prevented him from leaving the country.

The action was taken under provisions of a law published that day entitled the Departure from Rhodesia (Control) Amendment Act, which gave the immigration minister power to forbid the departure of persons whose journeys were deemed not to be in the public interest.

Acting under the new law, the government Sept. 8 confiscated the passport of Bishop Abel Muzorewa, leader of the African National Council, who had been under hospital observation in the Mtoko area for bilharzia and ulcers. Some accounts of the incident said Muzorewa had been on the point of leaving for the U.S. to obtain medical treatment unavailable in Rhodesia.

(Banana left Rhodesia illegally in May 1973 to study in the U.S. He was arrested May 24, 1975 on his return to Salisbury airport, and he was sentenced June 20 to three months at hard labor after he pleaded guilty to leaving the country without travel documents.)

Heavy fines authorized. A state-of-emergency decree published by the Rhodesian government Jan. 19, 1973 gave provincial commissioners in tribal areas the right to impose heavy fines on black communities suspected of aiding nationalist guerrillas infiltrating the country recently. News accounts did not give specific amounts for the fines, although one source said they were unlimited. The move followed by one day a speech in which Prime Minister Ian Smith had promised "tough action" against subversives.

A commissioner would be authorized to impose the collective fine "if he is satisfied" that persons in a tribal area had helped guerrillas, failed to report their presence, contravened security laws or committed murder, arson or "malicious injury to property." The new regulations added: "It shall be lawful for a provincial commissioner to exercise these powers without giving notice to the persons affected and without affording them any opportunity to make representations against the proposed exercise of these powers."

If officials could not collect money, they were entitled to take cattle or moveable property. Anyone who "refuses to disclose" property information would be subject to fines of about $270 and jailed for one year.

Political parties in Rhodesia opposed the fines Jan. 20. The Rhodesia party said they were "a terrible confession of failure and smack of panic. Hundreds of people, women and children included, may now be punished by a civil servant for the suspected offense of one man, without any recourse to the impartiality of the law." Pat Bashford, leader of the Center party, declared: "Rhodesia cannot hope to put an end to the terrorist incursions until she puts her house in order and demolishes the entire rotten edifice of racial discrimination erected by the [governing] Rhodesian Front." Bashford assailed the closing of the border with Zambia as a "tragic error."

Arrests. Edison Sithole, publicity secretary of the African National Council, said June 30, 1972 that "about 40" members of his organization had been detained by police for unknown reasons in the Mtoko area.

Two officials of the African National Council were arrested by the Rhodesian regime Feb. 26, 1973 and detained under emergency regulations. They were Charlton Ngcebetsha, the secretary general, and Arthur Chadzingwa, the organizing secretary.

Bishop Abel T. Muzorewa, the council's president, and the Rev. Canaan Banana, the vice president, attacked the government in a public statement Feb. 27, saying that by its "thoughtless actions" the Smith regime was creating a situation in which blacks, "denied expression of their legitimate political rights through constitutional means," would have no choice but to "attempt to change the present system through a violent revolution." The two leaders also indicated that because of the arrest of Ngcebetsha and Chadzingwa they were canceling plans for exploratory talks with the Rhodesian government.

Muzorewa Feb. 28 described as wrong reports that only two members of the ANC had been arrested Feb. 26. Muzorewa insisted that six had been seized. "There may not be official detention orders against the other four but they have disappeared," he said. The bishop identified the missing men as S. T. Bogoni, K. Bheope, Gabriel Chigwida and Peter Katsande.

Eleven black Africans in Sinoia were given prison terms March 15 ranging from 3½ to 10 years for assisting terrorists and failing to report their presence.

Penalties opposed. A Roman Catholic group dubbed the Commission for Justice & Peace in Rhodesia asked March 23, 1973 for a probe of the government policy of imposing heavy penalties on blacks accused of helping terrorists.

The commission declared: "Whole groups of people feel the punitive effects of measures taken in terms of the emergency regulations and security measures that look more like white protectionism. ... Schools have been shut at short notice and children sent home.... Furthermore, it is galling for the average man to be visited by the authorities, have a couple of beasts taken from his herd and be told this was part of a communal fine. The history of similar punitive measures of other countries indicates that the effect is to consolidate opposition."

Niesewand jailed, then cleared. Peter Niesewand, a Rhodesian journalist, was given a prison sentence under the Official Secrets Act April 6, 1973 but then was cleared by the Appellate Division of the High Court May 1 and freed May 3.

The April 6 sentence, to two years at hard labor, was imposed after Niesewand's conviction in a one-day trial in March. John E. T. Hamilton, serving as presiding magistrate, suspended one year of Niesewand's jail term on condition that the defendant not be convicted of a similar offense for three years because, he said, Niesewand had "acted openly and not in secret."

Although the charges against Niesewand were unspecified and his trial was held in secret, he was known to have been prosecuted under legislation making it a crime to publish information "calculated to be, or which might be, useful, directly or indirectly, to any enemy." The act defined "enemy" as including any "hostile organization." Niesewand, who pleaded not guilty, had worked for Reuters, the British Broadcasting Corp. (BBC) and the Manchester Guardian and had reported the incursion into Rhodesia of black guerrillas entering the country from Mozambique.

British Prime Minister Edward Heath said April 9 that the Niesewand trial and its verdict had damaged prospects for an early settlement of the Anglo-Rhodesian constitutional dispute. Heath was thought to have been replying indirectly to remarks made in the Rhodesian Parliament

April 5 by Prime Minister Ian Smith, who declared without further explanation: "The moment has come for the government to take positive action. Accordingly, we now go forward once again in an attempt to prove to the British government that the implementation of the agreed constitution would be in the best interests of Rhodesia and of all its people."

In another reaction to the Niesewand verdict, Harold Wilson, British Labor party leader, said April 5 that Rhodesia was governed under "a system of organized thuggery" and the trial had been "staged for the purpose of intimidating any other journalist who seeks to find and print the truth" about the country.

The Rhodesia Herald, a Salisbury newspaper, alleged April 7 that secret trials were "alien" to a way of life the government had pledged to defend.

Sir Alec Douglas-Home, British foreign secretary, sent Prime Minister Smith a telegram April 7 expressing "grave concern" over the issue.

Following his release May 3, Niesewand was put on a plane for London in exchange for a pledge of silence on the military situation in Rhodesia.

Chief Justice Sir Hugh Beadle ruled that the government had failed to show that the information published in Niesewand's articles was prejudicial to the interests or the safety of Rhodesia. In the first such procedure in its history, the court had heard arguments on the facts of the case in secret session on orders of the government.

Despite the acquittal, Niesewand was retained for two days in solitary confinement under the Feb. 20 detention order, which the government had said was not directly related to the subsequent official secrets charge. He had been detained in Gwelo Feb. 20 on the grounds that he was "likely to commit or incite the commission of acts which would disturb or interfere with the maintenance of public order." Niesewand, was a Rhodesian citizen born in South Africa.

Minister of Justice Desmond Lardner-Burke said May 3 Niesewand had been released because his "presence outside Rhodesia will not be detrimental to the interests of public safety or public order."

Niesewand, after his release, charged in London May 5 that his arrest had been designed "to intimidate the press into comparative silence about the official campaign being launched in tribal trust lands to persuade Africans to agree to the 1971 independence settlement proposals negotiated with Britain and rejected by the Africans." He said "scores of Africans" were detained on political charges in the two prisons where he was kept, some "held without trial or charge for a decade."

Briton jailed for plot—A Briton was sentenced April 10 to five years at hard labor (four years were suspended) for conspiracy to overthrow the government by "violence or forcible means."

According to the prosecution, Christopher Hewitson of Cambridge, who pleaded guilty, had conspired with 11 black schoolboys to obtain army trucks from a Salisbury drill hall and distribute weapons from a public armory to blacks in Harari township. Afterwards, military installations were to have been attacked and Cabinet members seized.

The magistrate said he had suspended most of the sentence because of the "stupidity of the whole plot" and the "improbability of its succeeding."

Students restricted. Ninety-eight African students who had been sentenced in an August riot at Salisbury University were freed from jail Oct. 31, 1973 but placed under restrictions that would bar them from the university campus. Thirteen others were still serving sentences, and 14 more were found guilty of riot charges Nov. 9. Nearly half the 370 black students at the university had been arrested in the Aug. 7 clash with police. The disturbances erupted after a university disciplinary committee recommended the expulsion of six students and the suspension of eight others after a mass protest Aug. 3 over alleged racial discrimination.

Church-state clash on brutality charges. Justice, Law & Order Minister Desmond Lardner-Burke accused Roman Catholic bishops April 4, 1974 of "trying to undermine lawful authority and the forces of law and order" and said they were trying to force a confrontation between church and state.

The bishops' conference had backed a full-page advertisement in the Rhodesia Herald April 2 by the Commission for Justice and Peace, a Roman Catholic organization, demanding a government inquiry into allegations of brutality by members of the security forces.

Lardner-Burke reiterated the government's refusal to open an inquiry into the alleged incidents on the grounds that it would be "harmful to the morale of the forces." The specific charges that Rhodesian and supporting South African forces had committed atrocities in December 1973 were leveled March 27 by a black member of Parliament. Lardner-Burke dismissed the allegations that day as "misguided and mischievous" and rejected the demand to convene a commission to investigate the claim.

The leaders of the Anglican, Roman Catholic and Methodist churches of Rhodesia circulated a report charging members of the Rhodesian security forces with 10 acts of brutality to blacks, it was reported Aug. 22.

International Sanctions

U.S. imports chrome. The importation of chromium (chrome) by U.S. industry despite the U.N.'s economic sanctions against Rhodesia proved to be a continuing source of controversy.

The U.S. State Department confirmed Jan. 4, 1971 that it had given a license to Union Carbide Corp. to ship 150,000 tons of Rhodesian chromium to the U.S. The department explained that the action did not constitute a change in policy toward Rhodesia, as Union Carbide had paid for the chromium before the imposition of U.N. sanctions against that country.

Bishop Abel Muzorewa, chairman of Rhodesia's African National Council, told the U.N. Security Council Feb. 16, 1972: "The African people of Rhodesia have been deeply shocked by the blatant disre-

gard for the U.N. Charter, for human suffering in Rhodesia and for international law by the United States in violating the Security Council resolution which imposed sanctions on Rhodesia. The purchase of chrome by the United States, in my opinion, had no other motives apart from encouraging and boosting the morale of the racist regime in order to make it defy the world. I was wondering whether it is not time someone investigated to establish whether or not the United States violated the law. If it did, it is time someone brought the United States before the International Court of Justice. Whatever the motives, the Africans believe it is an expression of bad faith."

The U.S. Treasury Department announced Jan. 25, 1972 that curbs on importing Rhodesian chrome, asbestos, silver, copper and nickel had been officially lifted as a result of legislation passed by Congress in 1971. The legislation, an amendment to a military procurement bill, ended the authority of the President to prohibit the importation of strategic materials also being imported from a Communist-dominated country. It thus prevented a ban against Rhodesian chrome since the U.S. imported chrome ore from the Soviet Union.

Opponents of the amendment contended importation of chrome from Rhodesia would be in violation of international law because of the U.N. embargo. Supporters argued against dependency for a strategic material upon the Soviet Union, which the other side claimed was a "false issue" since the U.S. reportedly held 1.3 million tons of chrome surplus in its strategic stockpile. The Nixon Administration maintained public neutrality on the amendment, although House GOP Leader Gerald Ford (Mich.) voted for it.

Former British Prime Minister Harold Wilson said April 19 at a lecture at Lehigh University in Pennsylvania that the decision of the U.S. Congress to lift the ban on Rhodesian chrome was "calculated to outrage moderate African feeling" and would give "new heart to the Rhodesian racialists."

George Bush, the U.S. representative at the United Nations, told an audience at Tulane University in New Orleans April 21 that the U.S. had violated U.N. sanctions by importing Rhodesian chrome because it "seemed the realistic solution" instead of paying "twice the price" for Soviet chrome.

Moves in U.N. Various moves were taken in the U.N. during 1972 to reinforce the sanctions against Rhodesia.

The U.N. Security Council Feb. 28 had voted 13-0, with the U.S. and Great Britain abstaining, to ask all countries to continue honoring its ban on trade with Rhodesia. Christopher E. Phillips, the U.S. delegate, argued that at least nine Security Council members had already violated the sanctions. He declared: "Let us be blunt about the problem. The sanctions are not going to work if there is a double standard about compliance with them." The Council's Committee on Sanctions against Rhodesia reported June 30 that the U.S. had purchased three shipments of nickel from Rhodesia. The shipments, which arrived in Baltimore in April and May, had been confirmed by the U.S. government.

The Security Council July 28 passed a resolution condemning "all acts violating" U.N. trade sanctions against Rhodesia. The measure, introduced by Guinea, Somalia and Sudan, passed 14-0 with the abstention of the U.S.

Later in 1972 the U.N. General Assembly voted Dec. 7 to approve a resolution calling on the Security Council to consider the urgent need to broaden the scope of sanctions against Rhodesia to include all measures envisaged under article 41 of the U.N. Charter. These included cutting off rail, sea, air, postal and radio communications with the country. The resolution, passed 93-8 with 23 abstentions, also urged the Security Council to consider imposing sanctions against South Africa and Portugal for refusing to observe the existing measures against Rhodesia.

The Security Council's Sanctions Committee recommended April 27, 1973 that the United Nations approve 13 regulations to tighten sanctions against Rhodesia. Fourteen members, including Britain and France, asked the world body to call for repeal of a U.S. law allowing the import of Rhodesian chrome and other strategic ores.

The new measures would include searches of cargo from South Africa and Portugal suspected of coming from Rhodesia, seizure of the cargo and use of revenue from its sale to pay the investigators. The U.S. said it interpreted the resolution as allowing each government to enforce the rules in accordance with its own laws, including the chrome import law.

The U.S. Senate May 31 voted to continue the importation of chrome. It acted by a 40-36 vote to remove from a State Department appropriation a provision to repeal the 1971 legislation under which Rhodesian chrome was imported.

Sen. Gale McGee (D, Wyo.), leader in the effort to reinstate the ban on Rhodesian chrome, said after the vote that the Administration was "basically dishonest" on the Rhodesian question. (McGee had received a letter May 20 from John N. Irwin 2d, a State Department undersecretary, apparently supporting McGee's amendment and noting that the import of Rhodesian chrome "put the U.S. in violation of its international legal obligations." Irwin had pointed out that the U.S. had a chrome surplus of 2.2 million tons.)

U.S. court on Rhodesian imports—The U.S. Court of Appeals for the District of Columbia ruled Oct. 31 that Congress could authorize the importation of Rhodesian chrome in violation of treaty obligations under the United Nations charter.

The court action affirmed an earlier dismissal by U.S. District Court Judge Aubrey E. Robinson Jr. of a suit filed by the Congressional Black Caucus. The group, led by Rep. Charles C. Diggs (D, Mich.), had argued that a 1971 amendment to the military procurement bill, introduced by Sen. Harry F. Byrd (Ind, Va.), had violated U.S. obligations to the U.N.

The Oct. 31 opinion declared: "We think that there can be no blinking the purpose and effect of the Byrd amendment. It was to detach this country from the U.N. boycott of Southern Rhodesia in blatant disregard of our treaty under-takings. Under our constitutional scheme, Congress can denounce treaties if it sees fit to do so and there is nothing the other branches of government can do about it."

Diggs had said that the chrome was not a strategic material because Union Carbide and Foote Minerals, the two companies importing the metal, were us-ing it "for consumer items, such as kitchen ware."

The Supreme Court April 16 rejected a petition that it overturn the 1971 law permitting imports of Rhodesian chrome.

U.S. imports $13 million. In the 12 months ended Jan. 12, 1973, the U.S. had bought from Rhodesia $13 million worth of "strategic and critical commodities," ac-cording to the London Times Feb. 24. The Times said information on the purchase of nickel cathodes, high carbon ferrochrome and chrome ore had been given to a House foreign affairs subcommittee by John Hennessy, assistant treasury secretary for international affairs.

Shortages reported. It was reported in 1973 that the international action against Rhodesia was having a noticeable affect on the country's economy.

According to the New York Times April 17, the United Nations sanctions imposed in 1966 after the country's white minority unilaterally declared its inde-pendence had caused chronic shortages of foreign currency, and a marked decrease in consumer goods imports in the past year, although Rhodesia was able to pur-chase goods abroad when currency was available. Shortages were reported in parts for farm machinery and automobiles and in raw materials for about 700 light industrial plants set up to replace imports.

Gasoline rationing—Rhodesia an-nounced a gasoline rationing program, ef-fective Feb. 1, 1975. This was needed, according to Commerce & Industry Minister Jack Mussett, to cope with the "spectacular" rise in the cost of petro-leum and the threat of supply cutbacks. However, speed limit curbs set in De-cember 1973 were lifted.

4 in U.S. admit violations. Four per-sons, including the Vermont state tax com-missioner, pleaded guilty April 12, 1972, in U.S. district court in New York, to violation of sanctions against trade with Rhodesia.

U.S. Attorney Whitney N. Seymour Jr. said the action was the first prosecu-tion for violations of the 1968 sanctions. (The U.S. was selectively violating them in order to import Rhodesian chrome, but otherwise, the country was maintaining a general embargo against trade with Rhodesia.)

The case involved an attempt on the part of IDI Management Inc. of Cin-cinnati, formerly C.&I. Girdler Inter-national, to operate a $50 million fer-tilizer plant at Que Que in Rhodesia. Also accused were the Margas Shipping Co. of Panama; Herbert H. Hamilton, IDI's president; David J. Paterson, a businessman living in the Bahamas; and Conrad E. Wysocki, an IDI engineer.

A separate information was filed against Edward H. Bartlett, the Vermont tax commissioner, charging him with conspiracy in the transaction. In a state-ment issued through his attorney, Bart-lett admitted having "instructed a bank in Switzerland to form a corporation which would be used for the purpose of trading with Rhodesia." He said that when sanctions were imposed in 1968 he had been an accountant with C.&I. Girdler and had worked to secure the shipment of $5 million worth of ammonia to Rhodesia, needed to operate the fer-tilizer plant his firm had helped build.

Bartlett added: "It comes as no small surprise that the Executive Branch should now seek to enforce the regula-tions with respect to one commodity and not the other. This kind of enforce-ment raises fundamental questions of fairness as well as constitutionality."

Penalties in the case were imposed June 16. Judge Charles L. Brieant Jr. fined the Margas Shipping Co. of Panama $100,000 and IDI Management Inc. of Cincinnati $200,000. Herbert H. Hamil-ton, IDI president, was fined $7,500 and put on probation for a year. David J. Paterson was assessed $2,500 and Conrad E. Wysocki, an IDI engineer, was fined $1,750.

Boycott violations charged—The Carnegie Endowment for International Peace said Aug. 25, 1973 that Pan American and Trans World Airlines had violated U.S. law and United Nations sanctions by doing business with Rhodesia, and said Avis and Hertz car rental companies might also have violated the law.

The German magazine Der Spiegel had charged July 16 that 138 companies, including about 40 German firms, had violated the sanctions, often by trading with Rhodesia via Mozambique or South Africa.

Foreign Secretary Sir Alec Douglas-Home of Great Britain had told the House of Commons June 12, 1972 that Rhodesian exports had reached 97% of the level they had attained before the colony declared its independence from Britain in 1965. Douglas-Home remarked that "a lot of exports are going to countries—members of the U.N.—who are supposed to be supporting sanctions.... But there is no need for new machinery. What is required is stricter enforcement by the international community of existing measures."

A chemical firm in Aarhus, Denmark and two of its directors were fined about $7,000 April 20 for illegal exports to Rhodesia.

Reynolds indicted—A U.S. grand jury indicted Reynolds International, Inc. Nov. 1, 1973 for violating bans against Rhodesia by importing Rhodesian ore for aluminum manufacture.

Australian action. Australian Prime Minister Gough Whitlam announced Dec. 14, 1972 a ban on exporting wheat to Rhodesia in accordance with United Nations sanctions. The former government had authorized wheat sales to Rhodesia on "humanitarian" grounds. The sales amounted to $A2.4 million in 1971–72.

Australia July 5 had said that it would not renew the expired Australian passport for Stanley O'Donnell, an Australian-born permanent secretary in the Rhodesian Ministry of External Affairs, on the grounds that Australia did not recognize Rhodesia.

Similar action was promised on the passports of two other Australian-born Rhodesian officials if the men were still working for the Salisbury regime when their passports expired. The action followed an official protest from Ghana over the use of Australian passports by the three officials.

Australia's Post Office April 18, 1973 halted phone, telecommunication and mail services from the Rhodesian Information Center in Sydney. Postmaster General Nigel Bowen said this was done in view of Rhodesia's "illegal regime."

The center, registered as a private company in New South Wales, claimed it did not officially represent the Rhodesian government.

A short time thereafter Australian airlines were told by the Department of Civil Aviation not to book tours through or to Rhodesia, it was reported June 8.

A Foreign Affairs Department spokesman said it was in accordance with the U.N. ban on trade relations with Rhodesia. The department said it considered tourism to come under terms of the sanctions.

The government July 31, 1974 closed the Rhodesian Information Center. Foreign Minister Donald Willesee said the government had always been concerned that the center might disseminate "propaganda material."

3 jets delivered. Three 12-year-old Boeing 720 jets were flown to Salisbury April 14, 1973 by Air Rhodesia crews. Transport Minister Roger Hawkins called this event "one of the biggest holes knocked in sanctions for a number of years."

The planes, reportedly purchased for not more than $1.5 million from a West German charter airline through Swiss and Liechtenstein intermediaries, were to be used to inaugurate jet service on Air Rhodesia.

U.K. eases curbs. The British House of Commons Nov. 9, 1972 had approved a bill submitted by Foreign Secretary Sir Alec Douglas-Home for the maintenance of economic sanctions against Rhodesia.

Douglas-Home's proposals, passed by a vote of 266–29, involved slight increases in the amount of cash gifts that could be sent to Rhodesia by Britons with relatives there as well as increases in travel allowances for the elderly. The House of Lords later that day ratified the sanctions order by a vote of 159–43. (Eighty members of the House of Lords had asked the government Oct. 30 to abandon sanctions on the grounds that Rhodesia's rebellion was "now no more than a technicality.")

A spokesman for the Rhodesian government described the British concessions Nov. 10 as "valueless," saying they were "designed to placate the back-benchers of the Conservative party rather than to bring comfort to Rhodesians."

The Rhodesian multiracial Center party approved the new order Nov. 10 but the Rev. Ganaan Banana, vice president of the African National Council, called the move an attempt to reduce the effectiveness of sanctions, explaining: "It would appear to us that the present position of the British government on sanctions amounts to a de facto recognition of the Smith regime."

Rhodesian Prime Minister Ian D. Smith said in a nationwide radio address Nov. 11, the anniversary of his country's unilateral declaration of independence from Britain, that Rhodesia had been "sorely tested" by sanctions but that conditions were improving. Smith declared: "These have been seven rewarding years which have left me more optimistic about the future than I have been at any time in the past."

Metal dealers fined—A firm of British metal dealers was fined $14,400 May 2, 1974 on the ground that it had illegally imported 300 tons of chrome from Rhodesia. It was reported to be the first prosecution for importing in violation of the trade embargo ordered by an earlier Labor government after Rhodesia's ruling white minority declared independence in 1965.

U.S. weighs chrome curb. The U.S. Senate voted 54-37 Dec. 18, 1973 to restore a ban on chrome imports from Rhodesia. The ban, supported by Sen. Hubert Humphrey (D, Minn.) and by the State Department, had to overcome a filibuster by Sen. Harry F. Byrd (Ind, Va.) and supporters with a successful cloture vote of 63–26.

The bill died because the House failed to act on it before the 1973 session ended. The measure had been scheduled for consideration Dec. 19 but was withdrawn by its backers because of lack of support.

In 1975, the House Sept. 25 defeated a bill to reinstate the prohibition on U.S. importation of chrome, ferrochrome and nickel from Rhodesia. The measure, rejected by a 209-187 vote, would have returned the U.S. to compliance with U.N. sanctions. The Ford Administration favored reimposition of the bans.

Rep. Donald Fraser (D, Minn.), manager of the bill, blamed its defeat on animosity toward the U.N. and lobbying by the steel industry, which said that it would have to rely principally on the Soviet Union if Rhodesian imports were cut off.

Rep. Edward Derwinski (R, Ill.), leader of the opposition, warned against damaging the U.S. economy by restricting the importation of vital raw materials.

Britain ends Beira patrol. British Foreign Secretary James Callaghan announced June 26, 1974 that London had ended the naval patrol that for more than nine years had prevented the landing at Beira, Mozambique of crude oil destined for Rhodesia.

The patrol, considered to have been completely effective, had prevented the pumping of oil through the only pipeline entering Rhodesia, connecting Beira to the Feruke oil refinery near Umtali. With the independence of Mozambique, Callaghan said, "such patrolling is no longer necessary. (According to a report by a Rhodesian nationalist source, Mozambique had pledged to respect United Nations resolutions and sanctions against Rhodesia and would close its ports to Rhodesian goods, it was reported June 29.)

Rail link with South Africa—The first direct rail link between Rhodesia and South Africa was completed Sept. 10, 21 months ahead of schedule. The railway provided Rhodesia with a major alternative to present outlets to the sea through Mozambique.

The new rail line connected Rutenga and Beitbridge in Rhodesia, linking the Rhodesian capital of Salisbury with Johannesburg.

Exclusion from Davis Cup tennis play. Rhodesia and South Africa were barred Jan. 15 from participating in the 1971 Davis Cup tennis competition as the drawing was completed for European zone play. Both countries were included in the 1970 draw, but did not play because many other nations threatened to withdraw if players representing South Africa and Rhodesia were allowed to participate.

South Africa was barred because of its policy of racial apartheid. Rhodesia was excluded because 23 European nations had advised the secretary of the Davis Cup nations that they could not accept Rhodesia as a participant because of United Nations restrictions.

(In a government action May 6, 1975, the French Tennis Federation banned Rhodesia from the women's Federation Cup held in Aix En Provence, France. According to United Press International May 6, highly placed sources said French Government officials pointed to the United Nations resolution boycotting Rhodesia for its racial policies. A plea to uphold the U.N. ban, according to the source, had come to the French Government from Great Britain.)

Rhodesia out of Olympics. Rhodesia, whose entry in the 20th Olympic Games in Munich, West Germany had led to boycott threats by black athletes, was voted out of the 1972 summer games Aug. 22 by the International Olympic Committee (IOC).

The IOC's action followed a week of ultimatums by black African nations that they would withdraw from the games if Rhodesia competed.

Rhodesia was voted out by the IOC, 36–31, with three abstentions. Announcement of the vote was made by IOC President Avery Brundage, who had offered strong statements of support for Rhodesia's participation.

Although the racial issue had triggered the dispute, the IOC said a technicality over the passports of the Rhodesian athletes had led to the expulsion. The reason given by the committee was that the Rhodesians had failed to produce passports to prove they were British subjects as well as Rhodesian citizens.

Rhodesia, which had been excluded from the 1968 games, had received an invitation to compete in Munich under a compromise by the Supreme Council for Sport in Africa, the sports governing body for the black African bloc. That compromise was based on Rhodesia's willingness to compete as British subjects under the British flag. When Rhodesia accepted those terms, the IOC extended an invitation and Rhodesia came to Munich with a 44-member team, including six black trackmen.

Rhodesia's entry had first touched off only token opposition from smaller African nations, including Tanzania, Sierra Leone and Sudan. But the protest took on a new shape Aug. 15–16 when Ethiopia and Kenya, the continent's two athletic powers, joined the boycott.

The threat of a boycott grew Aug. 18 when a group of U.S. black athletes pledged in an unsigned statement that if Rhodesia was allowed to compete, "we will take a united stand with our African brothers."

The boycott threat led the IOC to meet Aug. 21 to reconsider Rhodesia's invitation.

(As the 1976 Olympics approached, the IOC voted 41-26 May 22, 1975 to withdraw its recognition of Rhodesia and exclude it from the Games because Rhodesia did not comply with Olympic rules banning racial discrimination. Pressure for the expulsion had been brought by black African nations.)

Other Economic, Foreign & Political Developments

Economy up. The 1970 Economic Survey, released April 28, 1971 by the Ministry of Finance, showed that Rhodesia had been visited by 320,269 tourists in 1970, an increase of 7% over the figure for the previous year.

The survey listed the nation's growth rate at 4.5%, after allowing for price increases, and said that a net immigration of 6,340 was the highest in a decade.

The ministry reported April 18, 1972 that exports had risen during 1971 to about $416 million, described as "almost the presanctions level." Per capita earnings for "Europeans and Africans rose by 9% and 5.4% respectively." The dispatch said "preliminary estimates" indicated a growth rate for the economy during 1971 of "13.6% at current prices, or about 10% in real terms."

Addressing businessmen June 28, Prime Minister Ian Smith revealed balance-of-payments figures for the country for the previous three years. He said there had been a surplus of $3.4 million in 1969 and a surplus of $4.3 million in 1970 but that in 1971 there was a deficit of $18.6 million. The figure was "causing concern" but was normal for the Rhodesian economy, he said, during periods of "economic revival."

Rhodesia reported April 28, 1973 a visible trade surplus of $95 million in 1972, with exports at $483 million, higher than in 1965. Current accounts for 1972 showed a surplus of $5 million, compared with deficits in the previous two years. The figures did not reflect recent losses incurred by closing the Zambian border.

The visible trade balance was later described as a $4.725 billion deficit.

According to the yearly Economic Survey, the gross domestic product rose by 8% in real terms, somewhat less than the 1971 rate, which had been inflated by an unusually good agricultural season. Real average earnings for Africans had increased 19% over the past 10 years, compared with 17% for other groups. Net immigration of Europeans was 8,820 in 1972.

An April 23, 1974 report said Rhodesia had realized a $57.75 million balance-of-payments surplus in 1973. Economic growth was reported at 8.4% in 1972 and 6.5% in 1973.

African bus strike. Some 400 African bus drivers in Salisbury June 26, 1972 ended a strike which had begun 13 days earlier and had spread to Bulawayo June 21.

The drivers, who had asked for extra payment for shifts operated without conductors, returned to work when an emergency transport service run by Rhodesian army drivers went into effect. Ian McLean, minister of labor, had said June 25 that the drivers' claim for an increase in pay could not be negotiated until after the strike ended. In Bulawayo that day 71 drivers were reported arrested for taking part in the illegal strike.

Mine disaster. An explosion in the Wankie Colliery Co. coal mine in northwest Rhodesia trapped 468 men June 6, 1972 in a sloping shaft hundreds of feet beneath the surface. Rescue efforts were halted entirely June 7 by two small explosions and escaping poisonous gas. Sir Keith Acutt, chairman of the company, announced June 9 there was "no cause for hope." The final death toll was reported July 4 as 427.

Rhodesia debts paid. The Treasury said June 11, 1973 that it had paid nearly £18.3 million in compensation to the World Bank because Rhodesia had defaulted on loan payments. Britain had guaranteed the loans before Rhodesia unilaterally declared independence in 1965.

Farm output grows. The Agricultural Marketing Authority said a huge increase in the cotton crop in 1973 and higher world demand would enable the authority to pay a bonus of 6¢ a kilogram to farmers, it was reported Sept. 30. The government had reported July 24 and 25 that harvests of most crops and production of beef had exceeded expectations despite a drought early in the year.

Nonaligned nations' views. Foreign ministers of more than 60 nonaligned nations, mostly from Asia and Africa, met in Georgetown, Guyana Aug. 8–12, 1972 for wide-ranging discussions. The conference members said they would carry on the fight to eliminate all traces of colonialism and racial discrimination in Africa. Specifically, delegates pledged to work for establishment of a strong military, financial and training program to aid African liberation movements, and to act to prevent commerce between all countries and Rhodesia and its foreign investors.

Delegates from more than 50 countries met in Oslo in April 1973 to discuss racism and colonialism in Africa. The conference members demanded the recognition of the African nationalists in Rhodesia as that country's legitimate government, and called for the seizure of all cargoes for Rhodesia and awarding of their proceeds to the nationalists.

Politics. In 1973, the ruling Rhodesia Front (RF) party of Prime Minister Ian Smith defeated the new white moderate Rhodesia party in a by-election May 18 in a rural district seen as a test of the regime's popularity. The new party, led by Allan Savory, the only white opposition member of Parliament, received 22% of the votes. In another by-election, the African National Council won its third known supporter in Parliament May 24.

Opposition Center party spokesman Jack Humphries said Aug. 17 that African majority rule in Rhodesia was inevitable, but that the governing Rhodesian Front party was prepared to bring the country "crashing in ruins" rather than face the fact.

In 1974, the RF won an easy victory in the July 30 election, securing all 50 white seats in Parliament for the third successive time since 1962.

The RF won more than 70% of the vote cast. The liberal opposition Rhodesia Party (RP) won 18% of the vote from the 38 seats which it had challenged. RP leader Tim Gibbs was defeated, as was Allan Savory who had resigned his RP leadership June 4 and membership June 16 in an inter-party dispute and had run as

an independent. Nominees of the rightist Rhodesia National Party were also defeated.

Blacks elected eight of their 16 representatives to Parliament. (The other eight were appointed posts.) Seven of the victors were supporters of the African National Council (ANC) which had earlier called for a boycott of the elections by black Africans. No government-supported black candidates of the African Progressive Party were elected. Only 7,000 of the country's 5.7 million blacks were franchised to vote in the elections and barely 50% of them chose to do so.

Smith had called for the elections June 19 "to end the state of uncertainty in the country resulting from recent international and internal events."

Salisbury announced Aug. 27 that Rhodesia's new national anthem would be "Ode to Joy," the choral movement of Beethoven's Ninth Symphony. The previous anthem, "God Save the Queen," had been abandoned in 1969.

De Kock resigns—Wickus de Kock, minister of information, immigration and tourism, resigned from the cabinet Oct. 30, 1975. He said he was "out of step with the government." Often cited as a possible successor to Prime Minister Ian Smith, de Kock had reportedly taken strong issue with Smith's Oct. 12 criticism of South Africa's efforts to promote a constitutional settlement in Rhodesia.

One of the most influential members of the government, de Kock reaffirmed upon resigning his staunch support for pursuing a policy of detente in southern Africa and for finding an "equitable solution" to the constitutional dilemma confronted by the white minority government and the black majority population.

De Kock had held that a settlement should provide for a confederation of white and black states, rather than a single majority-ruled state as sought by the government.

Further anti-guerrilla moves. The Rhodesian government had initiated land resettlement and cash rewards programs in efforts to counter the growing momentum of rebel activities, it was reported by Salisbury radio March 21 and April 17, 1974. Northeast authorities had been empowered to order area residents to perform forced labor (for pay) on public security projects, it was reported Feb. 8.

New regulations reported Feb. 8 allowed that people detained for questioning could be held 60 days, twice the previous time limit.

The Ministry of Defense announced April 3 that new military call-ups had begun as part of the program to increase the size of the armed forces; financial incentives to encourage reenlistment were also instituted, it was reported April 10.

Inflation at 20-year high. Inflation during the first quarter of 1975 rose by an annual rate of 8.2%, the highest rate of inflation in 20 years, it was reported May 20.

Jamaica parley agrees to press Rhodesia ban. Leaders of the 33 Commonwealth nations held their biennial conference in Kingston, Jamaica April 20–May 6, 1975 and agreed to increase pressure on the white minority regime of Rhodesia to force it to negotiate with black nationalists.

A final communique issued May 6 announced a decision to give financial assistance to the new government of Mozambique, when it became independent in June, so it could join the United Nations trade blockade against Rhodesia.

The communique took note of the determination of African nationalists to use "peaceful means if possible" to achieve their objective of independence for Rhodesia on the basis of majority rule, but recognized "the inevitability of intensified armed struggle should peaceful avenues be blocked by the racist and illegal regime" of Rhodesian Prime Minister Ian Smith. The policy was in line with declaration on southern Africa policy recently adopted by the Organization of African Unity. The government of Britain, Canada, New Zealand and Australia had refused African demands to provide arms to Rhodesian nationalists should negotiations fail.

Bishop Abel Muzorewa, president of the African National Council (ANC), a coalition of Rhodesian black nationalists, had addressed the conference April 30. He warned that failure of Rhodesian nationalists to achieve their goal soon would lead to "a reintensified armed struggle." Another ANC leader, Joshua Nkomo, arrived in Kingston April 29 and stayed through May 6, when he met with British Prime Minister Harold Wilson and the presidents of Tanzania, Zambia and Botswana.

Trudeau shuns meeting. Canadian Prime Minister Pierre Trudeau refused Sept. 23, 1975 to participate in the opening of an international agricultural event in Ontario that day because two Rhodesians were competing. Trudeau said he had only learned of the Rhodesians' participation that very day and subsequently declined to attend the event, the international plowing championships, because Canada had no diplomatic relations with Rhodesia's "illegal" white government. He expressed concern that his attendance might imply de facto recognition of the regime.

Peace Efforts Fail

Ceasefire Is Unsuccessful

Black nationalist leaders and Rhodesia's white minority government reached a tentative truce toward the end of 1974. Peace efforts foundered, however, over the inability of the two sides to agree on the basic issue—the demand that Ian Smith's white regime turn over power to the country's black majority.

Accord to end warfare, detentions. Rhodesian Prime Minister Ian Smith announced Dec. 11, 1974 that an immediate truce had been agreed to by his white minority government and black nationalists after prolonged fighting in the northern frontier.

In a televised address, he said all detained black leaders and followers of the various nationalist movements would be released at once and that a constitutional conference would be held on the nation's political future to determine how the black majority would enter the government.

Smith made his announcement after a series of meetings in Lusaka, Zambia, between representatives of the Rhodesian nationalist groups, Rhodesian government officials and leaders of three black African nations. The talks, which began Dec. 4, had broken down Dec. 6. Salisbury Dec. 7 rejected demands for immediate acceptance of the principle of majority rule before any constitutional conference was held. In his Dec. 11 announcement, Smith said talks between the Rhodesian parties had continued, however, after the breakdown. According to the subsequent agreement reached, the conference would take place "without any pre-condition."

Rhodesia had released two jailed black nationalist leaders, Joshua Nkomo of the Zimbabwe African People's Union (ZAPU) and the Rev. Ndabaningi Sithole of the Zimbabwe African Nationalist Union (ZANU), both in prison for the past 10 years, and had flown them to Lusaka for the private meetings. Also attending the sessions were Bishop Abel Muzorewa of the African National Council (ANC), the only legal black political organization in Rhodesia, and Presidents Kenneth Kaunda of Zambia, Julius Nyerere of Tanzania and Sir Seretse Khama of Botswana. Two Rhodesian government officials, Attorney General Anthony Smith and Cabinet Secretary Jack Gaylard, participated in the Dec. 6 meeting at which the first set of proposals was presented.

South Africa pledges to withdraw forces—South African Prime Minister

John Vorster said Dec. 11 that his country would withdraw its paramilitary police forces from Rhodesia as soon as confirmation was received that hostilities had ended.

In his statement, delivered immediately after Rhodesian Prime Minister Smith's announcement of a cease-fire pact, Vorster also revealed that South African officials had flown to Lusaka to assist in averting a total collapse of the negotiations Dec. 6. Vorster had directed a program of secret diplomacy over several months that prepared the ground for the Lusaka talks, with private meetings and public statements aimed at marshaling the cooperation of black African nations in bringing an end to hostilities in southern Africa.

The South African leader had said Oct. 23 that both his nation and its black neighbors had to choose "between peace on the one hand or an escalation of strife on the other." In a strong statement of support, Zambian President Kenneth Kaunda Oct. 26 hailed Vorster's speech as "the voice of reason for which Africa and the rest of the world have been waiting."

The Afrikaans-language Cape Town newspaper Die Burger, closely linked to the government, had reported Nov. 30 that Vorster led a 15-man delegation to the Ivory Coast a month earlier for meetings with President Felix Houphouet-Boigny, Senegal President Leopold Senghor and Zambian President Kaunda.

Uneasy truce in Rhodesia. The Rhodesian government Dec. 30 threatened to call off plans for a projected constitutional conference with black nationalists unless guerrillas ceased their operations.

It had been announced Dec. 24 that guerrillas had killed four members of the South African police force serving in northeastern Rhodesia. The African National Council (ANC) issued an apology for the incident, blaming difficulties in communicating news of the cease fire to the field. ANC leader Bishop Abel Muzorewa had said Dec. 12 that the cease fire was to take place immediately; however, Robert Mugabe, executive secretary of the Zimbabwe African National Union (ZANU), asserted Dec. 15 that the cease

fire agreement had been an informal one.

The Rhodesian government began releasing black political detainees Dec. 16, and by Dec. 24 had released 80 of the 300–500 reportedly imprisoned, according to the French newspaper Le Monde Dec. 26.

Regime & nationalists harden positions. Rhodesian Justice Minister Desmond Lardner-Burke said Jan. 9, 1975 that because nationalist leaders had failed to halt guerrilla activity, the government would release no more political detainees. He charged that despite the agreed-upon cease-fire, hostilities had in fact increased in some areas of the country.

The black nationalist leaders issued a statement Jan. 12 declaring they would boycott a proposed constitutional conference until the Rhodesian government agreed to several conditions, including a demand that the conference be called by Great Britain and chaired by the British foreign secretary. Among the other demands was insistence upon the release of all political prisoners and removal of the ban on Rhodesia's guerrilla movements. The statement was issued through the umbrella group for the black movements, the African National Council (ANC), which also said that the conditions had been drawn up at the Lusaka meetings in December 1974.

Sithole arrested, talks halted. The Smith government March 4, 1975 arrested ZANU leader Ndabaningi Sithole. The African National Union immediately broke off the constitutional settlement talks with the white minority government until Sithole were released.

The turn of events was widely seen as seriously jeopardizing the possibility for a peaceful settlement between the government and the black majority. Robert Mugabe, second in command of ZANU, said March 4 that, with Sithole's arrest, "hopes of a peaceful settlement have been exposed as a pipe dream." He branded the arrest an intimidation and said guerrilla warfare would be intensified as a result.

According to reports March 4–5, the Rhodesian action was aimed at removing Sithole, the most militant leader with whom the government was dealing, from the settlement talks so as to negotiate a "better deal" with more moderate black leaders. The government alleged, however, that it had arrested Sithole "to protect the lives of his intended victims," after discovering that he was plotting to assassinate potential opponents within the black movements. Joshua Nkomo, leader of the Zimbabwe African People's Union, was believed to represent the most serious challenge to Sithole, but Nkomo March 5 declared the government allegation a fabrication and reiterated a unified black stance in refusing to participate in the constitutional talks as long as Sithole were detained.

The first direct talks between the black leaders and Prime Minister Ian Smith had taken place Feb. 5 in Salisbury and were followed by a second meeting Feb. 12. Representing the ANC bodies were: Sithole, Nkomo, and ANC officials Bishop Abel Muzorewa, Elliot Gabellah and Gordon Chavanduka. No progress was reported to have emerged from the meetings, but a third, cancelled as a result of Sithole's arrest, had been scheduled for March 6.

South Africa concerned over arrest— South African Foreign Minister Hilgard Muller March 7 expressed his government's concern at Rhodesia's arrest of the Rev. Sithole. Addressing the Parliament in Cape Town, Muller acknowledged that the action could be a serious setback to detente in southern Africa, but he expressed the hope that a public trial would be held. (Salisbury, however, reaffirmed March 8 that the trial would be closed "to protect the witnesses.")

According to a London Times report March 6, Rhodesian Defense Minister P. K. van der Byl had flown to Cape Town to inform South Africa of the arrest; the South African government, the report said, was displeased by the development.

Zambia March 4 condemned Sithole's arrest as "a deliberate act aimed at sabotaging black unity." Zambia, like South Africa, had figured significantly in initiating the Lusaka talks in December 1974 on a Rhodesian ceasefire agreement.

The British government March 4 expressed its "disappointment" in learning of the arrest.

Sithole jailing upheld. A special tribunal in Salisbury April 2 ruled that the Rhodesian government had been justified in its arrest of Sithole. The court said it had not investigated the charges of an assassination plot in connection with which he had been arrested because, to protect the identity of the witnesses, the inquiry would have had to be held in secret and the particulars withheld from Sithole.

However, the court found that as leader of ZANU and commander of its military wing, Sithole bore responsibility for rebel violations of the ceasefire. Sithole had withdrawn his case from the tribunal March 26, two days after it opened, because of the altered character of the inquiry, but the court proceedings continued despite his absence.

Sithole freed, quits Rhodesia. The Rhodesian government released Sithole April 4 and permitted him to be flown April 6, in a Zambian jet airliner with other Rhodesian nationalist leaders, to a meeting in Tanzania of the Organization of African Unity.

At the end of the Dar es Salaam meetings, Sithole decided not to return to Rhodesia and face possible reimprisonment, a spokesman for the African National Council (ANC) said April 14.

In announcing the release, Prime Minister Ian Smith said he had acted following a request from ANC leader Bishop Abel Muzorewa, supported by the South African government and "the four northern presidents." These, it was later learned, were Presidents Kenneth D. Kaunda of Zambia, Julius K. Nyerere of Tanzania and Sir Seretse Khama of Botswana, and the president-elect of Mozambique, Samora Machel.

Smith said Sithole's release was not a move to which Salisbury had readily agreed. "However," he added, "we were assured that to do so would significantly assist the cause of detente. This is therefore a further indication of our goodwill and serious endeavor to promote detente in southern Africa."

Guerrilla fighting continues. Salisbury made public Jan. 22, 1975 a communique reporting that government forces had killed at least 20 black nationalist guerrillas in clashes since the ceasefire was signed Dec. 11, 1974; 15 of the guerrillas had been killed since Jan. 13.

The release also reported that seven members of the South African police force had been killed in guerrilla confrontations in Rhodesia since the ceasefire accord.

The government reported fighting on the northern border Feb. 11. Two members of the Rhodesian security forces were reported killed near the Mozambique border March 7. Three guerrillas were hung in Salisbury Feb. 28.

Guerrillas slew three white civilians in northwestern Rhodesia, in the Zambezi valley region, the London Times reported April 13. Three Rhodesian soldiers were killed in a guerrilla confrontation April 2. According to the April 2 report, the deaths of two rebels in fighting the preceding week had raised the number of guerrillas killed since December 1972 to 550.

A government communique June 14 reported that 20 Africans had been killed in fighting between nationalist guerrillas and Rhodesian security forces June 12 in the northeast. The communique did not state whether the dead were rebels or villagers.

New guerrilla suppression drive slated— Salisbury announced July 11 that it was preparing to institute a secret plan to step up counter-insurgency measures against black guerrilla forces. "We will get back to the position where we are in total control of the security situation and dictating the course of events ourselves," a government spokesman said.

Rhodesia extended its 10-year-old state of emergency for another 12 months, it was reported June 26.

Border curfews imposed. Salisbury imposed dawn-to-dusk curfews along Rhodesia's eastern border with Mozambique July 25, 1975 and along the northern border with Botswana Aug. 5 to combat recruitment activities by guerrillas

crossing the borders. The Mozambique border action came after some 250 black students had reportedly disappeared from mission schools in the region. Four African National Council (ANC) officials were arrested in the northeast in connection with the alleged recruitment drives, Salisbury said July 17.

*Mozambique border clash—*Salisbury announced Oct. 10 that Mozambique soldiers had killed a white Rhodesian in a Rhodesian forest reserve near the Mozambique border Oct. 9. Rhodesian security forces later killed one of the members of the Mozambique force, the statement said. It was reportedly the first such clash between the two nations since Mozambique became independent June 25.

South African police pulled out. The Rhodesian government announced Feb. 11, 1975 that some of the units of the South African police in forward positions on the Zambezi River, the border between Rhodesia and Zambia, were being withdrawn; it was not made clear whether the troops were leaving Rhodesia entirely. The announcement followed assurances from the Zambian government that guerrilla incursions across the river into Rhodesia would cease.

South African Police Minister James T. Kruger announced in Pretoria Aug. 1 that an order had been issued for withdrawal of the remaining 200 members of its paramilitary police force stationed in Rhodesia.

"It has never been the purpose, nor has it been in the interests of Rhodesia or South Africa, to get involved in internal struggles between Rhodesians," Kruger said. Sent to Rhodesia in 1967 to stop terrorists from entering South Africa, Pretoria's police forces in Rhodesia at one point totaled 2,000. Since December 1972, 18 South Africans had been killed in Rhodesia.

Rhodesian Defense Minister P. K. van der Byl had announced the South African decision in Salisbury Aug. 1. Van der Byl, who had appealed July 27 for the South African forces to remain, said that the security situation in Rhodesia had deteriorated since the December cease-fire agreement.

U.S. probing mercenary recruitments.

The U.S. State Department announced June 22, 1975 that it had asked the Justice Department to investigate reports that Americans were being recruited to fight against black nationalist guerrillas in Rhodesia.

The department said the drive was being conducted by Phoenix Associates, a Boulder, Colo. firm established by Robert Brown, a former Special Forces major in Vietnam, who said June 23 that he sought to "merchandize information on mercenary opportunities abroad." A State Department spokesman said the company might be violating a law which required agents of foreign governments to register.

A spokesman for the Zimbabwe African National Union (ZANU), a Rhodesian black nationalist group, said that about 60 Americans were already fighting in Rhodesia, according to a June 24 report.

(An American-born Rhodesian army corporal, John Allan Coey, 22, was among four soldiers killed June 19 in a clash with guerrillas in northeastern Rhodesia.)

Talks Prove Fruitless

Negotiations criticized.

Settlement talks being conducted by the Rhodesian government with Bishop Abel Muzorewa of the African National Council had been subjected to broad criticism in early 1974. The ANC itself conceded Jan. 17 that no progress has been made.

The Zimbabwe (Rhodesia) African National Union had, since Jan. 16, repeatedly accused Muzorewa of being an agent of the British colonial "divide and rule" policy. Pro-settlement black groups, of which the most recent and vocal was the African Progressive Party (APP) headed by former Parliamentary Secretary Chad Chipunza, the bishop's uncle, sought without success to replace the ANC in the government negotiations.

The APP announced Feb. 3 that in rejecting the 1971 Constitution, the ANC was forcing Rhodesia to work under the 1969 Constitution which did not offer eventual majority rule.

Allan Savory, leader of the Rhodesia Party, provoked strong government condemnation when, in an election speech reported Feb. 23, he called for a constitutional conference attended by all responsible leaders in the country, including, "if all terrorist activity were to be stopped," representatives of the banned nationalist movements. Prime Minister Ian Smith described the proposal as "a most irresponsible and evil suggestion" and alleged that such pronouncements undermined the talks in progress.

ANC rejects settlement proposal—After months of negotiations between Bishop Muzorewa and Ian Smith, the ANC voted unanimously June 2 to reject the government proposals for political settlement. The government had reportedly offered to increase black representation in Parliament from 16 to 22 seats, a concession that the ANC deplored as falling "far short of demands," saying it would "deny the African people the acquisition of effective representation."

Smith said July 22 that the Rhodesia Party had harmed the talks by negotiating privately with the ANC's Edison Sithole and guerrilla groups. Bishop Muzorewa denied the contention later that day.

Sithole had been arrested along with 52 other ANC leaders June 20 and, as a result, the ANC suspended all further negotiations with the Smith government and called for a boycott of the July 30 elections.

(Two ANC leaders, Gordon Chavanduka and Elliott M. Gabellah met with British leaders in London June 29–July 8 to discuss the Rhodesian situation.)

In a related incident, police opened fire on rioting Africans in Gwelo, in the southwest, killing one person June 3. According to reports June 4, the demonstration broke out following erroneous reports that Bishop Muzorewa of the ANC had accepted the government's settlement proposals.

The ANC Aug. 8 rejected an invitation from Smith to a constitutional conference of African groups. Muzorewa said such talks should be convened only under Britain's chairmanship.

Three executive members of the ANC who ran as candidates in the Rhodesian elections July 30 resigned "voluntarily" from the organization, the ANC announced Aug. 5. The ANC had boycotted the elections.

A planned meeting with six leaders of the Rhodesian liberation movements failed to materialize when Salisbury Jan. 3 refused to permit them to fly to Lusaka.

Callaghan sees African leaders. British Foreign Secretary James Callaghan paid a 12-day visit to southern and eastern Africa Dec. 31, 1975–Jan. 11, 1975 for top-level meetings, chiefly on Rhodesia.

Speaking in Lusakà, Zambia, Jan. 1, Callaghan likened the government of Prime Minister Ian Smith to a man stranded in the middle of an icefield: "The ice looks very secure at the start, but then it starts to crack up all around . . . We have to help save them from themselves."

In a Jan. 8 assessment, Callaghan said: "We are now at a crunch point in the future development of southern Africa. If things go well, we could get a settlement in Rhodesia that would lead to peace and cooperation; to justice, to majority rule. . . . If things go wrong, then I believe we shall be in for a period of increasing armed struggle which will not be confined to one side. It will be fought out with growing bitterness on both sides. This is the measure of the responsibility we hold in our hands."

During his visit, Callaghan held talks with President Kenneth Kaunda of Zambia, Sir Seretse Khama of Botswana, Hastings Kamuzu Banda of Malawi, Julius Nyerere of Tanzania, Jomo Kenyatta of Kenya and Gen. Yakubu Gowon of Nigeria.

He also held an unscheduled meeting with South African Prime Minister John Vorster in Port Elizabeth. Emerging from the Jan. 4 talk, Callaghan said he had been left with "a clearer picture of South Africa's attitude on the question of Rhodesia."

Muller confers. South African Foreign Minister Hilgard Muller flew to Lusaka, Zambia Feb. 9, 1975 for a day of meetings with Rhodesian nationalists and black African leaders. The state-owned Zambian television called the visit "epochmaking" and other observers described it as one of the most important developments in the region since relations among the nations of southern Africa began thawing late in 1974.

OAU sets southern Africa policy. A special ministerial session of the Organization of African Unity (OAU) which opened April 7 in Dar es Salaam, Tanzania, concluded April 11 with the issuance of a document known as the Dar es Salaam Declaration on Southern Africa. The declaration represented a victory for the relatively moderate stance advocated by such nations as Tanzania and Zambia. It called for the peaceful solution of problems in the region; approved limited contacts with South Africa on the issues of majority rule in Rhodesia and independence for Namibia (South-West Africa); but otherwise urged the political, economic and cultural isolation of South Africa until it abandoned apartheid.

In his opening speech April 7, which sought to forge a bridge between the moderate and the more radical black African nations, Tanzanian President Julius K. Nyerere said: "This conference is not about so-called dialogue or detente with South Africa. This conference is about the liberation of southern Africa . . . [It] will have succeeded if it leaves South Africa in no doubt at all that we are still ready to use peaceful means to achieve independence in Rhodesia and Namibia. But if this is made impossible, we shall resume and intensify the armed struggle."

(A resolution introduced by Guinea, to end all contacts with South Africa, received little support at the meetings, although several nations, including Libya, Lesotho, Uganda and Kenya, denounced those nations—notably, Tanzania, Zambia, Botswana, and Mozambique—engaging in covert or overt contacts with the Rhodesian government.)

The Dar es Salaam declaration incorporated, according to the New York

Times April 16, large portions of a Tanzanian position paper that differentiated between colonial and racist issues in southern Africa. "Africa's strategy," the paper said, "should be to separate the two issues, as far as practical, and to give priority to ending the colonial situation in Rhodesia and Namibia." To these ends, negotiations with South Africa were "justified . . . as long as there was a chance that South Africa could help in ending the colonial problems," as recent developments had indicated.

Addressing the assembled delegations, Zambian Foreign Minister Vernon Mwaanga said that South African Prime Minister John Vorster had "kept his word" and contributed to progress on the Rhodesian front. Mwaanga also said that Vorster had "assured us that South African security forces will be withdrawn [from Rhodesia] by the end of May 1975."

Kaunda asks U.S. to shift its policy — Zambian President Kenneth D. Kaunda, in remarks made at a White House dinner given in his honor by U.S. President Gerald Ford April 19, urged the U.S. to re-examine and change its policy toward Africa. "You will forgive us, Mr. President, for our candor if we reaffirm on this occasion our dismay at the fact that America has not fulfilled our expectations."

His remarks were considered unusually blunt. President Ford and Secretary of State Henry Kissinger declined comment on the 20-minute remarks.

Kaunda said that U.S.-Zambian relations "are cordial, although there is room for improvement through more sound cooperation." But, he added, "What gives Zambia and Africa great cause for concern is America's policy towards Africa— or is it the lack of it, which, of course, can mean the same thing." Citing the U.S. practice of abstaining in United Nations votes, he noted that "a no-policy position may not be a neutral position."

Referring to the Dar es Salaam Declaration, he urged the U.S. "to support our efforts in achieving majority rule in Rhodesia and Namibia immediately and the ending of apartheid in South Africa."

"Peace is at stake," Kaunda said. "America must heed the call of the oppressed . . . If we want peace we must end

the era of inertia—in Rhodesia and Namibia and vigorously work for ending apartheid. America must now be in the vanguard of democratic revolution in southern Africa."

Black rule delay reportedly seen — Zambian President Kaunda was reported to have said that he thought it would take more than 10 years to achieve majority rule for the blacks of Rhodesia, according to a document, released in Salisbury April 23, which was prepared by two white Rhodesians who had recently interviewed the Zambian leader. Kaunda also reportedly said that any sudden move to majority rule could lead to a break-down in the economy of Rhodesia.

A copy of the report, which had not been intended for publication, had been released April 21 by Edson Sithole, publicity secretary of the African National Council. The Rhodesian government asked journalists to withhold publication, because of the "delicate state of affairs," the London Times reported April 23. ANC leader Bishop Abel Muzorewa joined in the appeal. Journalists agreed to withhold publication until the Zambian government offered comment. When no response from Lusaka was made, the newspapers printed the reports April 23.

ANC again rejects Smith call. The African National Council April 27, 1975 rejected an invitation from Ian Smith for talks on the convening of a constitutional conference. The ANC said such talks could not be held until Salisbury fulfilled the terms of the Lusaka cease-fire agreement.

ANC reaffirms unity, vows struggle. The leaders of the African National Council conferred in Dar es Salaam, Tanzania July 5-8, 1975 with the presidents of Tanzania, Zambia, Mozambique and Botswana. The leaders of the ANC ended their talks with a statement pledging "intensification of the liberation struggle" and reaffirming their unity in their common goal.

The ANC had been racked by dissension during the preceding weeks. A scheduled congress to elect new leadership was postponed June 16 due to "serious administrative and other extreme difficulties" as the constituent groups—the Zimbabwe African National Union (ZANU), the Zimbabwe African People's Union (ZAPU) and the Front for the Liberation of Zimbabwe (Frolizi)—exchanged mutual accusations of deceit.

The leader of ZAPU, Joshua Nkomo, vigorously attacked Bishop Abel Muzorewa June 30, accusing the ANC president of mounting a campaign against him. (Nkomo's majority on the ANC central committee would assure him victory when the organization's elections took place, it was widely acknowledged.)

Smith prefers pro-Nkomo group—Prime Minister Ian Smith indicated in a June 26 television interview that he favored the prospect of negotiating in a future constitutional conference with a group dominated by Nkomo. In his response to a question, Smith, 56, also conceded that majority rule in Rhodesia was possible in his lifetime, saying: "It may be, but this will be something for the conference table."

Charter talks set above Zambezi River. A government statement released in Salisbury Aug. 12, 1975 announced that Rhodesia's white leaders would meet with African National Council leaders before Aug. 25 to discuss a new Rhodesian constitution. The announcement said the meeting would "give the parties the opportunity to publicly express their genuine desire to negotiate an acceptable settlement" of the dispute over a new charter for the racially divided country.

The meeting would end a 10-year stalemate between Rhodesia's black and white leaderships on talks to pave the way for the country's transition from white minority rule to black majority rule. Efforts to begin the negotiations were set in motion by a December 1974 truce agreement which had been only partially respected.

The planned talks would be held in railway cars, provided by South Africa, on a bridge above the Zambezi River, just below the Victoria Falls, precisely between Rhodesia and black-ruled Zambia. Salisbury had insisted that the talks be held in Rhodesia; the ANC had demanded they be held outside the country. The Rhodesian government representatives were to enter the conference car from the Rhodesian side, while the black delegates would enter from Zambia.

The agreement, the precise terms of which were not revealed, was reached in Pretoria, South Africa during an Aug. 9–10 meeting between Rhodesian Prime Minister Ian Smith, South African Prime Minister John Vorster and a representative of the Zambian government, all of whom signed the document. Vorster had played a key role in prodding Rhodesia to agree to the meeting.

According to the Aug. 12 announcement, after the Victoria Falls talks, the conference would "adjourn to enable the parties to discuss proposals for a settlement in committee or committees within Rhodesia."

In a speech Aug. 13, Smith said the Victoria Falls bridge talks would be a perfunctory session, consisting merely of a signing ceremony. He also likened the ANC to "a decapitated chicken," a reference to the ANC's factional disputes. He sought to minimize the talks Aug. 14 in a TV broadcast in which he said: "It would be unwise to put too much faith in the prospects of a successful outcome to this initiative."

ANC leader Bishop Abel Muzorewa rejected Smith's interpretation Aug. 15, claiming the talks would be substantive. He also rejected the holding of subsequent meetings in Rhodesia. (Several ANC leaders were subject to arrest if they entered Rhodesia and Smith had strongly indicated Aug. 15 that amnesties would not be forthcoming.)

The Times of Zambia reported Aug. 17 that the ANC would attend the talks despite "the provocative utterances by rebel Ian Smith."

Preliminary charter talks collapse. Talks between Rhodesia's white minority government and black nationalist leaders of the African National Council broke down in and several other persons from the ANC in order to "protect the integrity, unity and security of the ANC and the future of the people of Zimbabwe." In a Sept. 14 statement, acknowledging the organization's split, the Lusaka-based ANC denounced the Nkomo faction as a "breakaway" group, but said that two black political parties could simultaneously exist. Both groups, however, persisted in claiming to represent the ANC, the only legal black political organization in Rhodesia.

Nkomo's ANC congress was held in Highfield, a black township outside of Salisbury, Sept. 28. It was attended by more than 3,000 representatives. In addition to electing Nkomo president, the congress also chose a new 69-member executive council.

Although Nkomo in his acceptance speech demanded continued negotiations with the Rhodesian government to secure majority rule "now, not tomorrow," the Highfield meeting was repudiated by the Lusaka-based ANC. Charging that Nkomo's congress was illegal and unconstitutional, it announced that it would hold an ANC congress in October to resolve the organization's problems.

(In a Sept. 22 statement, the Lusaka-based faction had charged that Nkomo had negotiated a secret pact with Rhodesian Prime Minister Ian Smith in which Nkomo would assume the premiership of Rhodesia and a multiracial cabinet would be formed.

(Nkomo, a former trade unionist and political prisoner, was the only one of the prominent ANC personalities to be functioning at present within Rhodesia.)

Muzorewa ANC faction meets—The ANC faction that remained loyal to Bishop Abel Muzorewa held a "national consultative meeting" in a sports stadium in Salisbury's Highfield African township Oct. 26.

More than 15,000 supporters attended the meeting, which had received a permit for only 6,000; police sources said a further 15,000–20,000 supporters had to be turned away.

Addressing the crowd, Elliott Gabellah, acting president of the ANC faction in the absence of Muzorewa who Oct. 6 had declared his intention to remain in Zambia, said the meeting itself would be cancelled due to the large turnout. He stated later in a news conference that the swell of support had demonstrated that the Rhodesian government would not be able to negotiate a constitutional settlement with the ANC faction of Joshua Nkomo alone.

A Nkomo-faction meeting, held in September, had been attended by fewer than 5,000 supporters. Nkomo Oct. 27 refuted the significance of the Muzorewa-faction ANC meeting, calling it a "circus." He said his group had not held a rally, but a "properly constituted annual congress."

Smith recants anti-Vorster remark—Ian Smith apologized Oct. 20 for having said in a recorded interview televised Oct. 12 that South African Prime Minister John Vorster had been responsible for the failure of the August attempt to reach a constitutional settlement.

Following four hours of talks with Vorster in Pretoria, Smith apologized for any embarrassment caused Vorster by the assertion and denied that he had meant to imply in the interview that South Africa was interfering in Rhodesia's internal affairs. South Africa had played a key role in organizing the now-defunct settlement talks and had actively intervened in an attempt to prevent them from collapsing.

In his television statement, which was aired in London and Salisbury, Smith had said he believed that "if this new initiative had not been taken by Mr. Vorster and the four northern [black African] presidents, I believe we would have had a [Rhodesian] settlement by now."

Smith's remark had provoked sharp criticism from the South African press and several cabinet ministers had expressed their anger and dismay at the comment, which threatened to rupture relations between the two nations. Vorster said Oct. 12 upon learning of the statement that, if accurately reported, it meant that "the many discussions in which the Rhodesians were involved in Pretoria, Cape Town, Salisbury and Lusaka had served no purpose at all." Smith had accused the media Oct. 13 of "gross distortion" of his remarks.

the early hours of Aug. 26. Each side blamed the other for the failure to make progress toward an agreement to hold formal negotiations.

The talks, held in a railroad car on a bridge straddling the Rhodesian-Zambian border, had begun Aug. 25 and continued throughout the day. The meeting had been arranged under the aegis of South African Prime Minister John Vorster and Zambian President Kenneth Kaunda, both of whom attended. The two leaders, the major proponents of detente in southern Africa, also held extensive talks, in Rhodesia as well as Zambia, while the Victoria Falls meeting was in progress.

Vorster and Kaunda indicated Aug. 26 that they would persist in efforts to get the Rhodesian settlement talks under way again. Vorster asserted in Pretoria that "certain hitches" had arisen, but that a deadlock had not been reached. Addressing the two delegations Aug. 25, Vorster and Kaunda had emphasized that bargaining in committees should begin within seven days and that a full new constitutional agreement should be reached within 60 days.

The breakdown in the talks was announced by Rhodesian Prime Minister Ian Smith, leader of his government's delegation to the talks, who returned to Salisbury Aug. 26 and told Parliament that the ANC leaders had been determined to make the talks fail.

ANC leader Abel Muzorewa asserted Aug. 26 that the talks had broken down because Smith refused to grant amnesty for council leaders who faced possible arrest in Rhodesia if they returned to participate in talks there.

According to conference sources, the ANC was under pressure from Zambia and South Africa to sign and adhere to the Aug. 9 Pretoria agreement providing for substantive constitutional talks in Rhodesia after the preliminary conference. Although the document had been signed by Mark Chona, Kaunda's envoy, on behalf of Zambia and the ANC, no ANC representative had signed.

The ANC leadership was split between moderates such as Muzorewa and Joshua Nkomo, leader of the Zimbabwe African People's Union (ZAPU), and militants—

including those who faced arrest in Rhodesia such as the Rev. Ndabaningi Sithole of the Zimbabwe African National Union (ZANU) and James Chikerema of the Front for the Liberation of Zimbabwe (Frolizi). Their disputes reportedly absorbed much of the time spent at the Victoria Falls meeting.

The Rhodesian delegation to the talks included Smith, Deputy Prime Minister John Wrathall, Minister of Defense and Foreign Affairs P. K. Van der Byl, Minister of Information Wickus de Kock and Cabinet Secretary Jack Gaylard. The ANC delegation comprised Muzorewa, Nkomo, Chikerema, Sithole, ANC Vice President Elliott Gabellah and seven other officials.

Nkomo emerges as leader in ANC split. Joshua Nkomo, who was leader of the moderate Zimbabwe African People's Union (ZAPU), was elected president of the African National Council Sept. 28, 1975 in a controversial and disputed national congress held in Rhodesia. Nkomo's election signaled the split of the organization into two distinct factions.

The long-simmering feud within the ANC groups had begun escalating Sept. 3 when Nkomo denounced the Rev. Ndabaningi Sithole, leader of the militant Zimbabwe African National Union (ZANU), one of the ANC movements. Sithole earlier had announced the formation of the Zimbabwe Liberation Council (ZLC) as an external wing of the ANC, in Lusaka, Zambia. Neither Sithole nor James Chikerema, who was leader of the third black movement, the Front for the Liberation of Zimbabwe (Frolizi), were legally permitted to enter Rhodesia, where both were subject to immediate detention.

It was in his Sept. 3 statement denouncing the Sithole move that Nkomo called a national ANC congress to be held later in the month to elect a new president for the organization. The current ANC president, Bishop Abel Muzorewa, who had in the past been criticized by Nkomo, was on an extended fund-raising tour of Europe at the time.

Upon his return to Lusaka, Muzorewa Sept. 11 ordered the expulsion of Nkomo

Smith & Nkomo agree to talks. Prime Minister Smith and Joshua Nkomo in Salisbury Dec. 1, 1975 signed a joint declaration of intent to hold talks in Rhodesia on a constitutional settlement.

It was the first indication of progress toward a settlement since the collapse in August of talks between Smith and a group of leaders of the black nationalist movement which had since split into two rival factions.

Despite an apparent government concession—the guarantee of full immunity from detention or restriction for any member of the ANC negotiating team and freedom to enter and leave Rhodesia as they wished (a crucial point which had contributed to previous failures to get talks under way)—the ANC exile faction, led from Zambia by Bishop Abel Muzorewa, repudiated the pact immediately. A prominent Muzorewa supporter, the Rev. Ndabaningi Sithole, asserted in Dar es Salaam, Tanzania Dec. 1 that "we intend shooting our way back into Zimbabwe until majority rule is eatablished in our country."

In a Salisbury statement, Nkomo declined to say whether he would invite the leaders of the exiled ANC faction to the proposed talks. Nkomo's position was that a constitutional agreement would have to result in the immediate appointment of an interim government reflecting black majority rule and the introduction within one year of one-man-one-vote elections.

Smith-Nkomo talks collapse. Prime Minister Smith and Joshua Nkomo opened constitutional settlement talks in Salisbury Dec. 15, 1975, but the talks broke down March 19, 1976.

A joint statement issued in Salisbury declared the parties had "reached an impasse and are therefore breaking off the talks. This will provide an opportunity for consultation and consideration."

In separate statements following the announcement, Smith and Nkomo attributed the talks' collapse to the intransigency of the other and each called upon Great Britain to assist in the resolution of the dispute.

Smith gave two reasons for the talks' breakdown: Nkomo's demand for the immediate resignation of the government and dissolution of Parliament and their replacement by an interim council headed by a British-appointed chairman; and Nkomo's insistence on lowering voting qualifications so that a black majority Parliament would be achieved in the first election. Both were rejected by the government as untenable.

"For our part," Smith said, "we offered far-reaching proposals involving power-sharing and embodying considerable constitutional advantages for the African people. These were rejected by the ANC.

"I believe that the British government should no longer avoid the responsibility which it claims and should now actively participate in resolving the constitutional issue in Rhodesia," Smith concluded.

Nkomo accused the government of "evasion and prevarication" and said the talks broke down "on the single and fundamental issue of majority rule now. This the regime was not prepared to contemplate, save in 15 years' time and when they are satisfied that the blacks have earned it. . . . We make no apologies for rejecting these racist and contemptuous proposals.

"It is the goal of Britain to decolonize this country," Nkomo asserted. "If she is not prepared to play her role, then Britain and the regime have left it to the people themselves."

The government delegation comprised the prime minister, Agriculture Minister David Smith, Foreign Affairs and Defense Minister P. K. van der Byl, Public Service Minister Reginald Cowper and Internal Affairs Minister Jack Mussett.

The nationalist team numbered 22 delegates and legal advisers, including two British lawyers and three representatives of the Zambian government.

UK envoy sees Smith & Nkomo. The British government Feb. 24, 1976 had dispatched Lord Greenhill, former head of the diplomatic service, to Rhodesia to meet with government officials and black nationalist leaders to assess the possibilities for progress and a British role in the constitutional talks then in progress.

Greenhill met with Smith and Nkomo during his three-day visit, but leaders of the external militant wing of the ANC which had boycotted the constitutional negotiations, refused to speak with him.

British Foreign Secretary James Callaghan reported to Parliament March 2, after receiving Greenhill's report on the meetings, that there were no grounds for hopes of an early transfer of power to the black majority in Rhodesia. Smith, Callaghan said, remained "his own man and he will go his own way."

The decision to send an envoy to Salisbury followed a Feb. 20 statement by Smith before Parliament in which he said Rhodesia had reached "a stage in our history where it could be beneficial to change our tactics. If the British government is prepared to make a constructive and realistic effort to assist in our settlement, then I believe we must give this consideration." Rhodesia had consistently resisted past attempts by Great Britain to mediate or participate in the constitutional negotiations on the transference of power.

Smith said he was responding to an earlier offer by Great Britain which followed meetings held in London in early February between British officials and Nkomo.

Muzorewa ANC backer killed in riot—One man was killed Jan. 12 by police who opened fired on a crowd of some 200 persons demonstrating in Gwelo's Mkobo township in support of the external faction of the African National Council (ANC) headed from Zambia by Bishop Abel Muzorewa. The police said the demonstrators had stoned the homes of supporters of the rival Nkomo ANC wing.

In another development, the Rhodesian government released the Rev. Canaan Banana, a former ANC vice president, from detention Jan. 15. He was restricted, however, from moving outside of a 12-mile radius of the center of his home town, Bulawayo.

Smith rejects British plan. A two-stage plan proposed by Great Britain March 22, 1976 to resolve the Rhodesian crisis in the wake of the collapse of the constitutional talks was rejected March 23 by Prime Minister Smith as "no less extreme" than the ANC's position.

The British proposal, outlined to the House of Commons in London by Foreign Secretary James Callaghan, called first for the Rhodesian government to accept several preconditions and, second, for the negotiation of the actual terms of a constitution for independence.

The preconditions were: acceptance of the principle of majority rule; election for majority rule within 18 months to two years; agreement that majority rule would have to precede independence; and assurance that the constitutional negotiations would not be unduly protracted and that the transition of power would be orderly.

Britain pledged to provide financial and diplomatic assistance to insure the transition and promised direct efforts at the United Nations to lift current economic sanctions against Rhodesia if the conditions were agreed to. There would, however, be no aid whatsoever if the preconditions were not accepted.

Callaghan several times directed his appeal to the white Rhodesian electorate, in effect circumventing the Smith government. If Smith were not to agree to the pursuit of a negotiated settlement as outlined in his address, Callaghan said, "I hope other leaders will emerge who recognize the realities of the hour." Smith, the foreign secretary averred, was "leading his country on the path of death and destruction."

After meeting with his cabinet March 23 Smith announced Rhodesia's rejection of the British plan, declaring that London had "chosen to disregard the realities and had come forward with proposals no less extreme" than the ANC's. In a March 20 press conference, in which he had pressed his appeal for British participation in efforts to resolve the Rhodesian crisis, Smith had said: "I don't believe in black majority rule in Rhodesia, not in a thousand years."

White popular opinion rallied behind Smith after the British announcement, even before Salisbury had officially rejected London's proposals. Tim Gibbs, leader of the liberal-leaning white Rhodesia Party, declared that Britain was forcing Rhodesia "to the brink of bloodshed" in advocating so brief a period as two years for the election of a majority government. The multiracial Center Party also rejected the British timetable.

Joshua Nkomo, leader of the ANC faction with which the government had been negotiating, said he had expected "a more positive move" from Britain.

Sithole quits ANC. The Rev. Ndabaningi Sithole Sept. 9, 1976 announced his withdrawal from the African National Council. Sithole deplored the ANC's failure to unify its rival factions, the Zimbabwe African People's Union (ZAPU) and the Zimbabwe African National Union (ZANU).

Following his resignation, Sithole claimed sole leadership of ZANU, but it was unclear whether all or part of ZANU had withdrawn from the ANC.

Sithole's claim to ZANU leadership was challenged by Robert Mugabe, who had close ties with ANC guerrilla forces known as the Zimbabwe People's Army (ZIPA), it was reported Sept. 10. According to the report, ZIPA was almost completely under the control of the ZANU military leadership. ZIPA had been formed from the remnants of the Third Force, a guerrilla organization run by representatives of ZANU and ZAPU in an effort to unify the guerrilla command.

Guerrilla-Rhodesia Fighting: Foreign & Domestic Effects

Smith predicts guerrilla offensive. Prime Minister Ian Smith Feb. 6, 1976 said in a nationwide broadcast address that guerrilla warfare along Rhodesia's border with Mozambique had recently intensified after a period of relative calm. Warning the nation to expect the most serious guerrilla incursions to date, he announced an increased military callup and told Rhodesians that they would be subjected to psychological warfare as well.

Clashes between Rhodesian security forces and black nationalist guerrillas had significantly risen during the preceding two weeks, Smith said, with 14 "terrorists" and one member of the Rhodesian forces killed.

The prime minister said the guerrillas, operating out of Mozambique, were supporters of the Zimbabwe African National Union (ZANU) faction of the militant external wing of the African National Congress (ANC). The guerrillas, he charged, were seeking to undermine current negotiations between his government and the internal faction of the ANC headed by Joshua Nkomo. (It was widely believed in Salisbury, reports indicated, that, if the Smith-Nkomo talks were to collapse, the militant faction headed by Bishop Abel Muzorewa would be impelled to launch a full-scale guerrilla war.)

Mozambique border clashes mount. At least 78 guerrillas and 10 members of the Rhodesian security forces were killed in confrontations in the operational zone along the 800-mile Mozambique-Rhodesia border between Feb. 6, 1976, the day on which Rhodesian Prime Minister Ian Smith warned of an impending nationalist offensive, and Feb. 29.

One of the most serious incidents occurred Feb. 24 when, according to a Salisbury military communique, Rhodesian forces lost one soldier and killed 24 guerrillas in a "follow-up hot pursuit" operation against a suspected guerrilla camp. This was the first reported foray across the border, as the "hot pursuit" designation was acknowledged to signify, since Mozambique became independent in June 1975.

Salisbury did not identify the location of the action, but in a March 3 announcement in which he closed his nation's border with Rhodesia, Mozambique President Samora Machel said the incursion had occurred at Pafuri, a Mozambique village on the Limpopo River, where the Rhodesian, South African and Mozambiquan borders met. Machel said seven Rhodesians had been killed in the operation in which Mozambique forces suffered two casualties and shot down two Rhodesian jet planes.

Rhodesian Defense and Foreign Affairs Minister Pieter van der Byl, in his March 3 comments on Machel's announcements, said that Rhodesian forces had "from time to time" entered Mozambique in "hot pursuit" of terrorists. Maputo invited the

Salisbury action, he maintained, by giving bases and assistance to Rhodesian nationalist guerrillas. He further defended the "hot pursuit" practice as being "time-hallowed" and sanctioned by international law.

In an earlier clash, Salisbury reported that security forces from Mozambique had battled Rhodesian troops Feb. 20 in a border incident at an undisclosed location. This was the first reported confrontation involving Mozambique troops since the former Portuguese colony became independent in June 1975.

Among other incidents, three black Rhodesian paramilitary policemen were killed in a guerrilla raid on a hotel near Inyanga, 70 miles north of Umtali, in eastern Rhodesia, Feb. 29 and 17 guerrillas and four security force members were killed in a clash in the northeastern operation zone near Mt. Darwin Feb. 28.

Mozambique girds for war, shuts border.
Mozambique President Samora Machel March 3, 1976 put Mozambique on a war footing against Rhodesia, describing a Feb. 24 attack by Rhodesian forces on the Mozambique village of Pafuri as "an act of war." Bishop Abel Muzorewa, leader of the militant external wing of the African National Council, the now-divided umbrella organization of Rhodesian black nationalist movements, was present as Machel made his broadcast announcement.

The Mozambique president closed the 800-mile border shared by the two nations, thus severing Rhodesia's critical access to the sea, and, in accordance with United Nations and Organization of African Unity resolutions, imposed sanctions, including the confiscation of Rhodesian property in Mozambique, against "the British colony of Southern Rhodesia," the territory's designation prior to its unilateral declaration of independence from Great Britain in 1965.

(The Financial Times of London reported March 4 that Mozambique's decision to impose sanctions had been agreed to at a meeting of the presidents of Zambia, Tanzania, Botswana and Mozambique in early February.)

The Marxist president called on Mozambiquans to build air raid shelters in all population centers and devote time to manning antiaircraft defenses. Earliest translations of Machel's address had been interpreted as constituting a virtual declaration of war and were so reported in the South African press that day, only to be corrected after an information official in Maputo (formerly Lourenco Marques), the capital of Mozambique, told a South African editor in Johannesburg in a telephone interview that Mozambique had not declared war.

In the only official Rhodesian reaction to Machel's announcement, Foreign Affairs and Defense Minister Pieter van der Byl said in a television statement March 3 that Machel was acting against Rhodesia in order to divert attention from Mozambique's internal difficulties.

Van der Byl charged that the earlier distortions of Machel's statement as a declaration of war were part of the "diabolical psychological war" being waged against Rhodesia. "Samora Machel has not declared war on us and we certainly have no intention of declaring war on him, but all this saber-rattling can only make an already difficult situation much more dangerous," he said. Van der Byl further asserted that the closing of the border would be "infinitely more harmful to Mozambique than to Rhodesia."

(According to the Financial Times of London March 3, from 20% to 30% of Rhodesia's trade was dependent upon Mozambique transportation links. This compared with approximately 70% dependence before June 1975 when Mozambique acceded to independence from Portugal. While exact figures were not available, Mozambique was known to be significantly dependent upon transit fees from Rhodesia and South Africa for the bulk of its foreign-exchange earnings, earnings that would halt with the imposition of sanctions.)

Prior to the Mozambique action, Salisbury Feb. 27 had suspended rail traffic between Rhodesia and Maputo, after Mozambique arrested 16 employes of the Rhodesian railroad at Malvernia, a train depot just inside Mozambique. The 16, eight white and eight black, were subsequently transferred to Maputo where officials refused to provide any details on the detentions.

UK lauds Mozambique, vows assistance—The British government March 3 acclaimed Mozambique's decision to apply full economic sanctions against the white minority government of Rhodesia.

The Commonwealth of Nations March 4 issued a communique in London indicating that its secretary general, Shridath Ramphal, would contact the Mozambique government in order to determine the black African nation's immediate economic aid requirements.

The Financial Times of London reported March 4 that the British government had previously made a definite offer of aid to President Samora Machel at the conclusion of the Kingston, Jamaica Commonwealth Congress in May 1975. Judith Hart, who was at the time Britain's minister for overseas development, confirmed that the amount of the aid "understanding" was £15 million ($30.2 million). British estimates made in May 1975 had put the cost to Mozambique of closing its border to Rhodesia at about £10 million, although some African sources had put the total as high as £40 million.

South Africa weighs response—South African Prime Minister John Vorster responded cautiously March 4 to Mozambique's imposition of sanctions and closing of the border against Rhodesia. He warned that the actions could cause "an escalation to something much more serious."

Vorster's statement failed to provide a commitment to guarantee full Rhodesian trade assistance, but left room for "adaptations" to compensate for the loss of Mozambique transportation links. With Mozambique's actions, South Africa was the only nation through which land-locked Rhodesia could import or export goods; rail links through Zambia had been closed in 1973.

Zambia vows to aid Mozambique—Zambian President Kenneth Kaunda March 3 welcomed the Mozambique decision to impose sanctions against

Rhodesia and said Zambia would cooperate fully with the moves. In a Feb. 15 address to officials of the United National Independence Party in Lusaka, Kaunda had said: "Before Zimbabwe is free, there is going to be a bloodbath in that country."

Zambia foresees war, asks U.K. force. Zambian President Kenneth Kaunda March 29, 1976 urged U.K. military intervention in Rhodesia to bring the war he predicted would engulf the country "to a quicker end." Upon the breakdown of the constitutional talks in Salisbury March 19 Kaunda had declared that Africa had no option but to help intensify the armed struggle of the Rhodesian nationalists.

In his March 29 remarks to foreign newsmen in Lusaka, Kaunda said that the Rhodesian guerrillas currently being trained in Mozambique and Tanzania (estimated to number about 12,000) could, for the time being, fight the war themselves, needing only arms, money and medicine from outside.

British intervention on the side of the nationalists would, he said enhance London's reputation in Africa. He called on Britain to arrest all the "rebels" (the members of the white minority Rhodesian government), dissolve the government and Parliament, and install an executive committee with a British chairman.

In a related development, Kaunda met in Lusaka with the presidents of Tanzania, Mozambique and the Ivory Coast March 24–25 to discuss the Rhodesian crisis in light of the collapse of the Salisbury talks March 19. In addition to Presidents Julius Nyerere, Samora Machel and Felix Houphouet-Boigny, Joshua Nkomo, head of the Rhodesian-based ANC faction, and Bishop Abel Muzorewa, leader of the external militant ANC faction, also participated in the talk. No communique was issued at the meeting's end, but sources said the leaders had discussed plans for the intensification of the guerrilla war and tried unsuccessfully to bring about a reconciliation between the two ANC factions.

Fighting & arrests. Serious incidents continued on through April 1976.

In clashes between Rhodesian security forces and nationalist guerrillas, Salisbury said April 5 that eight rebels had been killed in the preceding four days, bringing the total killed during 1975 to 128; 16 Rhodesian soldiers had been killed since the beginning of the year. Eight more nationalists were said to have been killed in four days of clashes reported April 15. Two Africans who had broken curfew regulations were also killed that day, Salisbury said. Four guerrillas and seven Africans had been listed killed in actions reported by Salisbury April 1. Four of the civilians had apparently been slain in crossfire and three during the curfew.

Rhodesia had also intensified arrests of nationalists in the capital region during April. Police arrested 158 Africans for taking part in an illegal meeting April 4 in Sinoia, 60 miles north of Salisbury. Among those held was Morton Malianga, national chairman of the external faction of the African National Council headed by Bishop Abel Muzorewa. Another 38 Africans were arrested in Tafara township, six miles east of Salisbury, April 11 after clashes between supporters of the two rival ANC factions.

Guerrillas kill tourists, transit halts. Rhodesia shut its main road to South Africa and transit on the newly-completed Rutenga-Beitbridge railway was interrupted April 19, 1976 after attacks by guerrillas that day near Nuanetsi, in the southern ranchlands region. The guerrilla actions, more than 60 miles inside Rhodesia, were the deepest such penetrations to date.

Service on the rail line was interrupted for 24 hours after the rebels blew up a section of the track. Rhodesian police sealed off a 178-mile section of the Fort Victoria-Beitbridge road to South Africa after guerrillas shot and killed three South African motorcyclists near Nuanetsi.

Salisbury April 20 announced tighter security measures to protect tourists and the railway. Tourism was one of Rhodesia's main sources of foreign exchange, with receipts of more than $40 million in 1975, according to an April 20 report. Moreover, the Rutenga-Beitbridge

line was Rhodesia's only direct rail link to South Africa, the sole nation through which Rhodesia continued to evade international economic sanctions.

Rhodesia's main road to South Africa opened to traffic May 3 with paramilitary convoys in escort.

Guerrilla forces May 5 tried to sabotage the rail line which entered South Africa via Botswana, Salisbury announced May 6. The attempted sabotage occurred at Plumtree in western Rhodesia near the Botswana border.

Military service extended. The Rhodesian regime May 1, 1976 extended indefinitely the service terms of its territorial forces. Four days later it extended the length of service for regular troops from 12 months to 18 months. The actions were taken in the wake of increasing guerrilla activity and were part of a new security offensive.

The May 1 announcement came in a nationwide speech by Lt. Gen. Peter Walls, armed forces commander. It affected young men who had completed within the last three or four years or who were completing their compulsory one-year service. Previously these persons had faced 55-day call-ups. The May 1 action extended the period indefinitely.

Rhodesia had 10,000 territorials and 5,000 active army and air force personnel. The nation's economic activity would be seriously impaired if all the territorials were withdrawn from the workforce simultaneously by a call-up. (Rhodesia's paramilitary forces numbered about 8,000 active and 35,000 reservist and civil police totaled 5,000.)

In his speech, Walls warned that the armed forces would persist in "hot pursuit" operations across the Mozambique border. "Where our terrorists take refuge across the border when we are closing in on them to destroy them, we will, if necessary, follow them across the border," he said.

Walls said that the nation's security forces had advised the government to extend tours of active duty for regular units to 18 months, the action ordered on May 5.

In a related development, A. J. Smith, Rhodesian secretary for African education, said Oct. 30 that 340 black high school students had quit school to join guerrilla forces during October.

State of emergency renewed. Citing increased guerrilla warfare, "hostility" from neighboring countries, factional fighting among black nationalists and continuing United Nations sanctions, Minister of Law and Order Hilary Squires June 24, 1976 announced a renewal of the state of emergency. Emergency rule had been imposed in 1965 and extended periodically.

Death penalty extended—An amendment to the Law and Order (Maintenance) Act Sept. 8 made the death penalty mandatory for those who recruited and trained guerrillas within and outside Rhodesia; for those who failed to report terrorist suspects or who harbored known terrorists, and for those who gave false information about terrorists to officials. Children under 16 and pregnant women were excluded from the penalty.

Casualties rise in guerrilla strikes. The intensified guerrilla campaign on the eastern frontier with Mozambique claimed the lives of 291 black nationalist insurgents and 39 Rhodesian troops, both blacks and whites, since Jan. 1, according to data released June 10, 1976 by Edward Sutton-Pryce, deputy minister in Rhodesian Prime Minister Ian Smith's office.

In May alone, according to releases from Salisbury, clashes along the Mozambique border had resulted in the deaths of 104 guerrillas, 18 members of the Rhodesian security forces (plus five who died as a result of accidents), 29 curfew-breakers (civilians who were shot during the dawn-to-dusk curfew imposed in parts of the region) and 80 other civilians (including those succumbing to landmine injuries and those killed while in the company of terrorists).

The following eastern Rhodesia incidents were among those reported in communiques issued by the Rhodesian Defense Ministry. The communiques generally referred to the actions as having taken place in "the operational zone," the

designation for the Mozambique border region.

May 6–12—Clashes claimed 34 lives: eleven guerrillas, two members of the security forces, six curfew-violators and 15 civilians who stepped on land mines.

May 13–14—Nine unspecified deaths were reported.

May 21—Five guerrillas and one black civilian accompanying them were killed and one white soldier died in action; a second soldier died of injuries sustained in fighting that had taken place weeks earlier.

May 24—One guerrilla and three curfew-breakers were reported killed and one black woman was killed by cross fire. Two white civilians traveling in the mountainous district north of Umtali on the Mozambique border were reported to have been fired upon by black Africans. Salisbury announced a dawn-to-dusk curfew in the Umtali region.

May 25—Eight guerrillas and three civilians were killed and three members of the security forces were injured in reported clashes.

May 27—Reports said black guerrillas had penetrated to within 32 miles of Salisbury, the deepest thrust yet toward the Rhodesian capital. Two guerrillas were shot and a black woman was killed in cross fire between nationalist and government forces.

May 28—Eight nationalists and four black civilians were killed.

May 29—Seven guerrillas were killed and one member of the security forces was injured.

May 30–June 1—Twenty-three guerrillas and one member of the security forces were killed in clashes.

June 3—Twelve guerrillas and two curfew-violators were reported killed.

June 5—Two white civilians and a black schoolmaster were reported killed by guerrilla insurgents.

June 6—A white woman and her two daughters were killed in a land mine explosion near Chipinga and a black policeman was reported killed in an engagement with rebel forces.

June 10—Eleven guerrillas were killed in an incident which was also reported in the London Times June 14 by its correspondent who accompanied the Rhodesian forces on the operation. The Times report said that the dead included "a Marxist political commissar who is attached to every guerrilla section and two terror experts trained in Russian-run camps in Tanzania."

June 13—Eleven guerrillas were reported killed in two incidents in the "operational zone." Also reported that day was the sabotage of the Salisbury-Umtali railroad line at Macheke, 60 miles east of the Rhodesian capital. (Transit on the line had been seriously hampered and uncertain since a May 15 attack which prompted a government statement advising that safety guarantees could no longer be provided on the railroad.)

Among developments in regions other than the Mozambique border area, two white civilians were killed by guerrillas May 23 at Kezi, 45 miles north of Bulawayo, near the Botswana border. The railroad connecting Rhodesia to South Africa via Botswana was derailed that day in the second major sabotage incident on the line. A further attack on the rail line took place June 13.

Two Rhodesian soldiers died May 17 in an attack at Ugundi, on the Fort Victoria-Beitbridge road. Salisbury May 23 ordered a compulsory convoy system along 90 miles of the road from West Nicholson to Beitbridge, on the South African border, replacing the voluntary armed convoy patrol instituted three weeks earlier when the road was reopened.

Zambia OKs guerrilla raids on Rhodesia. Zambian President Kenneth Kaunda said May 28, 1976 that his government would permit Zimbabwe guerrillas to use Zambia as a base for raids in Rhodesia.

Kaunda previously had supported continued efforts to secure a negotiated settlement in the Rhodesian conflict. In his May 28 statement, Kaunda said that guerrillas were already in training in Zambia for the opening of the front.

Of Rhodesia's white minority, Kaunda said: "If only they could follow the example of whites in Zambia, it would have given us a chance to do something better for them in Rhodesia. Now, instead of peaceful change there is war. . . . The [black] people will take over because there will be a revolution."

Rhodesian Defense Minister Pieter K. van der Byl confirmed June 10 that black nationalist guerrillas had opened a third front along the 600-mile northwestern border with Zambia. The other fronts were along Rhodesia's 200-mile northern border with Mozambique and on its 600-mile eastern border with that nation.

Van der Byl said blacks operating from Zambia had been responsible for explosions that several days earlier had damaged three planes at a remote Rhodesian airstrip near the Zambian border. There were, he said, an estimated 400 guerrillas poised for attack in Zambia. About 1,300 black nationalists had launched attacks on Rhodesia from Mozambique, he added.

In a related development, Kaunda charged June 13 that "rebels in Rhodesia"—his designation for the white minority government there—were responsible for planting bombs in Lusaka's central post office and the high court building. The bombs extensively damaged both buildings that day. Asked to comment on Kaunda's charge, a Salisbury government spokesman said: "We do not know to whom Dr. Kaunda is referring when he refers to Rhodesian rebels."

Mozambique base is bombed by jets. Rhodesian planes destroyed a Mozambican army post at Espungabera June 10, 1976 in retaliation for a 3-hour mortar-and-rocket barrage earlier that day against a tea plantation in southeastern Rhodesia near the Mozambique border.

The attack on the plantation was believed to have been conducted by Mozambique government forces, rather than by Rhodesian black nationalists who had also been operating from Mozambique bases, the London Times reported June 12. The artillery fired in the attack on the plantation included Soviet-made 122-mm. rockets which caused damage but no injuries, a Salisbury spokesman said.

The air strike, the first major attack on a Mozambique army base since that nation's president, Samora Machel, closed the border with Rhodesia, knocked out an ammunition dump and guerrilla mortar positions, the Rhodesian government spokesman said. The incident took place in the border region, about 20 miles from the Rhodesian town of Chipinga, site of earlier guerrilla attacks. The area is about 250 miles southeast of Salisbury.

The Rhodesian spokesman also warned Zambia, where a spokesman had said earlier that Rhodesian guerrillas would be permitted to open up a new military front along the Rhodesia-Zambian border. "The attack on Espungabera can be seen as a warning to Zambia and as an indication that Rhodesia is prepared to step up the pace and extent of the war if provoked," the Salisbury spokesman said.

Violence continues on Mozambique border—A Rhodesian military communique reported a gunfight between Rhodesian and Mozambique troops July 10 in which one Mozambique soldier was reported killed.

An eight-year-old white girl was reported killed by a guerrilla ambush of three cars on the Rhodesia-South Africa road July 13.

Rhodesia raids Mozambique. For the second time since June, Rhodesian forces entered Mozambique Aug. 8, 1976 in purported retaliation for attacks being launched against the Salisbury regime from there by Rhodesian black nationalists. An official announcement said that 300 guerrillas were killed in the raid as well as 30 regular Mozambique troops and 10 civilians.

The statement, released Aug. 10, said the raid had taken place two days earlier in retaliation for a mortar attack that day on a Rhodesian army base from a camp about three miles inside Mozambique and 20 miles south of Umtali. Five Rhodesian soldiers were reported to have been killed by the mortars. "As a result of this unprovoked aggression across our border," the

announcement said, "and in accordance with the accepted international practice of hot pursuit" Rhodesian security personnel moved against the camp.

The account, which did not specify whether the air force had been used, said that the Rhodesians destroyed a roadblock and a bridge on their way to the camp, suffering only "a few minor injuries" in the operation. They attacked the camp, the official statement said, on the basis of "irrefutable evidence" that it was being used for guerrilla activities and after "repeated warnings" to the government of Mozambique about the dangers of supporting terrorists.

"It has consistently been made clear that Rhodesia has no quarrel with the people of Mozambique or their armed forces, with whom they wish to live in harmony," the statement said.

"In the absence of any restraining influence from the outside world, Rhodesia has had no option but to strike at the centers of organized terrorism on her borders in the interests of her own self-preservation. These terrorists owe allegiance to nobody save themselves and acknowledge no Rhodesian political leadership. They are not motivated by any desire to improve the lot of their fellow Rhodesian Africans, but solely by a lust for power and self-enrichment at the hands of any victim they care to choose."

Attack on refugee camp charged—An aide to the United Nations High Commissioner for Refugees (UNHCR) accused Rhodesia Aug. 20 of having destroyed a U.N. refugee camp in Mozambique Aug. 8, killing at least 675 civilians.

Hugo Idoyaga, a Uruguayan representative of the UNHCR in Mozambique, reported to UNHCR headquarters in Geneva Aug. 20 that he had found 10 mass graves of men, women and children in the Nyazonia camp Aug. 18. He also reported that on a May 28 visit to the camp he had seen no signs of guerrilla activity, as alleged by the Rhodesians.

In his report to the UNHCR, Idoyaga said that Rhodesian soldiers had disguised themselves as Mozambicans, using Mozambican uniforms and weapons and riding in vehicles marked with Mozambican registration numbers. White Rhodesian soldiers painted their hands and faces black to aid in the deception, he added.

According to Idoyaga's report, the Rhodesian convoy split into three groups. One sabotaged the main bridge across the River Pungue near the camp, another prepared an ambush on the road leading to the camp, and the third entered the camp itself.

Edward Sutton-Pryce, a deputy minister to Prime Minister Ian Smith, held a televised news conference Aug. 28 and exhibited documents which he said represented proof that the camp had been a base for guerrilla activities. Among the papers shown were: a map of the camp, labelling some buildings "barracks"; information on recruits' backgrounds which gave their reasons for joining the guerrilla movement, and a list of names and personal information of over 2,000 Africans with "revolutionary" code names.

Pieter van der Byl, Rhodesia's minister of foreign affairs and defense, challenged the U.N. Aug. 24 to send a commission of inquiry to investigate the raid. He said that the bodies of women and children reportedly seen by Idoyaga could have been bodies of persons executed by guerrillas or on the order of Mozambican President Samora Machel and placed in the camp to mislead the U.N. about the camp's real purpose.

A subcommittee of the U.N. Human Rights Commission unanimously approved a resolution Aug. 30 asking for a full U.N. investigation of the attack.

Border & guerrilla activity. Cross-border violence, guerrilla activity and anti-guerrilla actions continued on into the second half of 1976.

Rhodesia accused Mozambique regular troops Aug. 11 of having carried out simultaneous mortar bombardments that day against Umtali and a police post 250 miles south of there. "Minor damage was caused to government installations, with more serious damage to civilian property," the official announcement said.

There was no indication how Rhodesian authorities knew the mortars had come from Mozambique troops and not Rhodesian guerrillas. The attack on Umtali hit the Greenside suburb, damaging a military barracks and several houses and

injuring two black civilians. Officials estimated that the shells had come from the town of Machipanda just across the border.

Rhodesian security forces issued a communique Aug. 15 charging Mozambique with having mounted a mortar and rocket attack on the border post of Nyamapanda Aug. 15 in which two Rhodesian policemen were killed.

Botswana reported Aug. 12 that Rhodesian troops had crossed into northern Botswana Aug. 6 and had questioned villagers at gunpoint about the presence of guerrillas in the area.

A government spokesman confirmed Aug. 18 that Rhodesian authorities had ordered the closing of a Congregational Church mission in the town of Chipinga about nine miles from the Mozambique border, as part of a crackdown on missionaries who allegedly aided black guerrillas.

Black nationalist guerrillas attacked a military camp in northeastern Rhodesia Aug. 30, wounding six soldiers, according to an Aug. 31 government statement.

A government communique released Sept. 1 put the guerrilla death toll in Rhodesia for August at 131, the highest reported monthly figure since the guerrilla war started in December 1972. The total did not include guerrillas reported killed in the Aug. 8 raid.

A government communique Sept. 2 reported that a helicopter pilot and his gunner were killed in action near the Mozambique border and one guerrilla and two policemen were fatally shot in a black township outside the city of Bulawayo.

An elderly white woman was killed Sept. 7 by guerrillas in Plumtree, six miles from the Botswana border.

Security officials reported Sept. 10 that two black government officials had been killed by guerrillas and that 12 guerrillas had been killed Sept. 8-10.

The government said Sept. 14 that guerrillas had killed five Rhodesian security officers in a surprise attack on their field camp. This was the greatest number of Rhodesian deaths suffered in a single engagement since the guerrilla fighting had started in 1972.

The security forces said Oct. 1 that

troops had killed 28 members of a guerrilla group that had infiltrated Rhodesia from Mozambique.

An Oct. 9 military communique said that the farm of a high official of the Zimbabwe African People's Union had been burned by guerrillas.

An Oct. 11 communique reported that a white worker had been injured and an African youth killed by guerrillas Oct. 9. The communique also reported that 10 guerrillas and four African women accompanying them had been killed in an attack on a government camp.

The government Oct. 15 reported that two white security-force corporals had been killed since Oct. 14. Their deaths brought to 95 the total of white deaths since January, 1976. Official statistics revealed that 1,059 guerrillas had been killed since the beginning of the year.

Security forces Oct. 17 reported that the brother of a member of Bishop Abel Muzorewa's delegation to the Geneva talks on Rhodesian majority rule had been killed by guerrillas.

The government Oct. 18 reported a Mozambique rocket and mortar attack in southeastern Rhodesia Oct. 16–17.

—Security forces said Oct. 27 that 11 persons, including Africans, had been killed by guerrillas since Oct. 24.

The military reported Oct. 28 that 19 guerrillas had been killed in the previous 24 hours and that an elderly white couple and a white rifleman had been victims of guerrilla attacks.

Guerrillas wreck rail bridge—Guerrillas Oct. 6 blew up a railroad bridge over the Matetsi River about 32 miles south of the Zambia border and 18 miles east of Botswana.

A freight train carrying ore (presumably copper) was crossing the bridge at the time of the explosion. No one was injured, but 11 cars plunged into the river. The train had been carrying goods between Zaire, Zambia and South Africa.

ANC militants convicted—Eight members of the African National Council (ANC) were sentenced to death Aug. 30 by the Salisbury High Court on charges of sabotage and urban guerrilla warfare.

They had been convicted of causing explosions on railroad tracks near Salisbury and at a beer hall in a black township, and of carrying out grenade attacks on a restaurant and nightclub in Salisbury in which two people were injured.

Mozambique camp attacked. Rhodesian forces Oct. 31, 1976 struck at guerrilla bases in Mozambique in apparent retaliation for Oct. 30 attacks that left four persons dead.

The Rhodesian forces spent two days in Mozambique territory and reportedly destroyed seven guerrilla camps before returning to Rhodesia Nov. 2. The troops had penetrated 50 miles into Mozambique at Tete Province in the north and Gaza in the south.

Mozambique charged Nov. 1 that Rhodesia had used tanks, aircraft and heavy artillery. Rhodesian officials called the charge "highly imaginative."

At a Nov. 3 press briefing, assistant police commissioner Mike Edden said that the raids had set back by two months plans for a major offensive of more than 1,000 guerrillas of the Zimbabwe African National Union. Edden said that the major military operations had taken place only in Tete Province and that the Gaza action had been in retaliation for earlier firing on a Rhodesian town. He did not release casualty figures, except to say that no Mozambican soldiers or civilians were killed.

The city of Umtali was hit in retaliation by Mozambican rocket attacks Nov. 3, but sustained no serious damage. Mozambique Nov. 4 said that Rhodesian soldiers had attacked a border post, suffering heavy losses.

The raid on Mozambique was generally believed to have been a response to perceptions of a hardening in the nationalists' position at Geneva. A government source quoted Nov. 3 in the New York Times accused nationalists of "threatening . . . war while they're supposed to be talking peace." The source said that the raid was meant to show "that we are not weakening our military position."

Todd house arrest lifted. The government June 5, 1976 lifted its restrictions on former Prime Minister Garfield Todd who had been under house arrest since February 1972.

Presented with the unheralded order, signed by Hilary Squires, minister of law and order, Todd said he had no immediate plans to return to politics. Earlier in the year, Joshua Nkomo, leader of the Rhodesia-based faction of the African National Council (ANC), had said he would seek Todd's counsel if the ANC resumed talks with the Rhodesian government.

Bishop jailed, then deported. Donal Lamont, Roman Catholic bishop of Umtali, was sentenced Oct. 1, 1976 to 10 years' hard labor on two counts of failing to report guerrillas and two counts of counseling others to do the same. He was deported the following year.

Lamont, an outspoken critic of the Rhodesian minority government, had pleaded guilty at the start of his trial Sept. 21. The 65-year-old bishop was accused of having advised a nun on duty at a medical mission near the Mozambique border in April not to report an African who had requested and received medical supplies. The bishop also was charged with failure to report another incident in June, when two armed guerrillas demanded and received supplies from the mission.

A Vatican spokesman announced Oct. 2 that Pope Paul VI had sent Lamont a message of sympathy. The spokesman praised Lamont's "dedication to the cause of racial equality."

Lamont was president of the Catholic Commission for Justice and Peace in Rhodesia, an organization which charged the Rhodesian army with using abduction, torture and murder against African civilians. In a report released Sept. 30, the commission accused Rhodesian security forces of making little distinction between guerrillas and innocent villagers in conducting security operations.

Lamont was stripped of his citizenship and deported March 23, 1977 as "an undesirable inhabitant of or visitor to Rhodesia," according to a government statement. He had won an appeal Feb. 24 of his 10-year prison sentence. The term had been reduced to four years in prison, with three years suspended.

Zambia charges guerrilla in Chitepo murder. A Rhodesian guerrilla commander, Josiah Tongogara, was charged in a Lusaka magistrate's court April 21, 1976 with murder in the March 1975 slaying in Lusaka of Herbert Chitepo, the Rhodesian nationalist leader.

Tongogara, 35, was supreme military commander of the Zimbabwe African National Union (ZANU) before the movement merged in December 1974 with other Rhodesian nationalist groups within the African National Council. Chitepo had been ZANU chairman.

Tongogara had been detained by Zambian authorities for about a year before he was formally charged. The charge was filed following the release April 9 of a report by an international commission appointed in 1975 by Zambian President Kenneth Kaunda to investigate Chitepo's murder. The commission report concluded that the ZANU executive committee and its military high command had "carried out" Chitepo's assassination. The commission also determined that the motive for the slaying was "the erroneous belief by the Karanga tribe elements that Mr. Chitepo and other Manyika tribe leaders in the [executive committee] had master-minded" a political imbroglio that resulted in many deaths in November-December 1974.

Members of the rebel group and Chitepo backers were killed in the plot, which was led by Thomas Nhari, a Chitepo opponent.

Another former ZANU guerrilla, Tyupo Shumba Chigowe, was sentenced to death by the Lusaka High Court April 14 for the murder of Edgar Madekurozwa, one of the Chitepo supporters slain in the aftermath of the Nhari rebellion.

ANC rift. A meeting of five African heads of state Sept. 6–7, 1976 in Dar es Salaam, Tanzania failed to reconcile the opposing factions of the African National Council.

The conference had been called to determine a common strategy for dealing with the governments of Rhodesia and South Africa. Attending were Presidents Julius K. Nyerere of Tanzania, Kenneth D. Kaunda of Zambia, Samora M.

Machel of Mozambique, Agostinho Neto of Angola and Seretse Khama of Botswana; Sam Nujoma, president of the South-West Africa People's Organization, and the leaders of the ANC factions. The presidents issued a joint statement Sept. 7 agreeing "to further intensify the armed struggle" in Rhodesia.

The main topic of the conference had been the widening ANC split between the moderate Zimbabwe African National Union (ZANU), led by Joshua Nkomo, and the more militant Zimbabwe African People's Union (ZAPU), led by Bishop Abel Muzorewa.

The two factions had split along ethnic lines, and their friction had been aggravated by Nkomo's decision to enter into negotiations with the Rhodesian government.

Muzorewa called for armed struggle as a "last resort" to achieve black majority rule. "We have been left with no choice but to take up arms," the Methodist minister said Aug. 19, before returning to his exile residence in Mozambique.

The ANC conflict had flared up June 6 when ZANU forces attacked a ZAPU military training camp in southern Tanzania, the Washington Post reported Aug. 23.

According to a ZAPU spokesman, Chinese military instructors had actively participated in the ZANU attack, which left 21 People's Union guerrillas dead and 28 others missing. (The ZAPU was backed by the Soviet Union, while the ZANU reportedly received Chinese assistance.)

The formation of a new black Rhodesian nationalist movement, the Zimbabwe Reformed African National Council, was announced Aug. 23 by a splinter group of the Muzorewa faction. Its leader, Robert Mugabe, in self-exile in Mozambique, said that the group would be willing to participate in talks with the Rhodesian government if other guerrilla leaders were invited to attend.

U.S. Seeks Solution

In 1976 the U.S. assumed the leadership in the effort to resolve the Rhodesian dilemma and to bring majority rule to the troubled African land.

Kissinger states principles in Lusaka. The U.S. opening was made by Secretary of State Henry A. Kissinger in a major policy statement delivered in Lusaka, Zambia April 27, 1976. In his address, Kissinger pledged to take steps "to usher in a new era in American policy" toward southern Africa.

Kissinger, on a two-week tour of African nations, spoke at a luncheon given in his honor by Zambian President Kenneth Kaunda.

The Kissinger statement declared U.S. support for majority rule in Rhodesia, an independent Namibia (South-West Africa) and the termination of apartheid in South Africa. Throughout his speech, Kissinger stressed the urgency of these goals. He reiterated U.S. warnings against foreign intervention in southern Africa and offered U.S. proposals for broad economic development programs in the region.

In his most emphatic remarks, Kissinger told the white minority regime in Rhodesia that it would face "the unrelenting opposition" of the U.S. until a negotiated settlement were achieved with the black majority. He later offered Washington's good offices in negotiations for a swift and peaceful transfer of power.

Endorsing British proposals for a two-year transition to majority rule, Kissinger pledged U.S. assistance to "the people of Rhodesia" during that period and vowed continued aid to "a newly independent Zimbabwe" under black rule.

Underscoring the U.S. commitment to a Rhodesian settlement, he said he would ask Congress to repeal the Byrd Amendment that permitted Rhodesian chrome to be imported in contravention of United Nations sanctions and he pledged U.S. efforts to insure strict global observance of those sanctions.

The African nations suffering hardship as a result of imposing the sanctions were promised U.S. aid as well. A specific offer to Mozambique, which had recently shut its border with Rhodesia, was announced. In a further pledge, Kissinger vowed to cooperate with the presidents of black African nations, including the Marxist

Mozambique government, in carrying out U.S. Rhodesian policy.

Kissinger said in his address:

President Ford has sent me here with a message of commitment and cooperation.

I have come to Africa because in so many ways, the challenges of Africa are the challenges of the modern era. Morally and politically, the drama of national independence in Africa over the last generation has transformed international affairs. More than any other region of the world, Africa symbolizes that the previous era of world affairs—the colonial era—is a thing of the past. . . .

Of all the challenges before us, of all the purposes we have in common, racial justice is one of the most basic. . . .

. . . Here in Lusaka, I reaffirm the unequivocal commitment of the United States to human rights, as expressed in the principles of the United Nations Charter and the Universal Declaration of Human Rights. We support self-determination, majority rule, equal rights and human dignity for all the peoples of southern Africa—in the name of moral principle, international law and world peace.

On this occasion I would like to set forth more fully American policy on some of the immediate issues we face—in Rhodesia, Namibia and South Africa—and then to sketch our vision of southern Africa's hopeful future.

The U.S. position on Rhodesia is clear and unmistakable. As President Ford has said, "The U.S. is totally dedicated to seeing to it that the majority becomes the ruling power in Rhodesia." We do not recognize the Rhodesian minority regime. The U.S. voted for, and is committed to the U.N. Security Council resolutions of 1966 and 1968 that imposed mandatory economic sanctions against the illegal Rhodesian regime. Earlier this year we co-sponsored a Security Council resolution, which was passed unanimously, expanding mandatory sanctions. And in March of this year, we joined with others to commend Mozambique for its decision to enforce these sanctions even at great economic cost to itself.

It is the responsibility of all who seek a negotiated solution to make clear to the Rhodesian minority that the world community is united in its insistence on rapid change. It is the responsibility of those in Rhodesia who believe in peace to take the steps necessary to avert a great tragedy.

U.S. policy for a just and durable Rhodesian solution will therefore rest on 10 elements:

First, the U.S. declares its support in the strongest terms for the proposals made by British Prime Minister [James] Callaghan on March 22 of this year; that independence must be preceded by majority rule which, in turn, must be achieved no later than two years following the expeditious conclusion of negotiations. We consider these proposals a basis for a settlement fair to all the people of Rhodesia. We urge that they be accepted.

Second, the Salisbury regime must understand that it cannot expect U.S. support either in diplomacy or in material help at any stage in its conflict with African states or African liberation movements. On the contrary, it will face our unrelenting opposition until a negotiated settlement is achieved.

Third, the U.S. will take steps to fulfill completely its obligation under international law to mandatory economic sanctions against Rhodesia. We will urge the Congress this year to repeal the Byrd Amendment, which authorizes Rhodesian chrome imports to the U.S., an act inconsistent with United Nations sanctions. In parallel with this effort, we will approach other industrial nations to insure the strictest and broadest international compliance with sanctions.

Fourth, to insure that there are no misperceptions on the part of the leaders of the minority in Rhodesia, the U.S., on the conclusion of my consultations in black Africa, will communicate clearly and directly to the Salisbury regime our view of the urgency of a rapid negotiated settlement leading to majority rule.

Fifth, the U.S. government will carry out its responsibility to inform American citizens that we have no official representation in Rhodesia nor any means of providing them with assistance or protection. American travelers will be advised against entering Rhodesia; American residents there will be urged to leave.

Sixth, as in the case of Zambia a few years ago, steps should be taken—in accordance with the recent U.N. Security Council resolution—to assist Mozambique, whose closing of its borders with Rhodesia to enforce sanctions has imposed upon it a great additional economic hardship. In accordance with the U.N. resolution, the U.S. is willing to provide $12.5 million of assistance.

Seventh, the U.S.—together with other members of the United Nations—is ready to help alleviate economic hardship for any countries neighboring Rhodesia which decide to enforce sanctions by closing their frontiers.

Eighth, humanitarian provision must be made for the thousands of refugees who have fled in distress from Rhodesia into neighboring countries. The U.S. will consider sympathetically requests for assistance for these refugees by the U.N. High Commissioner for Refugees or other appropriate international organizations.

Ninth, the world community should give its support to the people of Rhodesia as they make the peaceful transition to majority rule and independence, and should aid a newly independent Zimbabwe [Rhodesia]. To this end, we are ready to join with other interested nations in a program of economic, technical and educational assistance, to enable an independent Zimbabwe to achieve the progress and the place in the community of nations to which its resources and the talents of all its people entitle it.

Finally, we state our conviction that whites as well as blacks should have a secure future and civil rights in a Zimbabwe that has achieved racial justice. A constitutional structure should protect minority rights together with establishing majority rule. We are prepared to devote some of our assistance programs to this objective.

In carrying out this program we shall consult closely with the presidents of Botswana, Mozambique, Tanzania and Zambia. . . .

Our proposals are not a program made in America to be passively accepted by Africans. They are an expression of common aspirations and an agenda of cooperation. Underlying it is our fundamental conviction that Africa's destiny must remain in African hands.

No one who wishes this continent well can want to see Africans divided either between nations or between liberation movements. Africans cannot want outsiders seeking to impose solutions, or choosing among countries or movements. The U.S., for its part, does not seek any pro-American African bloc confronting a bloc supporting any other power. Nor do we wish to support one faction of a liberation movement against another. But neither should any other country pursue hegemonial aspirations or bloc policies. An attempt by one will inevitably be countered by the other. The U.S. therefore supports African unity and integrity categorically as basic principles of our policy. . . .

Africa in this decade is a testing ground of the world's conscience and vision. That blacks and whites live together in harmony and equality is a moral imperative of our time. Let us prove that these goals can be realized by human choice, that justice can command by the force of its rightness instead of by force of arms.

These are ideals that bind all the races of mankind. They are the mandate of decency and progress and peace.

This drama will be played out in our own lifetime. Our children will inherit either our success or our failure. The world watches with hope, and we approach it with confidence.

So let it be said that black people and white people working together achieved on this continent—which has suffered so much and seen so much injustice—a new era of peace, well-being and human dignity.

Four African nations visited—Kissinger had begun his two-week trip to Africa in Kenya April 24. En route, he stopped in London April 23-24 for talks on southern African developments with Foreign Minister Anthony Crosland.

Launching his first trip to any black-ruled nation of Africa since he became secretary of state, Kissinger said on arrival in Nairobi: "I have come here to make clear that the U.S. associates itself with the two great aspirations of Africa—the aspiration to human dignity and racial equality and the aspiration to economic progress."

Before leaving Nairobi for Tanzania, Kissinger expressed Washington's support for majority rule in Africa and pledged that while the U.S. "does not plan to give military aid in any form to the nationalist movements in Africa . . . it will use its political and economic influence to bring about these objectives."

Arriving in Dar es Salaam April 25, Kissinger said the U.S. "welcomes the efforts Tanzania has made as mediator and conciliator" in southern Africa. Tanzania, opposing U.S. policy, had supported the victorious Soviet-backed Angolan nationalist movement. Kissinger April 26 said his talks with Tanzanian President Julius Nyerere had marked "a new beginning in the relations between Tanzania and the U.S."

In an April 26 press conference, Nyerere welcomed Kissinger's assurance of U.S. support for majority rule in southern Africa, but warned that war had already begun in Rhodesia. Anyone speaking of majority rule by peaceful means, he said, was "talking about something that is not there." The Tanzanian president said he had not sought U.S. arms aid to support the Rhodesian guerrillas, but noted that he did not get the impression that Kissinger "would use American might to oppose us in the war."

(Presidents Kenneth Kaunda of Zambia and Samora Machel of Mozambique issued a statement in Maputo April 26 declaring their governments' military support for the nationalist guerrillas in Rhodesia.)

In Zambia, where he delivered his major policy address, Kissinger met with Kaunda and also with Joshua Nkomo, leader of the Rhodesia-based faction of the African National Council.

Reaction to Lusaka speech—Zambian President Kaunda praised the Kissinger statement April 27. He assured Kissinger that he would have the support of Zambia and the governments of Tanzania, Mozambique and Botswana, as well. Zaire April 29 joined those nations and Kenya in endorsing the speech.

Britain also supported the Kissinger statement, which had backed the British proposals for resumption of constitutional talks in Rhodesia. Foreign Minister Anthony Crosland told Parliament April 28 that if Britain and the U.S. "had not taken the line we have taken, we would have undermined every moderate black leader on the entire continent of Africa."

Rhodesia April 27 denounced the speech, accusing Kissinger of "attempting to make decisions on our behalf."

U.S. would mediate in Rhodesia—Kissinger April 28 offered the good offices of the U.S. in constitutional negotiations on swift progress toward black majority rule in Rhodesia. He made the statement in Kinshasa, Zaire, the fourth stop on his African tour.

"The U.S. is willing to assist the parties, in so far as they request," he said, "to bring about the result mentioned in my Lusaka speech—rapid achievement of majority rule and guarantee of minority rights."

In a statement later that day, Kissinger added that he would not necessarily embark on the "shuttle diplomacy" which marked his personal mediation efforts in the Middle East. He said, however, that the U.S. was prepared to play a mediating role in the event of an escalation of combat between the nationalist guerrillas and Rhodesian soldiers: "The combat will have to be ended by negotiations. The more rapidly that takes place, the more lives will be saved."

U.S. travel discouraged. The U.S. embassy in South Africa May 13 "strongly" advised Americans not to travel to or within Rhodesia.

(The warning was issued in South Africa because the U.S., which did not recognize the white minority government in Rhodesia, had no diplomatic representation there. No country, except South Africa, which had a diplomatic mission in Salisbury, maintained diplomatic relations with Rhodesia.)

The U.S. announcement cited the "potential in the foreseeable future for increased violence" in Rhodesia and urged those Americans already there to make "contingency plans" for leaving.

Salisbury responded to the warning by asserting that the U.S. State Department was "completely out of touch" with the situation in Rhodesia.

Vorster, Kissinger hold parley. South African Prime Minister John Vorster and U.S. State Secretary Kissinger discussed the situation in Southern Africa June 23-24, 1976 at meetings in Bodenmais and Grafenau, remote villages in West Germany's Bavarian Forest. The discussions were the first high-level meeting since World War II between representatives of Pretoria and Washington.

"We hope ...," Kissinger said at a Munich news conference June 24 after the meetings "to contribute to a resolution that is achieved by negotiation and not by violence and which respects the dignity of all the peoples in the area, and this process is in motion." In separate comments, Vorster described the talks as

"worthwhile" and "outspoken, but friendly."

Kissinger was questioned about a remark he had made before leaving for Europe, to the effect that he would try to "determine whether South Africa is prepared to separate its own future from Rhodesia and Namibia [South-West Africa]." At the Munich press conference Kissinger said:

"The problem is whether it is possible to start an evolution in southern Africa in which sufficient guarantees are given to the minority so a system can evolve that the majority of the people want and [that] is bearable for the minority. This is the essence of the problem and [it] should not be viewed in terms of separating oneself from any particular group."

(Kissinger's earlier remark on the issue had prompted South Africa June 22 to reiterate its rejection of any suggestion that it impose economic or political sanctions "against Rhodesia or any other nation." The Kissinger-Vorster meetings, Pretoria said, "can only at this stage be an exchange of views.")

For the U.S., the meetings represented an opportunity to begin efforts toward achieving a negotiated solution in Rhodesia that would lead to black majority rule before the guerrilla war in that white-minority-ruled nation became more explosive.

For the South Africans, the meetings represented a major diplomatic achievement and a step toward an end to Pretoria's ostracism by much of the world. Before leaving for Germany, Vorster had said that he wanted to secure U.S. cooperation against Communist encroachment in southern Africa, as well as an end to U.S. military embargoes and to curbs on government credits to South Africa.

With Vorster in the South African delegation to the talks were Foreign Minister Hilgard Muller; Branx Fourie, secretary of the Foreign Office; Rolf Botha, ambassador to the U.S., and Gen. Hendrick Van Den Berg, head of the Bureau of State Security (BOSS). Included in Kissinger's delegation were William E. Schaufele, assistant secretary of state for African affairs, William G. Bowdler, ambassador to South Africa and Peter Rodman of the National Security Council.

U.S. follow-up—In a follow-up to the U.S.-South African conversations, William Schaufele, U.S. assistant secretary of state for African affairs, began a two-week trip to six African countries July 7 to discuss the Kissinger-Vorster talks.

William Scranton, U.S. ambassador to the United Nations, said July 9 that the U.S. would support majority rule in Rhodesia even if it were achieved by violence. He ruled out military aid to the African nationalists and expressed hope that a peaceful solution would be found.

U.S. Rep. Stephen Solarz (D, N.Y.) reported that guerrillas in Mozambique had told him July 8 that they refused to negotiate any settlement with the Rhodesian government that did not provide for immediate transfer of power to the black majority. The guerrillas had also ruled out accepting help from foreign troops and had refused to offer any guarantees of power-sharing with, or compensation for, white Rhodesians, Solarz said.

U.S. blacks criticize Kissinger—Black members of the U.S. Congress Sept. 2 criticized Kissinger's trip to Europe. The Black Caucus issued a statement saying that Kissinger should not meet with Vorster unless the talks resulted in a trip to South Africa and an announcement that all American ties with South Africa would be abolished until apartheid was ended.

A spokesman for the State Department said in reply Sept. 2 that such statements "fail to recognize the complexity of the problems involved" and "do not serve the cause of effective discourse."

Rhodesia asks U.S. talks. Rhodesian Prime Minister Ian Smith appealed Aug. 4 for direct talks with the U.S. over the constitutional issue that had kept his government at odds with Great Britain for more than a decade. Smith appeared to be responding to a speech given Aug. 2 by Kissinger.

In an address at Que Que, about 150 miles southwest of Salisbury, Smith emphasized his disagreement with "some views expressed recently by certain American leaders." Smith added: "It is quite clear to me that these views have been expressed because of ignorance of the position of our country. However, at least they are now thinking about us, talking about us, and if they make the daring decision to actually talk to us, I believe that will be a tremendous breakthrough and give us the opportunity to put over the facts and the truth." The Rhodesian leader noted that if U.S. officials wanted to influence events in Rhodesia "then they have no option other than to talk to us. Failing this, then surely their sincerity is in question."

Smith repeated his government's view that a "premature" handover of power to blacks would cause greater bloodshed than occurred in Angola because of the "deep tribal and ideological divisions among black politicians and the equally deep schisms in the ranks of the terrorists." Claiming his regime could hold out indefinitely, Smith said: "If need be, we can go on as we have been going on for the past decade ad infinitum. But this is not the answer. Our wish and our aim is to return to a position of normality as a participating member of the free world."

In a speech in Boston Aug. 2 to the National Urban League, Kissinger had given support to proposals advanced in March by British Prime Minister James Callaghan to solve the Rhodesian deadlock. He said that U.S. awareness of Africa's importance to foreign affairs "grew out of painful experience" and that the U.S. would "pursue our new Africa policy with conviction and dedication."

Kissinger had talks on Rhodesia Aug. 5 in London with Prime Minister Callaghan and with Anthony Crosland, the British foreign secretary.

Smith elaborated on his government's position in an interview reported Aug. 25 in the Washington Post. According to Smith, the U.S. demand that Rhodesia set a timetable for majority rule was "illogical." Majority rule had been the "ultimate goal" of Rhodesia since 1923, Smith said, but progress could be measured only by achievement, "not by a clock or calendar."

Smith added: "We find ourselves in the incredibly stupid position that we are fighting against other members of the free world more than we are fighting our natural enemies, the Communist world."

Speaking to Parliament Sept. 2, Smith decried negotiations being carried out on Rhodesia's behalf by outsiders, but said that "for a long time it has been very difficult for us to find local political leaders who are prepared to negotiate with us," referring to the African National Council.

Kissinger hits minority rule—Kissinger warned Aug. 31 that the "white populations of Rhodesia and Namibia must recognize that majority rule is inevitable," and he called South Africa's internal structure "incompatible with any concept of human dignity."

Speaking in Philadelphia at a national conference of the Opportunities Industrialization Centers of America, a manpower training group for the U.S. and Africa, Kissinger said: "We will continue to use all our influence to bring about peaceful change, equality of opportunity, and basic human rights in South Africa."

Prime Minister Vorster reacted strongly to Kissinger's speech in a Sept. 1 statement. Without mentioning the secretary by name, Vorster said, "South Africa's internal policy is determined by South Africa itself and is not prescribed to her by any person or country from outside."

Kissinger & Vorster in Zurich. Kissinger & Vorster met in Zurich, Switzerland Sept. 4–6, 1976 for a second round of talks on the southern African situation.

After the conference, Vorster agreed to a U.S.-British plan to provide financial guarantees of $1.5 billion to $2 billion for white Rhodesians, it was reported Sept. 9 in the New York Times. The plan was designed to assure Rhodesian whites their rights in an independent Rhodesia as well as the choice of emigrating with financial compensation.

In separate news conferences after their talks, both Kissinger and Vorster said "progress" had been made.

Kissinger said, "It is our view that a basis for further negotiations exists, though work still remains to be done." Kissinger said that he was "ready to continue negotiations in Africa if the parties should desire," referring to a meeting Sept. 6–7 in Tanzania of heads of the five black

African countries. Kissinger had originally planned to fly to southern Africa to meet with black leaders after talks in Zurich and London, but he changed his plans to await the results of the Tanzania conference.

Vorster made no detailed statement on the talks, saying that Kissinger had covered everything in his press conference. Vorster added only that he and Kissinger "had free and frank exchanges," and "resulting from that, progress has certainly been made."

(After leaving Zurich, Kissinger conferred with several European leaders on the Zurich talks. He met with British Prime Minister James Callaghan in London Sept. 6, and with French President Valery Giscard d'Estaing in Paris Sept. 7. He then flew to Hamburg, West Germany for talks with Chancellor Helmut Schmidt before returning to Washington Sept. 7.)

Mission scored, supported—Representatives of Rhodesian and Namibian liberation movements scored Kissinger's mission Sept. 9, at a conference of African specialists held in the Senate caucus room in Washington. Representatives of both factions of the African National Council said they saw no possibility of a peaceful solution.

United Nations Secretary General Kurt Waldheim said Sept. 16 that he hoped for a peaceful solution and endorsed Kissinger's efforts. (In a Sept. 2 discussion with Kissinger, Waldheim had said that the southern African war threat was a threat to international peace and security.)

Both West Germany and France expressed support for the U.S. position on Namibian independence and Rhodesian majority rule, it was reported Sept. 8. Chancellor Helmut Schmidt added that West Germany would also contribute to underwriting a compensation fund for white Rhodesians after majority rule was achieved.

Kissinger meets black leaders. Kissinger went to Dar es Salaam, Tanzania Sept. 14, 1976 to begin talks with African leaders aimed at finding a peaceful solution to southern Africa's racial crises.

Before his departure, Kissinger had said

Sept. 11 that his goal was not a permanent settlement, but the creation of a basis for negotiations involving all parties. He expressed little hope at finding a solution to the Rhodesian problem as a result of his trip.

Kissinger's arrival at Dar es Salaam was greeted with a statement by the Tanzanian government calling for the U.S. to declare its support for the liberation forces in Namibia and Rhodesia should efforts at peaceful negotiations fail. The statement was said to represent the views not only of Tanzanian President Julius Nyerere, but also of leaders of Botswana, Zambia, Angola and Mozambique.

After meeting with Kissinger Sept. 15, Nyerere said that he felt more pessimistic than before on the prospects for peace. Nyerere said he would have liked Kissinger to tell him that the Rhodesian white minority would accept majority rule within two years.

Nyerere warned the U.S. against accepting South African and Rhodesian claims that they were fighting the spread of communism. He said that black fighters used Soviet-made arms because no other arms were available to them.

Kissinger, in a news conference after the talks, said that his views of the situation had not been changed by his discussion with Nyerere and that he was still hopeful. Kissinger said that he had a clearer idea of the positions of the black leaders but refused to say in advance what the U.S. would do if the talks failed.

Kissinger conferred with President Kenneth Kaunda of Zambia in Lusaka Sept. 16. Kaunda told Kissinger that he had only "a few days, not weeks, to succeed." Kaunda said that war, although a "tragedy," was the only alternative if Kissinger's mission failed. Kissinger said that he was "conscious of the responsibility." The U.S. shared Kaunda's view that "time is running out," Kissinger said.

(William E. Schaufele Jr., U.S. assistant secretary of state for African affairs, had arrived in Dar es Salaam Sept. 8 to brief President Nyerere on the Kissinger-Vorster talks in Zurich and to prepare the groundwork for Kissinger's discussions with Nyerere. He then met with President Kaunda Sept. 9.)

Soviets score Kissinger mission—The Soviet press denounced Kissinger's efforts, accusing him of attempting to protect the white minority regimes in southern Africa, and warning Africans that similar "shuttle diplomacy" tactics in the Middle East had caused the Lebanese civil war, it was reported Sept. 17.

Vorster, Smith meet in Pretoria. South African Prime Minister John Vorster and Rhodesian Prime Minister Ian Smith met in Pretoria Sept. 14 for a five-hour discussion on the Rhodesian situation.

The two leaders had no comment on their meeting, but a communique released after the talks stated, "Mr. Vorster was able to convey various points of view bearing on the problems of the region to Mr. Smith. This was followed by a full and frank exchange of views."

Smith left Pretoria immediately after conclusion of the talks for a closed session of a congress of Rhodesia's ruling Front Party at Umtali.

Before leaving for Pretoria Sept. 13, Smith had released a statement saying that his government "can have no truck with some of the political gimmicks that are so much in credence today, things such as one man-one vote or majority rule."

Vorster, in a Sept. 13 speech to a National Party congress in Pretoria, had said that the South African government would not put pressure on Rhodesia to change its internal policies. Speaking in English before a cheering crowd, Vorster said, "I'm not prepared to prescribe to any of my neighbors what their policy should be. . . . The Rhodesians won't accept orders from South Africa or anybody else, for that matter."

South African Foreign Affairs Minister Hilgard Muller said Sept. 14 that South Africa would not force the Rhodesian government to yield power to its black majority. Speaking at the University of Pretoria after attending the Smith-Vorster talks, Muller said that "the Rhodesians themselves" must solve their problems.

South Africa's "attitude," Muller said, "has always been to avoid the escalation of violence, to create a climate for negotiation, to give advice whenever possible and to point out the alternatives and the dangers therein."

Rhodesian party congress backs Smith— The ruling Rhodesian Front Party Sept. 16 gave Prime Minister Ian Smith full power to decide Rhodesia's future in negotiations with Kissinger.

In a closed session of the party congress held Sept. 15–17 in Umtali, Smith said that a settlement of the Rhodesian crisis must take into account "the legitimate aspirations of the Africans" but also leave government in "civilized hands."

Desmond Frost, the party chairman, said in his opening speech Sept. 15 that U.S. and British compensation plans for Rhodesian whites would serve only to make a handful of blacks rich and would plunge the rest into abject poverty. He praised Smith's refusal to "negotiate on Kissinger's terms," referring to Smith's public refusal to accept any package deal worked out by Kissinger.

The congress issued a policy statement Sept. 17 that called Kissinger's proposals for compensation guarantees to whites unacceptable and repeated official opposition to black majority rule.

Ex-ministers propose solutions—Two former Rhodesian prime ministers Sept. 19 outlined proposals for U.S. and British roles in solving the Rhodesian crisis.

Roy Welensky called for a conference of black and white Rhodesian leaders and U.S., British, South African and Zambian delegates to draw up a constitutional settlement, with the U.S. and Britain to guarantee that the settlement terms were heeded.

Garfield Todd said that any efforts to find a solution had to be preceded by a commitment from the white minority government to black rule.

Kissinger confers with Smith & Vorster. Kissinger met in Pretoria Sept. 17–20, 1976 with Prime Ministers Smith of Rhodesia and Vorster of South Africa.

Kissinger's first talks with Vorster took place Sept. 17. The five-hour session was described as "constructive," but no further details were released.

After the second session, held Sept. 18,

it was reported that further progress had been made on the issues of Namibian independence and Rhodesian majority rule.

Kissinger met with Smith for eight hours Sept. 19, after which Kissinger said that they had discussed the U.S.-British proposals for establishing majority rule in Rhodesia within two years, with compensation for whites who lost property or chose to emigrate. Kissinger said that he was "satisfied that Mr. Smith and his three close collaborators will report favorably to their other colleagues." (Smith had been accompanied in Pretoria by David Smith, who was both deputy prime minister and finance minister, Commerce Minister Desmond W. Lardner-Burke, and Internal Affairs Minister Bernard H. Musset.)

Smith did not comment on his discussion with Kissinger and left immediately afterward to consult with leaders of Rhodesia's ruling Front Party.

In a short radio interview Sept. 20, Smith said that his talks with Kissinger had "concrete results" and that he felt there was "a chance of settlement."

After Cabinet consultations Sept. 21, Smith said that the proposals required cautious deliberation and that he had urged his ministers to take all the time they needed before making a decision.

(A spokesman for Joshua Nkomo, leader of the more moderate faction of the African National Council [ANC], said Sept. 21 that Nkomo had told him that while he did not like everything contained in Kissinger's proposals, "it was a package and as a package we can take it." Nkomo had said Sept. 19 that majority rule would have to be established in Rhodesia within nine to 12 months.)

Kissinger's meeting with Smith had been in doubt until Sept. 18. Kissinger had said in Lusaka, Zambia Sept. 17 that he would meet with Smith "only under the condition that this was the final element in reaching a satisfactory conclusion." After his first round of talks with Vorster Sept. 17, Kissinger said that he had still reached no decision regarding a meeting with Smith.

Smith arrived in Pretoria Sept. 18, officially to watch a Rhodesian-South African rugby match, and it was announced that evening that Kissinger might see him the next day.

(Kissinger refused to be photographed with Smith the day of their meeting, and referred to the Rhodesian leader in public as "Mr. Smith," not prime minister. The U.S. did not recognize the Rhodesian government.)

Vorster said Sept. 20 that Kissinger's proposals to Smith had laid the basis for a solution, and he said that neither he nor Kissinger had pressured the Rhodesian prime minister into accepting the proposals.

(Earlier, Rhodesian Transport Minister Roger Hawkins had set forth conditions for a U.S. role in solving the Rhodesian crisis. They included a visit to Rhodesia by Kissinger or his "trusted officials." At the opening of a regional agricultural show Sept. 10, Hawkins had said that Rhodesia would not accept a "package deal" imposed upon it by outside powers.)

Kissinger met for three hours at the residence of the U.S. ambassador Sept. 18 with representatives of the black Colored (mixed race) and Asian populations to discuss the South African situation. The meeting was denounced by militants who said that the representatives—chiefs of tribal homelands (bantustans) and leaders of legal nonwhite organizations—supported the South African government.

Kissinger also met with white opponents of apartheid and with the editor of the black newspaper The World.

Kissinger met again with Prime Minister Vorster Sept. 19 to discuss the independence of Namibia (South-West Africa).

Britain skeptical of Rhodesia success—Officials at the British Foreign Office said Sept. 21 that Prime Minister Smith's apparent agreement to consider Kissinger's proposals might be a move to gain time for the white minority government. They said that Smith had twice before agreed to concessions, only to reject them later.

The Foreign Office had said Sept. 19 that it was ready to call a constitutional conference on Rhodesia "if and when it seems appropriate."

2nd round with black presidents. Kissinger Sept. 20–23 again conferred with black African presidents, to whom he reported on his earlier talks with Prime Ministers Vorster and Smith in Pretoria.

Kissinger conferred with President Kaunda of Zambia in Lusaka Sept. 20; with President Nyerere of Tanzania in Dar es Salaam Sept. 21; with Zaire President Mobutu Sese Seko in Kinshasa Sept. 22, and with Kenyan President Jomo Kenyatta in Nairobi Sept. 23.

Few details of the talks were given. However, Nyerere indicated Sept. 21 that there was a basis for negotiations for a peaceful settlement in Rhodesia, and Mobutu said Sept. 22 that he was "convinced" a Rhodesian solution was possible.

Nyerere warned Sept. 22 that any departure from the British proposal for majority rule in Rhodesia within two years would be "totally unacceptable." Reporters on Kissinger's airplane had been told Sept. 21 that Kissinger and Smith had discussed the possibility of an extension of the two-year deadline.

Smith accepts plan. Rhodesian Prime Minister Smith Sept. 24, 1976 accepted Kissinger's proposal for the transfer of power to Rhodesia's black majority.

The proposal, first set forth by British Prime Minister James Callaghan March 22 and endorsed by the U.S. Aug. 2 provided for:

■ The attainment of majority rule within two years.

■ The immediate formation of an interim government by current Rhodesian government representatives and African leaders, which would function until majority rule was attained. The interim government would comprise two bodies—a council of state made up of equal numbers of blacks and whites and a council of ministers appointed by the council of state. The council of state would be led by a white chairman who would have no special vote. The council of ministers would have a black majority and a black first minister. The council of state would draft a constitution and supervise elections for majority rule. The council of ministers would be responsible for government departments, but the ministers of defense and law and order would be white.

■ British legislation to permit the elections for majority rule and the transition to independence (Rhodesia had "illegally" declared its independence and was still considered a British colony by the U.K. and African nationalists).

■ The end of world economic sanctions against Rhodesia and the cessation of guerrilla activities upon formation of the interim government.

■ A program of foreign economic support to insure continued Rhodesian economic growth.

Smith expressed general disagreement with the program Sept. 24 but said that he had been pressured into accepting it by the U.S. and South Africa. He said that "it was made abundantly clear ... that as long as the present circumstances in Rhodesia prevailed, we could expect no help or support of any kind from the free world."

A Kissinger aide said Sept. 25 that the Rhodesian agreement would not have been possible without South African Prime Minister John Vorster's persuasion during his meeting with Kissinger and Smith in Pretoria Sept. 19. Kissinger had shown Smith reports by three U.S. intelligence agencies which confirmed South African intelligence reports that Rhodesia faced imminent political and economic collapse, according to a Sept. 27 Washington Post report. The report added that Vorster had told Smith that he could expect no more help from South Africa. Earlier, Vorster had said that he would not pressure Smith into accepting any majority-rule agreement.

Smith's acceptance of the proposal followed several days of secret high-level talks with parliamentary leaders. The Cabinet met for two days Sept. 21–22, and while no details were released, Smith said that the ministers had reached a consensus on a reply to the Callaghan proposal as outlined by Kissinger in Pretoria. Smith then met with a caucus of 50 members of parliament Sept. 23 to discuss accepting the proposals. Smith had said that a two-thirds majority in favor of acceptance was needed in the 66-member House of Assembly.

Kissinger welcomed Smith's acceptance Sept. 24, saying that it was "only the beginning" of the negotiating process, but was "an encouraging development." He said that the black negotiating team that would help form the interim government would be selected by the presidents of the key black African states involved in the southern African crisis.

At a news conference in London with British Foreign Secretary Anthony Crosland, Kissinger said that American, British and South African representatives would meet in Washington to discuss the financial guarantees contained in the Callaghan proposals.

After Kissinger's departure for Washington Sept. 24, the British government issued a statement calling Smith's acceptance "a victory for realism and common sense."

Britain announced Sept. 29 that it would convene a conference to discuss the formation of a Rhodesian interim government. Crosland said that the meeting would be held within the next few weeks "anywhere in southern Africa acceptable" to the Rhodesians and the Africans. He stressed that Prime Minister Smith must be included. (African leaders had hinted earlier that they might bar Smith from attending any conference on an interim government.)

Britain initially had indicated that it preferred not to take part in forming an interim Rhodesian government, it was reported Sept. 23. London had stated that it would not send British officials to oversee or legislate arrangements for the transfer to majority rule because it was an internal Rhodesian matter.

The Foreign Office reversed its position and announced Sept. 25 that it would send an advisory team to Rhodesia to oversee the transition to independence. Britain's subsequent pledge to convene a conference on an interim government followed an appeal for British action by five African presidents.

Moscow scores Kissinger—The Soviet Union Sept. 25 called the Kissinger negotiations a "fraud" that was giving "breathing space" to white majority regimes in Africa. The denunciation was issued by the Soviet news agency Tass.

'Front-line' states score Rhodesia plan—Nyerere, Kaunda and the pres-

idents of Angola, Botswana and Mozambique criticized the Callaghan plan at a meeting in Lusaka Sept. 26, saying acceptance of the scheme would mean "legalizing" the white Rhodesian power structure.

The African leaders (whose countries were called "front-line" states because they bordered on South Africa or Rhodesia) did not mention Kissinger's diplomatic mission. They credited Smith's acceptance of majority rule in Rhodesia to armed struggle by Rhodesian liberation groups.

The presidents called on Britain to convene a conference outside Rhodesia to establish a black-majority transitional government, to discuss a future constitutional conference and to establish the basis for "peace and normalcy" in Rhodesia. Britain's subsequent pledge to convene a conference on an interim government was hailed Sept. 29 by the "front-line" leaders at a meeting in Gaborone, Botswana with British and U.S. officials and representatives of the African National Council (ANC).

The Callaghan plan also was criticized by the ANC's feuding factions, the Zimbabwe African People's Union (ZAPU) and the Zimbabwe African National Union (ZANU). ZAPU leader Joshua Nkomo said Sept. 23 that the plan contained "very serious flaws." Parts of the proposal were ambiguous and vulnerable to distortion by Prime Minister Smith, Nkomo warned. Ndabaningi Sithole, who claimed leadership of ZANU, said Sept. 25 that the plan would create a "puppet" regime in Rhodesia.

Nevertheless, the U.S. State Department issued a statement Sept. 26 saying that the black African leaders had accepted the basic proposals for majority rule in Rhodesia within two years and the establishment of a transitional government. The statement said that the U.S. would consult with Britain on organizing the meeting to form the interim government and added that the "road to a negotiated solution is now open."

A State Department official reported Sept. 27 that several African "front-line" leaders had sent messages to Washington saying that the negotiations for a Rhodesian settlement were still "on track." The leaders, who were not identified by the State Department, reportedly expressed "gratitude" for the U.S. efforts and said that they had not meant their Lusaka statement to be a rejection of the Callaghan plan. They indicated that they were willing to discuss details of the interim government at a conference set up by the U.S. and Britain.

Confusion mounted over the proposal and its terms Sept. 26–28.

President Nyerere objected to the proposal Sept. 27 because the structure of the interim government had been determined without consulting black leaders. He denied Sept. 28 that he had agreed to the Callaghan plan in advance of Kissinger's meeting with Smith in Pretoria. He said that he had avoided discussing details of the proposal with Kissinger Sept. 15 and 21 because he wanted the details to be worked out in a conference attended by Rhodesian nationalists.

The State Department acknowledged Sept. 27 that "major details" of the proposal had not been previously accepted by African leaders. The Africans had accepted the majority-rule plan as a basis for further negotiations, while Smith had presented the program to the Rhodesian public as a concrete settlement.

Rhodesian Foreign Minister Pieter van der Byl said Sept. 26 that in light of the African presidents' apparent rejection of the Callaghan proposal, it was up to the U.S. and South Africa to resolve the impasse. He said it was "unreasonable" to expect the Rhodesian government to change its stand when both sides had already agreed to the proposals. Van der Byl added that the U.S. and Britain should allow Rhodesia to negotiate with black representatives of its choosing if the African leaders refused to meet with the Rhodesian government.

The Rhodesian government issued a statement Sept. 28 accusing Kissinger of having misled Smith during their Pretoria talks. The statement said that Kissinger had sent Smith a secret communique Sept. 22 assuring Smith that "no new demands would be raised from the other side." The statement said that Smith had been told that the proposals were a package deal, to be accepted or rejected in their entirety with minimal negotiation.

Rhodesia requested Sept. 28 that

Britain send Edward Rowlands, minister of state, Foreign Commonwealth Office, to Rhodesia to help clear up the confusion. (Rowlands was in Botswana conferring with black leaders and with William Schaufele, U.S. assistant secretary of state for African affairs.)

Kissinger said Sept. 28 that he expected negotiations on the formation of the interim government to begin soon, and that a "breakthrough" had been achieved in spite of the conflicting claims of Rhodesians and Africans. He said that both sides wanted to start discussions on forming an interim government as soon as possible.

Nyerere said Sept. 28 that African leaders expected to force black rule in Rhodesia within four to six weeks instead of the two years specified in the Callaghan proposal. He said that when the interim-government conference convened it would create an interim government with a black majority instead of the equal black-white council envisioned in the proposal.

Gromyko & Kissinger at U.N.—Soviet Foreign Minister Andrei Gromyko and Kissinger addressed the U.N. General Assembly in New York Sept. 28 and 30, trading charges on the southern Africa issue and other matters.

Gromyko Sept. 28 delivered a sharp attack on Kissinger's diplomatic efforts in Africa. Gromyko said they were aimed at containing "the just struggle of the peoples of Zimbabwe (Rhodesia) and Namibia (South-West Africa) and of the indigenous population of the Republic of South Africa for their legitimate rights."

"Every possible method is being brought into play," Gromyko declared, "from direct suppression and violence to attempts to divert the national liberation movement away from genuine independence and freedom through political gimmickry and financial handouts." This presumably referred to the U.S.-British plan for a transitional government in Rhodesia and for financial compensation to white Rhodesians who chose to emigrate rather than live under majority rule.

Responding in his address to the assembly Sept. 30, Kissinger denounced Moscow's "crude attempts to distort the purposes of diplomacy and to impede hopeful progress toward peaceful solutions to complex issues." These efforts "only foster tension," Kissinger said. "They cannot be reconciled with the policy of improving relations."

"We have been concerned by the continuing accumulation of Soviet armaments and by recent instances of military intervention to tip the scales in local conflicts," Kissinger continued, apparently referring to the Soviet-Cuban intervention in Angola. "There may be some countries who see a chance for advantage in fueling the flames of war and racial hatred. But they are not motivated by concern for the peoples of Africa, or for peace. And if they succeed, they could doom opportunities that might never return."

Kissinger declared that the U.S. was impartial in southern Africa and he urged black leaders to devise their own political future without the interference of outside powers.

"Many obstacles remain," Kissinger admitted. "But let us not lose sight of what has been achieved: a commitment to majority rule [in Rhodesia] within two years; a commitment to form immediately a transitional government with an African majority in the Cabinet and an African prime minister; a readiness to follow this with a constitutional conference to define the legal framework of an independent Zimbabwe." (This was Kissinger's first recorded public reference to Rhodesia by its African name.)

Geneva Conference Deadlocks

British Foreign Secretary Anthony Crosland had announced Sept. 29, 1976 that Britain would convene an international conference "in southern Africa" to plan the creation of an interim Rhodesian government that would end white minority rule. After black African objections were expressed to southern Africa as a locale, the British shifted the site to Geneva, and the conference opened there in late October. But it adjourned in deadlock in December 1976 with Rhodesian Prime Minister Ian Smith charging that the British pandered to all black nationalist desires but disregarded white Rhodesian interests.

Smith accepts British conference plan. Rhodesian Prime Minister Smith agreed Sept. 30, 1976 to the British plan to convene a conference of black and white Rhodesians to prepare the transition to majority rule.

Details of Smith's confidential acceptance note to British Foreign Secretary Anthony Crosland were not revealed, but a spokesman said that Smith would probably lead the white delegation to the conference. The spokesman reaffirmed the Rhodesian government's position that the conference was not to write a Rhodesian constitution but was to form the interim government that would write it.

(Smith had said earlier that he would not accept a constitutional conference held outside Rhodesia. Black nationalists rejected attending any conference within Rhodesia while the white minority government was still in power.)

Smith met with British Minister of State Edward Rowlands and U.S. Assistant Secretary of State for African Affairs William Schaufele Oct. 4 in Salisbury. They discussed arrangements for the conference, to be chaired by Ivor Richard, British representative to the United Nations. No details of their talks were released, but the officials were said to be "encouraged" that plans were "moving ahead." After their session with Smith, Schaufele and Rowlands spoke with business representatives, members of white opposition parties and leaders of two African National Council (ANC) factions, Joshua Nkomo and Bishop Abel Muzorewa.

At a news conference Oct. 5, Rowlands said that both sides in the Rhodesian dispute had agreed on a date and location for their conference. He added that "one or two final consultations" were necessary before the details of the conference were announced.

Africans meet—An obstacle to the interim-government conference was the failure of the black nationalist groups to agree on common representation. Joshua Nkomo, leader of the Zimbabwe African People's Union (ZAPU), had indicated Sept. 25 that he was willing to meet with other nationalist leaders to resolve some of their differences.

ZAPU representatives met with Robert Mugabe, head of the Zimbabwe African National Union (ZANU) in Lusaka, Zambia Sept. 27 to discuss a unified stand. Nkomo apparently did not attend.

Nkomo met with Abel Muzorewa, president of the officially recognized ANC remnant (minus the ZAPU and ZANU factions), in Gaborone, Botswana Oct. 1. Both men described their talk as "friendly." The meeting was arranged at the urging of Rowlands and Schaufele, who were in Gaborone meeting with African leaders.

Muzorewa returned to Salisbury Oct. 3 after 14 months of self-imposed exile. He was greeted enthusiastically by an estimated 100,000 blacks. (Nkomo had been greeted by only 2,000 during a brief visit to the city Sept. 25.) Muzorewa accused the U.S. of promoting Nkomo as a future Rhodesian leader and said that he would not have accepted the Callaghan-Kissinger plan if Britain had not offered to sponsor the interim-government conference. Muzorewa objected to the parts of the proposal that called for a white chairman of the council of state, white ministers of law and order and defense and a transition period of two years to majority rule. He called this "negotiable."

Nyerere, Machel score conference plan—Tanzanian President Julius Nyerere criticized the British conference proposal Sept. 30, saying that Britain alone must negotiate with black representatives and that Smith's delegation could be included only as a "special-interest group," not as a negotiating party. Nyerere met with Schaufele and Rowlands Oct. 2, after Rowlands met Oct. 1 with Mozambican President Samora Machel.

Machel said Sept. 29 that guerrilla war in Rhodesia would not end until a concrete timetable for black majority rule was established and the details of the transfer of power worked out. (Most of the black nationalist guerrillas operated from bases within Mozambique and were supplied with Soviet arms by Mozambique.)

Rhodesia fund discussed. U.S., British and South African representatives met in Washington Oct. 5-7 to discuss setting up an international fund to aid the transition to majority rule in Rhodesia.

The Zimbabwe People's Army (ZIPA), the guerrilla faction of the ANC, rejected the Callaghan-Kissinger proposal Sept. 30 and pledged to continue fighting.

A statement issued after the talks said that the fund, which had been described as compensation for white Rhodesians, would be used to develop the skills of the black population and provide "economic security" for all citizens.

The size of the fund was not revealed, but previous estimates had put the figure at more than $1 billion, with the U.S. expected to contribute between $400 million-$500 million.

The meeting was attended by William D. Rogers, U.S. undersecretary of state for economic affairs; Sir Antony Duff, British deputy under secretary of state at the Foreign Commonwealth Office; and Roelof Botha, South African ambassador to the U.S.

Donald Jamieson, Canadian state secretary for external affairs, indicated Oct. 15 that Canada was ready to contribute to an international Rhodesian aid fund. After meeting with Kissinger, Jamieson said that "the Canadian public would be supportive as long as the result was a peaceful transition to black majority rule."

In a related development, the U.S. State Department was seeking ways to involve U.S. businesses in the transition to majority rule, according to an Oct. 18 Wall Street Journal report. Meetings were reported to have taken place between State Department representatives and businesses with major interests in southern Africa to coordinate policy and promote stability in the area.

Mugabe, Nkomo reject fund—ZANU leader Robert Mugabe Nov. 4 rejected Western proposals for an international fund to aid Rhodesian development and to compensate white Rhodesians who chose to leave the country after majority rule was established. In a New York Times interview, Mugabe said that the fund would "bind Zimbabwe politically and economically and . . . compromise our independence."

ZAPU leader Joshua Nkomo Nov. 8 also rejected the foreign-aid fund and indicated that he would favor ties with the Soviet Union rather than with the West.

Conference scheduled in Geneva. Britain announced Oct. 16, 1976 that the conference on Rhodesian majority rule would open formally in Geneva Oct. 28, with preliminary sessions beginning Oct. 21.

The conference originally had been planned to begin Oct. 25, but it was postponed at the request of the leaders of two factions of the African National Council (ANC)—Joshua Nkomo, head of the Zimbabwe African People's Union (ZAPU) and Robert Mugabe, chief of the Zimbabwe African National Union (ZANU).

Nkomo and Mugabe Oct. 9 announced the formation of a "patriotic front," or joint leadership of their separate committees at Geneva. They demanded immediate majority rule in Rhodesia and issued a list of preconditions for the conference, including release of all Rhodesian political prisoners and detainees, abolition of protected villages (army-occupied hamlets near Rhodesia's borders), abolition of restrictions on political activity, lifting of the Rhodesian state of emergency, suspension of all political trials, release of imprisoned guerrillas and permission for all nationalist exiles to return to Rhodesia. They also demanded that Britain name a Cabinet minister to chair the Geneva conference in place of Ivor Richard, Britain's representative to the United Nations (Nkomo specified British Foreign Secretary Anthony Crosland Oct. 17). Nkomo and Mugabe indicated that they would deal only with Britain at the conference and would regard Rhodesian Prime Minister Ian Smith's delegation "as an extension of the United Kingdom delegation."

The Rhodesian government reacted with pessimism to the black leaders' demands Oct. 9, blaming the "Russians" for urging the Africans to set conditions guaranteed to make the conference fail. However, Minister of Information Elly Broomburg said Oct. 11 that Rhodesia was willing to go ahead with the talks and would do all it could to bring about a rapid and successful conclusion. Smith warned black nationalists Oct. 13 that if they refused to abide by the terms he had accepted Sept. 24, he would form an interim government with moderate Africans who, he said, were willing to cooperate.

(Nkomo had indicated Oct. 10 that the preconditions were not meant to be adhered to strictly. A spokesman for U.S. Secretary of State Henry Kissinger Oct. 14 denied reports that Kissinger had given Smith assurances of a change in the U.S. attitude towards Rhodesia if black nationalists rejected the Sept. 24 settlement plan.)

Smith and Crosland exchanged different interpretations of the purpose of the Geneva conference. Crosland said Oct. 5 that the Sept. 24 agreement would serve as a basis for negotiations. Smith replied Oct. 6 that the points he had accepted were not negotiable and would have to be accepted or rejected as a whole.

Crosland repeated his position at a news conference in Washington Oct. 7 and said that the essential task was to get both sides to the conference to begin talks. He indicated that the less details were discussed beforehand, the easier it would be to set up the conference. The Rhodesian government repeated Oct. 11 that the Geneva conference would set up an interim government and would not write a constitution or plan majority rule, as black nationalists had demanded.

Britain Oct. 12 formally announced the Geneva conference participants. Besides Nkomo, Mugabe and Smith, ANC president Bishop Abel Muzorewa was invited.

Smith named his delegation Oct. 12: Deputy Prime Minister David Smith, Foreign Minister Pieter van der Byl, Minister of Justice and Law and Order Hilary Squires, and Minister of Lands, Natural Resources and Water Development Mark Partridge.

Nkomo announced the composition of his 18-member delegation Oct. 14. Included were ZAPU vice president Josiah Chinamano, ZAPU secretary general Joseph Msika and publicity secretary Willy Musarurwa. Nkomo also named Garfield Todd, a former Rhodesian prime minister, as one of his political advisors.

Muzorewa named a 21-member delegation Oct. 15, including several members who were in detention or serving prison sentences in Rhodesia. He added that if no separate invitation were issued to Rev. Ndabaningi Sithole, Mugabe's rival for ZANU leadership, he would invite Sithole to be part of his delegation. (Sithole had denounced the Mugabe-Nkomo alliance Oct. 10, saying that it was an attempt to exclude him from power. A ZANU faction meeting in Zambia Oct. 10 reportedly had endorsed Sithole as its leader.)

Leaders of some "front-line" states (Botswana, Mozambique, Tanzania and Zambia) met in Dar es Salaam, Tanzania Oct. 17 and urged Britain to invite Sithole, and Britain complied the next day. Sithole had arrived in Dar es Salaam Oct. 13. He said that he was not "irrelevant" to a Rhodesian political settlement, despite his apparent lack of a strong political base.

Talks open in Geneva. The Geneva conference on Rhodesian majority rule held its opening session in the Palais des Nations Oct. 28. Black and white delegations faced each other silently for 20 minutes while Ivor Richard, Britain's chief United Nations delegate who was chairman of the conference, read the opening statement.

No official report was released, but Richard said the session had been "strange and rather moving." He had included in his address a statement from British Prime Minister James Callaghan urging "all concerned not to let this opportunity slip."

The conference opening had been delayed more than two hours while Rhodesian nationalists threatened a boycott. Two African National Council (ANC) faction leaders, Robert Mugabe, leader of the Zimbabwe African National Union (ZANU), and Joshua Nkomo, leader of the Zimbabwe African People's Union (ZAPU), Oct. 27 had accused Britain of "collaboration with [Rhodesian Prime Minister] Ian Smith ... to wreck the conference." They demanded "a representative of ministerial rank with full powers to grant Zimbabwe its independence" to serve as the conference chairman. Nkomo and Mugabe agreed to attend after London promised to send a written explanation of its role at Geneva.

Mugabe arrived in Geneva Oct. 24 and repeated his rejection of U.S. Secretary of State Henry Kissinger's proposals for majority rule. "Armed struggle shall continue . . . until total power is transferred . . . [to the black majority]," Mugabe said. (Mugabe was chief spokesman for the Zimbabwe People's Army [ZIPA], the Rhodesian guerrilla force.)

Nkomo also arrived Oct. 24. He said that the interim government "must reflect clearly majority rule" and that he expected a transition period of less than two years. Speaking in London Oct. 22, Nkomo had said that Kissinger "has prepared an agreement in outline only" and the "form and shape of the new government" would have to be decided by the conference and not according to the terms Smith specified Sept. 24.

Bishop Abel Muzorewa, ANC president, and Rev. Ndabaningi Sithole, Mugabe's rival for ZANU leadership, arrived in Geneva Oct. 25. Muzorewa said after his Oct. 26 meeting with Richard that he was "very much encouraged" and predicted that the nationalists were "going to get a settlement." He joined the other nationalists in rejecting the Kissinger proposals as a framework for a Rhodesian solution.

(The Rhodesian government Oct. 19 had released from detention one man whom Muzorewa had named as part of his delegation and had allowed another, Rev. Canaan Banana, to join the Geneva talks.)

Smith arrived in Geneva Oct. 21 and repeated his stand that the proposals he had accepted were not negotiable. He warned that it was possible that the talks might reach a point where "the whole concept which brought us here has been undermined." But he said his delegation would not quit the talks as a protest. He indicated that he was prepared to be "eminently reasonable and patient" and would "lean over backwards to try to make the conference succeed."

Smith met with Richard Oct. 22, and in separate news conferences both men described their session as "constructive." They met again Oct. 23, and Smith reported that there were still "big problems to solve." Smith explained that the basic issue was observing the terms of the Kissinger proposals, and he stressed that

the changes proposed by black nationalists were unacceptable. He indicated that the air had been "cleared . . . over some points" that he called minor.

Richard said that Smith's "views about the proposals . . . are not entirely shared by the British government," but that there was "scope for an agreement."

Smith Oct. 25 denied that Kissinger had deceived him about whether or not the majority-rule proposals would be negotiable. Smith said that Kissinger had indicated that he had received "confirmation" from presidents of the "front-line" nations (the African countries bordering Rhodesia) that they had accepted the plan, a claim the presidents later denied. Smith suggested that "maybe we should ask Dr. Kissinger to come along . . . and set the record straight."

In an Oct. 24 television interview, Kissinger had said that "the essence of the framework" had been accepted by both sides. He said that Smith "added a few considerations of his own," which Kissinger had thought best to publicize, to avoid giving the impression that a secret deal had been made. Kissinger added that he did not regard the Sept. 24 agreement as "non-negotiable," saying "There must be some room for negotiation."

(The conflict involving Smith, the nationalists and Kissinger arose from two points of the proposal that dealt with the chairman of the council of state and the ministers of law and order and defense in the transitional government. During his negotiations with Kissinger, Smith had urged that those positions be retained by whites. Kissinger had discussed Smith's requests with Tanzanian President Julius Nyerere and Zambian President Kenneth Kaunda and had reported to Smith that they had not objected to the inclusion of the two points in the proposal which Smith announced Sept. 24.)

Kissinger was reported Oct. 27 to have ordered William E. Schaufele, assistant secretary for African affairs, to join Frank Wisner, a State Department desk officer for African affairs who was the U.S. Geneva observer. The U.S. was weighing moves to take a more direct role in the negotiations, should the parties reach a deadlock, according to the Oct. 24 New

York Times. Schaufele arrived in Geneva Oct. 30 to serve as Kissinger's Geneva contact.

According to an Oct. 26 New York Times report, U.S. diplomats had urged Nyerere and Kaunda to use their influence with the nationalists to prevent them from making extreme demands which would wreck the conference.

(The U.S. was pressing for increased British involvement in the Rhodesian situation. Britain was opposed to further involvement. African nationalists were demanding that Britain appoint a governor who would exercise control in Rhodesia during the transition period. They insisted that since Rhodesia had illegally declared its independence in 1965, Britain was still officially responsible for the colony. Britain's refusal to take over in Rhodesia stemmed from its reluctance to send troops into the area to quell guerrilla violence.)

In foreign reaction, South African Prime Minister John Vorster said Oct. 31 that "a settlement . . . can only be reached within the framework" of the Kissinger proposals that Smith had accepted. The U.S. Oct. 29 warned the Soviet Union against interfering in the progress of negotiations in southern Africa. (Soviet press and government statements had repeatedly denounced the U.S. efforts as preserving racist rule in the area.)

Smith delegation rejects independence proposal. The Rhodesian government delegation in Geneva Nov. 2 rejected nationalist demands for an early Rhodesian independence date.

Black nationalist delegates to the informal session had demanded independence by the end of 1977 while Rhodesian Prime Minister Ian Smith had insisted upon independence within two years. (Two nationalist representatives, Joshua Nkomo and Robert Mugabe, went a step further and proposed independence by Sept. 1, 1977.)

Smith announced Nov. 1 that he would return to Rhodesia Nov. 3, leaving Foreign Minister Pieter van der Byl in charge of the government delegation.

Smith said that he would return to Geneva "as soon as they [the nationalists] are ready to . . . talk about what we have come to talk about." He was referring to U.S. Secretary of State Henry Kissinger's proposals for majority rule, which Smith had accepted but the nationalists had rejected.

The Nov. 2 session followed several days of private talks between Ivor Richard, British conference chairman, and the various delegates. The first session of the conference had been adjourned Oct. 29 after Smith had denied accusations by Bishop Abel Muzorewa, ANC president, that Rhodesian security forces were guilty of torture and atrocities against civilians. Muzorewa had called for the election of an interim government on a one-man, one-vote basis and for the representation of political parties in the government on the basis of their electoral strength.

Smith leaves Geneva—Ian Smith left the Geneva conference Nov. 3 and returned to Rhodesia's capital. He expressed dissatisfaction with the lack of progress at the talks and blamed Britain for being "too ready to appease and to back down to the demands of the extremists."

Smith said that he had come "to discuss the Anglo-American proposals" but had failed "to get the others around the table to do it." He accused some of the nationalist delegates of "stupid puerile behavior" and said that he would return when he was satisfied that progress was being made.

At a Nov. 5 news conference in Salisbury, Smith said that even if the Geneva talks failed, majority rule would come to Rhodesia. He explained that he was prepared to work with "moderate, reasonable blacks" to implement the Kissinger proposals. "There is no way forward for us now if we cannot take black Rhodesian opinion with us," Smith said. In his view, he said, there was "still a chance" for the Geneva conference to succeed because "there is a will on the part of the major countries of the free world to bring peace to southern Africa."

Talks continue—Rhodesia's Pieter van der Byl, who had replaced Smith as delegation leader, expressed cautious optimism despite the deadlock. After a second session Nov. 4 on the legal aspects of majority rule (the first had been held Nov. 3) van der Byl said that there were "still certain disagreements" but that he was "a little more optimistic than a few days ago."

Britain Nov. 4 proposed March 1, 1978 as the date for Rhodesian independence and the establishment of majority rule. Ivor Richard of Great Britain, conference chairman, met Nov. 5 with all delegates and separately Nov. 6–7 with the factions in an effort to reach a compromise.

Richard conferred in London with British Prime Minister James Callaghan and British Foreign Minister Anthony Crosland. They were reported to have discussed a "flexible formula" for negotiating Rhodesian independence. The formula would concentrate on substantive issues of elections and government organization without fixing a specific date for majority rule. Upon returning to Geneva later that day, Richard denied that the talks had produced "a fresh initiative."

Richard Nov. 10 met separately with each of the four delegation representatives—van der Byl, Bishop Abel Muzo-wera, president of the African National Council (ANC), Robert Mugabe of the Zimbabwe African National Union (ZANU) ANC faction, and Joshua Nkomo of the Zimbabwe African People's Union (ZAPU) ANC faction. While no details of their talks were released, the nationalists reported no progress; however, van der Byl commented that the conference was "looking a bit better."

(According to Nov. 11 reports, Washington diplomatic sources said that Rhodesian nationalists were privately prepared to accept an 18-month transitional period as a compromise.)

The U.S. stepped up its behind-the-scenes efforts to resolve the conference impasse. The State Department Nov. 4 had announced that William Schaufele, undersecretary of state for African affairs, would return to the U.S. for consultations. John Reinhardt, U.S. assistant secretary of state for public affairs, met Nov. 5–6 with Zambian President Kenneth Kaunda and Tanzanian President Julius Nyerere.

Front-line nations back war—Representatives of the five "front-line" nations (near or bordering Rhodesia) Nov. 6 endorsed guerrilla war as the only means of achieving black majority rule in Rhodesia.

The black leaders, at a meeting in Tanzania, called upon friendly nations to increase their arms support for the struggle, but they did not counsel the nationalist leaders at the Geneva conference to walk out of the negotiations. The New York Times reported Nov. 7 that observers from the "front-line" nations and from the Organization of African Unity at Geneva had advised the nationalists to let Smith's delegation be the first to quit the conference.

Tanzanian President Julius Nyerere Nov. 10 said that British "reluctance to play their full role" at Geneva was the main reason for the conference impasse. He called upon Britain to assume responsibility for the ministries of foreign affairs and defense in the interim government.

Tentative date set for Rhodesian independence. Ivor Richard, British chairman of the Geneva talks on Rhodesian majority rule, Nov. 23 tentatively fixed March 1, 1978 as the date for Rhodesian independence.

Short of an unconditional commitment (which the nationalists wanted and which Britain wished to avoid until the details of the interim government were settled), the statement Richard presented to the conference delegates reportedly affirmed Britain's plan to "fix 1 March 1978 as the latest date by which Rhodesia will become independent," according to sources quoted Nov. 23 by the New York Times. Richard had returned to Geneva Nov. 23 after talks in London Nov. 22 with British Foreign Minister Anthony Crosland.

Rev. Ndabaningi Sithole, one of the nationalist delegates, left Geneva for talks with Tanzanian, Zambian and Mozambique leaders, the Nov. 20 London Times reported. The Times reported Nov. 23 that Tanzania, considered influential with the more militant Rhodesian nationalists, and Nigeria had issued a communique requesting Britain to set the March 1 date as the latest that Rhodesia would become independent.

Two of the militant leaders, Joshua Nkomo and Robert Mugabe, had met Nov. 19 with representatives of Angola and Mozambique, thought to be the more militant of the "front-line" African states.

(Nkomo's ZAPU office in Francistown, Botswana, Nov. 19 was bombed, killing one child and injuring four other persons. An official statement charged Rhodesian security forces with the bombing, but there was speculation that factionalist fighting between Rhodesian nationalist refugees in Francistown had been responsible.)

The U.S. State Department Nov. 19 denied that Kissinger had given Ian Smith assurances that the U.S. would supply military support if the Geneva talks broke down. Kissinger repeated the denial Nov. 20 in a conversation with President-elect Jimmy Carter. Smith had made the assertion in a TV interview in Salisbury Nov. 19.

Nationalists accept British plan. A month-long deadlock in Geneva was broken Nov. 26 when nationalist leaders Mugabe and Nkomo accepted the British proposal for independence on March 1, 1978.

They agreed to a British formula that allowed for independence earlier if the transition process was completed before the March 1 deadline. Their prior insistence on scheduling independence no later than Dec. 1, 1977 before discussing the interim government had delayed the conference since it opened Oct. 28. Two other nationalist representatives, Bishop Abel Muzorewa, ANC president, and Rev. Ndabaningi Sithole, Mugabe's rival for ZANU leadership, had been willing to turn to the details of the interim government before fixing the independence date.

Nkomo and Mugabe, who had formed a united "patriotic front" of their factions at Geneva, reportedly had disagreed on a joint response to the British proposal, presented Nov. 23, with Nkomo favoring acceptance and Mugabe opposed. They agreed to the proposal after two unspecified changes were made in its original wording. As accepted by the nationalists, the proposal read: "It is the British govern-

ment's firm position that all the agreed processes in Rhodesia will be completed in time to enable independence to be granted by March 1, 1978. They therefore fix March 1, 1978 as the latest date by which Rhodesia will become independent."

Formal discussions began Nov. 29 on the creation of the interim government. Rhodesian Foreign Minister Pieter van der Byl, who led the white delegation in the absence of Prime Minister Ian Smith, Nov. 30 repeated his government's insistence that the interim government be based on the plan outlined by the U.S. and Britain and presented to Smith by U.S. Secretary of State Henry Kissinger.

The nationalist leaders rejected the Kissinger proposals entirely. At the Nov. 30 session they presented counter-proposals which included appointment of:

■ A Council of Ministers to be established by the Geneva conference to rule Rhodesia during the transition period. The council was to have a "clear majority" of "liberation movement" (ZANU and ZAPU) representatives, with decisions to be made by simple majority or two-thirds majority votes as specified in an interim constitution.

■ A British resident commissioner responsible for overseeing the implementation of the Geneva conference agreements.

In apparent response to nationalist demands, Britain reversed its policy Dec. 2 and offered to play "a direct role" in a transitional government "if it is the general view that this would be helpful." Since the nationalists did not recognize the Rhodesian regime, they held that Britain still was responsible for Rhodesia as the colonial power. (The Rhodesian government opposed a British interim-government takeover and would accept only British diplomatic representation, with no special governing powers.)

Former Rhodesian Prime Minister Garfield Todd, an adviser to Nkomo's delegation, Dec. 1 called upon Britain to appoint a governor-general to take charge of the interim government and a general to take charge of the armed forces if the Geneva talks failed to produce an agreement.

ANC charges pro-Nkomo plot. ANC Secretary General Gordon Chavunduka Nov. 28 accused Britain, the U.S. and Zambia of conspiring to appoint Joshua Nkomo as head of the future Rhodesian interim government. Claiming that Britain was indifferent to the establishment of democracy in Rhodesia, Chavunduka warned: "The seven million people of Zimbabwe will not allow their leaders to be imposed on them."

ANC officials Nov. 27 had charged that the "front-line" nations (Angola, Botswana, Mozambique, Tanzania and Zambia) were conspiring with Britain to appoint Nkomo. British officials in Geneva Nov. 28 described the charges as "speculative," and Zambia Nov. 29 called Chavunduka's claims "unfounded" and "unfair."

Nationalist rivalries. Some of the issues troubling the Geneva conference were problems stemming from rivalries among the nationalist groups.

A delegation of the Zimbabwe People's Army (ZIPA), the guerrilla force, had arrived in Geneva Dec. 1. It was believed ZIPA's presence would strengthen the more militant black-nationalist factions at the conference, the Zimbabwe African National Union (ZANU) and the Zimbabwe African People's Union (ZAPU).

Bishop Abel Muzorewa, president of the African National Council (ANC), Dec. 4 condemned ZANU leader Robert Mugabe and ZAPU leader Joshua Nkomo for opposing elections for the interim Rhodesian government. He accused the two nationalists, who had united their delegations in a "patriotic front," of creating an "anti-democratic front" along with the white minority-government delegation. (The three delegations Muzorewa condemned favored an interim government composed of ministers appointed by agreement at the conference, although they disagreed on which positions would be held by whites and where executive power would lie.) Muzorewa Dec. 5 called upon Rhodesian whites to join the ANC. Although other nationalist factions accepted support from individual whites, Muzorewa's call was the first appeal for general white participation with a black faction.

Smith returns to Geneva. After a four-week absence, Rhodesian Prime Minister Ian Smith Dec. 8 returned to the Geneva conference on Rhodesian majority rule.

Smith conferred with Ivor Richard, British chairman of the conference, upon his return. Contrary to prior speculation that Smith's decision to return might produce a new initiative in the stalled talks, no progress was reported after the meeting. (In Salisbury Dec. 5, Smith had accused Richard of "complete disregard for the interests of white Rhodesians" and of "pander[ing] to the every want of the extreme black politicians who represent only a small fraction of Rhodesian opinion."

(The conference stalemate made conclusion by the agreed deadline, Dec. 20, highly unlikely, the London Times reported Dec. 9. If no agreement were reached by then, the Rhodesian independence date of March 1, 1978, would have to be renegotiated because Britain had insisted on a 15-month transition period to effect a transition to a multiracial government. The New York Times reported Dec. 3 that the black delegations increasingly were convinced that a U.S. role was necessary to achieve progress.)

Smith leaves Geneva, talks adjourned. Ian Smith left the Geneva conference Dec. 12, 1976, asserting that he saw "virtually no change" in the deadlocked meeting.

He had said Dec. 10 that he had been "misled by the parties who arranged this conference" (a reference to Britain) into believing that a change in the strategy of the black nationalist delegates in Geneva was imminent.

Upon his departure Smith repeated his objections to a British role in the transition to majority rule. He described as "ghastly" proposals that a British governor-general be appointed and that a Briton hold the combined ministries of justice and defense in the interim government. (The proposals had been discussed during Dec. 10–11 talks between British

Foreign Minister Anthony Crosland and U.S. Secretary of State Henry Kissinger. They were presented to the House of Commons by Crosland Dec. 14.)

In Salisbury Dec. 13, Smith said that he would negotiate with various black delegations during the planned conference recess. He did not rule out consultations with Bishop Abel Muzorewa, who was the African National Council (ANC) president and also a conference delegate, the Dec. 14 London Times reported. (Sources quoted by the Times said there was a possibility of an alliance between Smith and Muzorewa, considered the most popular nationalist figure among Rhodesian blacks. Such an alliance would be lined up against the more militant "patriotic front" of Robert Mugabe and Joshua Nkomo.

The Geneva conference was adjourned Dec. 14 until January 1977. Conference chairman Ivor Richard, Britain's chief delegate to the United Nations, termed the talks "a modest success," a view that was shared by neither the Rhodesian government nor the nationalist delegates.

Upon his return from Geneva, Muzorewa criticized Smith Dec. 12 for what he called delaying tactics at Geneva.

After a rally of more than 100,000 of his supporters in a black township outside Salisbury, Muzorewa called "patriotic front" objections to elections for the interim government "an insult to our people."

Britain offers Rhodesia alternatives. Before beginning his shuttle through southern Africa, Ivor Richard, British chairman of the adjourned Geneva conference on Rhodesian majority rule, Dec. 22 outlined several new alternatives that Britain proposed to help solve the transitional-government impasse.

At a Washington, D.C. news conference, Richard said that the posts of minister of justice and minister of defense in the transitional government could be filled by direct control of the two ministries by a Briton, control of the ministries by a committee of blacks and whites with a British chairman, control of one ministry by a black and one by a white, or control of both ministries by a Rhodesian white

who was not a member of the ruling Rhodesian Front party. (Richard had discussed the plans Dec. 21 with U.S. Secretary of State Henry A. Kissinger and had visited with Secretary of State-designate Cyrus Vance.)

The Rhodesian government Dec. 23 branded the four proposals "impractical."

Government, Politics & Racial Problems

Cabinet changes, new president sworn. Prime Minister Ian Smith made changes in his cabinet Jan. 13, 1976 to accompany the swearing-in Jan. 14 of Finance Minister John Wrathall, 62, as Rhodesia's second president. Rhodesia's first titular head of state, Clifford Dupont, retired at the end of 1975 after five years in the post.

In the cabinet shifts, David Smith, the minister of agriculture, was named to succeed Wrathall in the finance ministry and Rollo Hayman, a former deputy minister, assumed the agriculture post. Desmond Lardner-Burke, the controversial, hard-line minister of justice, law and order, was appointed minister of commerce and industry. He succeeded Elly Broomberg who was given the information, immigration and tourism portfolio. The justice, law and order post was left vacant, as was the position of deputy prime minister, formerly held by Wrathall.

Smith announced Sept. 9 the removal of Pieter van der Byl as minister of defense and the appointment of Reginald Cowper, minister of public service and co-ordination, in his place.

Smith said that he had removed van der Byl from his post because of the minister's increased work load (van der Byl was also minister of foreign affairs). However, Smith appointed van der Byl minister of public service in place of Cowper. Cowper remained leader of the House of Assembly and minister of coordination.

Smith appoints blacks to cabinet, assails Kissinger. Prime Minister Smith April 27, 1976 announced a new "initiative" to include blacks in his white minority government. The action was deplored by black nationalist leaders as "irrelevant."

Four tribal chiefs named by Smith took oaths of office April 28 to become the first black members of the Rhodesian Cabinet. They were Jeremiah Chirau, who was president of the Council of Chiefs, Tafirenyika Mangwende, Kayisa Ndiweni, and Zefania Charumbira. All four already were members of the Senate and, as tribal chiefs, were paid by the government. Three of six scheduled black deputy ministers were also named. Their specific posts were not announced, but all 10 would have responsibilities for African affairs, it was reported.

In a televised address, Smith restated his government's view on the question of majority rule:

Providing we are able to preserve our policy of the maintenance of standards—i.e., government by the best people, irrespective of color—I believe the vast majority of thinking Rhodesians will support this philosophy of responsible majority rule.

Any question of deviating from this standpoint, especially when we live cheek by jowl with the chaos and disaster which results from lowering standards, is out of the question. Therefore, let me make it crystal clear that neither I, nor any of my colleagues in government, are in any mood for appeasement.

Smith deplored the policy toward Rhodesia stated earlier that day in Lusaka by Secretary of State Kissinger who, Smith said, had joined "in the campaign to exert psychological pressure on Rhodesia." Smith said:

It is clear that both the American and British governments, having been caught on the wrong foot in Angola by the Russian intervention there, are in mortal dread of a recurrence in Rhodesia.

They believe, quite wrongly, that if the whites in Rhodesia could be persuaded to surrender, the Russians would then have no excuse to intervene here.

Therefore, they are prepared to sacrifice the whites of Rhodesia—and if necessary of the whole of southern Africa—in order to buy time for themselves, in order to avoid being confronted by further Russian aggression in the subcontinent. . . .

Let me say in the strongest terms that we have no intention whatever of surrendering our country as part of a policy of appeasing the Communists. We have no intention of allowing our country to degenerate into the sort of shambles which we see in Mozambique and Angola today.

Smith said his government would make a "supreme effort . . . on the security front." Noting the guerrilla offensive in southeastern Rhodesia, Smith said he had appointed a special Cabinet-level committee to deal with the problem of terrorism.

He said the government had decided to introduce "special criminal courts to deal solely with trials arising from terrorist activities."

Smith stressed the government's need to control the mass media. Referring to new censorship regulations published April 26, Smith said they were designed "to prevent the dissemination of information which could prejudice the security of the state and be harmful to Rhodesia."

Cabinet change scored—Widespread opposition to Smith's appointment of black chiefs to the Cabinet was reported by the New York Times May 4. According to the Times, blacks, liberals, conservatives and elements of Smith's party, the Rhodesia Front, reacted with hostility to the action.

Among those deploring the move was Joshua Nkomo, leader of the Rhodesia-based faction of the African National Council. He said May 7 the action had "no political significance."

Nkomo, the nationalist leader whose talks with Smith on a constitutional settlement had collapsed in March, also hardened his position on future dealings with the white minority regime. He said the concessions he had offered in the unsuccessful negotiations would not be presented again if the talks resumed.

Smith, Nkomo charged, had rejected "the most reasonable political agreement that could end the war. Now we couldn't even offer the same terms. They're out of date." Nkomo, who had been regarded as a moderate, added, "In turning down our agreement, they opted for war."

As an ostensible solution to the problem of political power for blacks, Deputy Minister Edward Sutton-Pryce had outlined a plan to separate Rhodesia into three provinces along racial and tribal lines, it was reported July 7. Two provinces would be inhabited by the two major African tribes composing Rhodesia's black population, and the third province would be white. Each province would have its own government, but Sutton-Pryce was unclear about the ultimate degree of central control.

Smith rejects reform plan. Prime Minister Smith July 23, 1976 dismissed as impractical the three main proposals of the Quenet Commission on Racial Discrimination, which his government had appointed. A preliminary version of the commission's findings had been rejected by an official spokesman earlier in the month.

The main findings of the commission report were that land set aside for whites should be opened up to all races, that a common electoral role should be reintroduced and that a declaration of rights should be adopted and made enforceable in the courts. Smith rejected these proposals in an address to Parliament, where his Rhodesian Front Party held the majority of seats.

"The importance of maintaining maximum productivity in our white farming areas" was, he said, "vital to our economic survival." Smith said that the productivity would be threatened if Africans were to take over any of the white farms. The "extension of African farming areas would represent an unacceptable security risk," Smith said, because black farmers were less able than whites to defend themselves against terrorist attacks.

Reintroduction of a common electoral roll would lead to racial friction, according to Smith, if whites and blacks were running for the same parliamentary seats. (In the Senate and the House of Assembly, which together made up the Parliament, most seats were filled by white candidates elected by white voters. The remaining seats were filled by black candidates elected by black voters.) Smith said that the commission had "failed to give this most involved question adequate consideration and I believe that their case is unconvincing."

The third main proposal, that a bill of rights having legal force should be adopted, was unacceptable to Smith because it ran the danger of making the courts a political institution.

On the whole, Smith said, he found the commission's findings "balanced and reasonable" and many of them would be adopted by the government. He did not, however, indicate which these would be or when they would be acted upon.

In the earlier action, Reg Cowper, House of Assembly leader, had presented in Parliament July 2 the regime's refusal to replace racially segregated voting rolls with common rolls and to end the ban on the purchase by blacks of white-owned land. On minor points, the government expressed willingness to change policies. While rejecting a plan to desegregate restaurants and hotels within two years, the government agreed that new establishments should be integrated. The government also agreed to lift a ban on multi-racial sports in schools and it accepted in principle the idea of compulsory armed service for blacks.

Bishop Lamont indicts regime. Roman Catholic Bishop Donal Lamont of Umtali, later jailed by the Rhodesian government, wrote an open letter dated Aug. 11 (made public Aug. 15), 1976 in which he assailed the Smith regime for its "clearly racist and oppressive policies" and "its stubborn refusal to change." Lamont held that these government policies were "largely responsible for the injustices which have provoked the present disorder...." His letter also said:

On whatever dubious grounds you may at one time have based your claim to rule, much argument no longer has any validity. You may rule with the consent of a small and selfish electorate, but you rule without the consent of the nation—which is the test of all legitimacy. All the legalistic quibbling in the world cannot alter that fact.

Neither can you deny that the world community of nations rejects your claim to legality. Your administration is an outcast from and stands condemned by the civilized world. Justification for this condemnation is set out with the most detailed, objective and incontrovertible clarity in the legal study recently published and distributed throughout the world by the International Commission of Jurists. This important document which you dare not neglect and cannot refute, supports my considered belief that the dangers which threaten Rhodesia have their roots in the repressive legislation which you have enacted in an effort to maintain the power and the privilege of the white minority, reckless of the rights of the rest of the population.

To summarize in its briefest form your abuse of power, I can do no better than to quote the words of Pope Paul VI when addressing the United Nations on the subject of racial discrimination. The Pope said: "Within a country which belongs to each one, all should be equal before the law, find equal admittance to economic, cultural and social life, and benefit from a fair share of the nation's riches." In every single detail of that magisterial statement your administration fails. The non-European people of Rhodesia are by your law denied every one of these rights which are theirs as from nature.

No wonder the oppressed people, made marginal to society in their own country, have welcomed and continue to welcome those whom they call "freedom fighters" and whom you call "terrorists." This is readily understandable. It is understandable too that such a force should have arisen and that it should daily be on the increase. Your oppression has called it into existence and given the young men and women who belong to it an attractive cause to espouse. They feel themselves compelled in conscience to fight for the elimination of all the discrimination which has degraded their people and make them second-class citizens in the land of their birth.

While I say this I must make it absolutely clear that, as in the past, I deplore and denounce with all the power which I have to command, all acts of violence which may have been perpetrated by these or by any other individuals or groups. The Church can never condone such violence, no more than it can turn a blind eye to its causes. At the same time I must repeat—no matter what the consequences for myself—that the institutional violence sanctioned by your administration and made respectable by acts of parliament, is itself the root cause of most of the physical violence which Rhodesia has experienced during the past ten years.

Prescinding from the long-standing discrimination practiced against the non-white population of this country, and lest I should seem to speak in vague generalities, let me record here some of the grave injustices which your administration has introduced since it came to office. Oppressive legislation has been multiplied, even when publicly rejected by your own Senate Legal Committee. The African civilian population has been clearly made to feel that it is now the deliberate target for what would normally be called "the forces of law and order." The army and police have been officially accorded excessive powers and guaranteed indemnity against the abuse of them.

Approval has been granted for the bombing and destruction of villages, even though these should contain innocent people. Obstacles of all kinds have been placed in the way of those who seek either legal justice or compensation for death or brutal treatment or loss of property. The media of communication have been placed almost entirely under the control of one political party, your own, and are manipulated constantly to suppress or to distort the truth.

Nor is this all: In a state which claims to be democratic, people are restricted or imprisoned without trial, tortured or tried in camera, put to death by secret hanging, and justification for all this barbarity is sought by you in the name of Christianity and of Western civilization and for what you call the "maintaining of Rhodesian standards." Surely this is the final absurdity.

In spite of their limited vision and of their consequent denial of integral development to all the people of Rhodesia, the efforts of previous governments had indeed brough many of the benefits of Christianity and of Western civilization to this country. You, however, by your total insensitivity to the rights of the human person and by your inability to read the signs of the times, have undone much of what had previously been accomplished. Yet you refuse to recognize your sorry condition and appear satisfied to continue your oppressive policies even though they should bring ruin to Rhodesia. Your reaction to the recent Quenot Report on Racial Discrimination is eloquent proof of this. . . .

If intensification of racial hatred, widespread urban guerrilla activity, increased destruction of property and fearful loss of life are to be avoided; if the whole sub-continent of Africa is not to be engulfed in a cruel war, you must without delay change your present tragic course of action. To continue Pope Paul's remarks: "As long as the rights of all the peoples, among them the right of self-determination and independence, are not duly recognized and honored, there cannot be true and lasting peace, even though the abusive power of arms may for a time prevail over the reactions of those opposed. All men must participate in the life of the nation. Power, responsibility and the decision-making cannot be the monopoly of one group or race segment of the people" Undoubtedly this will involve for some the sacrifice of privileges based solely on race, but being a work of justice it should eliminate the sources of discontent and violence and bring about that peace that we all long for.

It is up to you to give the lead. The fate of Rhodesia and its people is in your hands.

Government expenditures increase. The government announced a 40% increase in defense expenditures July 6, from $R60.3 million in 1975 to $R84.4 million. The police budget was also increased, from $R35.2 million to $R44.1 million. Government subsidies to the tobacco industry increased to $R10 million from $R3.1 million, and $R28.4 million was provided to Rhodesia Railways to meet operating losses. Other loans to industries brought the total government budget for 1976 to $R702.8 million, a 15.6% increase over 1975, with defense accounting for 12% of the total. A slow growth rate had been predicted because of lagging exports, although mining and agriculture output was high.

Tobacco subsidies cut—The president of the Rhodesia Tobacco Association announced a cut in tobacco subsidies and other measures to reduce Rhodesia's tobacco output for 1976–77 because of a larger-than-expected 1976 harvest, the Journal of Commerce said Aug. 25.

To discourage farmers from increasing tobacco acreage, the government set up a three-level price system. A certain amount of the crop would be maintained by government price supports, a further amount could be sold at unsupported (market) prices, and any tobacco produced in excess of the national target would result in forfeiture of government price support in proportion to the excess.

Emigrants' currency cut. In a move believed designed to reduce the flow of white emigrants from the country, Finance Minister David Smith July 15 announced drastic cuts in the sum of money those leaving Rhodesia permanently would be allowed to take with them.

The amount of money emigrants could take with them was reduced from $R5,000 ($8,100) to $R1,000 ($1,611). Vacation allowances were cut nearly in half, from $R400 to $R250.

Figures released Aug. 1 showed that in the first six months of 1976 the country had a net loss of 2,280 white persons compared with a net gain of 1,590 whites in the same period of the previous year.

Other Foreign Developments

EEC backs 'self determination.' In a policy statement adopted Feb. 23, 1976, the nine European Community foreign ministers underlined their governments' support for "self-determination and independence for the Rhodesian and Namibian peoples" and condemned South African apartheid.

Roy Hattersley, British minister of state, who participated in the policy deliberations, commented Feb. 23 that the EC declaration should be a signal to Rhodesian Prime Minister Ian Smith that his country was expected to conform to the "normal standards of civilized behavior."

The European Council, comprising the heads of government of the nine European Community nations, met in Luxembourg April 1–2. In the session's only agreement, the leaders restated a prior EC foreign policy position supporting British demands that the ruling white minority in Rhodesia accept inclusion of the black majority in the government.

Moscow denies role in Rhodesia. Soviet Foreign Minister Andrei A. Gromyko asserted March 25, 1976 that the Soviet Union was not involved with nationalist movements in either Namibia (South-West Africa) or Rhodesia. He made the assertion in London at the conclusion of an official visit to Great Britain for talks with Prime Minister Harold Wilson and Foreign Secretary James Callaghan.

Callaghan had called on the Soviet ambassador to London, Nikolai Lunkov, three times March 15–19 to express Britain's concern over foreign intervention in southern Africa.

South Africa bars military role in Rhodesia. South African Secretary of Information Eschel M. Rhoodie, an influential member of the government with close links to Prime Minister John Vorster, said May 13, 1976 that South Africa definitely would not intervene militarily to preserve Rhodesia's white minority government.

Rhoodie's remarks were the most unequivocal government statement to date on military aid for South Africa.

"We will not under any circumstances undertake an upholding operation," he said in an interview with a New York Times correspondent in Pretoria. "Military intervention by South Africa to uphold the Rhodesian government is absolutely out of the question."

The Times report also cited other South African officials who confirmed and amplified Rhoodie's statement, saying that Pretoria had informed Salisbury that the most Rhodesia could expect, in an extreme crisis, would be a "rescue operation" by South African forces to evacuate white Rhodesians.

Soviet influence in area feared—South African Foreign Minister Hilgard Muller Aug. 13 pledged support for American efforts to solve the Rhodesian problem and expressed fear of Soviet intervention in southern Africa unless a solution was reached.

Speaking at the congress of South Africa's ruling National Party at Durban, Muller said, "It would be disastrous for South Africa and the free world if a situation was allowed to arise which would give the Russians a justification to intervene elsewhere on the pretense that they were acting as champions of black Africans."

(Rowan Cronje, Rhodesia's minister of health, labor and social welfare, disagreed with Muller. According to an Aug. 20 London Times report, Cronje said in Parliament that "if they [the Soviets] want to get involved they will, whatever we do or do not do.")

South African Information Minister Cornelius Mulder denied that Muller had favored majority rule in Rhodesia, the London Times reported Aug. 20. In the same report, Prime Minister Smith was quoted as having said Aug. 16 that it was a "complete distortion" to claim that the South African minister had advocated majority rule for Rhodesia within two years.

Mobil accused on Rhodesia sanctions. A U.S. church group accused the Mobil Oil Corp. June 21, 1976 of involvement over a 10-year period in an elaborate scheme by which oil sanctions against Rhodesia were broken by as much as $20 million annually.

The charges were made by the United Church of Christ in a report drawn up by its Center for Social Action. The Rev. Larold K. Schulz, the center's executive director, released the document at a joint press conference with the Peoples Commission, a radical left-wing organization. Schulz explained that because previous disclosures about Rhodesia had been ignored by the news media, a joint announcement seemed the best way "to get the kind of impact necessary." He said that the information had come originally from a group called Okhela, which was composed of white South Africans who gave clandestine support to black nationalists.

As outlined by Schulz, the scheme involved the sale of petroleum products by Mobil (South Africa) to Genta, a purchas-

ing agency owned by the Rhodesian government, which then resold these goods to all the oil firms in the country, including Mobil (Rhodesia). Afterwards, in order to "make it look as if Mobil (South Africa) was not involved in any trade with Rhodesia," Schulz said, a "paper chase system" was devised "whereby sales and payments would be passed through various South African companies which acted as intermediaries." Schulz claimed that "similar procedures" had been worked out by the Royal Dutch/Shell Group, British Petroleum, Caltex and Total. He said that three U.S. citizens had acted simultaneously as directors of Mobil (South Africa) and executives of Mobil (U.S.A.).

A spokesman for Mobil denied the charge June 21, noting that the "management of our international division has gone to considerable effort to make sure that all of our affiliates, particularly those in southern Africa, have been informed of U.S. law," which forbade the sale to Rhodesia of most products.

Mobil said Aug. 27 that its efforts to investigate charges that its South African affiliate was supplying Rhodesia with petroleum had been blocked by South African law.

In a letter to the United Church of Christ, Mobil said that the South African official secrets act prohibited any dissemination of information relating to storage, distribution and sale of petroleum products. The company also wrote that attempts to get information from its Rhodesian affiliate had met with no response because of similar legal restrictions.

The South African affiliate, according to Mobil, had not supplied Rhodesia with petroleum since 1966, but the affiliate said it was powerless to prevent its customers from selling there.

The United Church Board for World Missionaries, the overseas arm of the United Church of Christ, said in an Aug. 30 Wall Street Journal report that it had notified the Securities and Exchange Commission Aug. 27 that it was filing a shareholder resolution calling upon Mobil to "take every measure immediately" to insure that petroleum supplies did not reach Rhodesia, including refusal to make bulk sales to buyers unable to verify that the products were not destined for Rhodesia. (According to a church official, the church and its affiliates owned about 85,000 shares of Mobil.)

Zero-growth economy seen. U.S. analysts predicted that Rhodesia's economy would experience no growth in 1976, despite good harvest and mining prospects, the New York Times reported Oct. 17.

According to the analysts, Rhodesian exports were unable to reach shipping points because of rail bottlenecks in South Africa, Rhodesia's only outlet to the sea. In addition, increased guerrilla activity forced Rhodesia to move shipments during daylight hours only, further reducing Rhodesia's export volume. An outflow of skilled labor was also cited as a serious economic problem. The analysts estimated that 1,000 skilled whites and professionals emigrated each month.

The report added that oil reaching Rhodesia from South Africa had been supplied by subsidiaries of Mobil Oil Corp. but said that there was no evidence of direct involvement of the U.S. oil company in defying the international blockade.

British seize tobacco. British customs authorities announced Aug. 18 the confiscation of 165 tons of Rhodesian tobacco under Britain's embargo on Rhodesian products. The tobacco, destined for a Canadian company, had been seized during a stopover in Dover in April 1975. The order of confiscation had been issued July 15, 1976, after tests showed the tobacco was Rhodesian. The Canadian company did not appeal the order within the one-month deadline after the order.

Zambia used Rhodesian railroad. The Rhodesian and South African press had reported that Zambia had exported thousands of tons of copper abroad through the Mozambique port of Lourenco Marques via Rhodesian railways, the London Times had reported Nov. 16, 1975. The action, which would negate the Zambian sanction against dealing with Rhodesia's white minority government and defy the border closing Salisbury imposed in 1973, was apparently taken to compensate for the nonfunctioning of the Benguela railway which linked Zambia with the already overburdened Angolan port of Lobito, from which export activities had all but ceased.

1977: Increasing Pressures

Warfare Intensifies

Pressures on the Rhodesian government mounted during 1977 as the international community increased its demands for the transfer of rule to the black majority. As the year's end approached, there seemed to be evidence that the white minority regime, however reluctantly, was preparing to compromise if possible and to capitulate if necessary on the best terms it could negotiate. This development was accompanied by—and probably at least a partial result of—a heightening of the intensity of the fighting between black nationalist guerrilla and Rhodesian government forces.

4th guerrilla front, wide action. A fourth military front in the war in Rhodesia was reported Jan. 6, 1977 to have appeared in northwestern Rhodesia, near the Zambian border.

Previous fronts were established by guerrillas infiltrating from Mozambique in the east and north and from Botswana and Zambia in the west. The new guerrillas were reported by Rhodesian security forces to be members of the Zimbabwe African People's Union, a nationalist faction headed by Joshua Nkomo. It was thought that Nkomo was mounting the offensive to compete for influence in the militant nationalist movement · with Robert Mugabe's faction, the Zimbabwe African National Union.

The Jan. 6 military communique reporting on the new front also said that 13 guerrillas and seven black civilians had been killed since Jan. 4. A Jan. 3 communique reported four guerrillas killed since Jan. 1.

The Jan. 3 communique also reported a guerrilla attack on a "consolidated" village Dec. 31, 1976, in which guerrillas set fire to more than 200 huts grouped together near the Mozambique border northeast of Mount Darwin. The report said nearly 1,000 Africans were made homeless by the attack, but there were no casualties.

("Consolidated" villages were formed by grouping several smaller African villages together for safety without military guard. In contrast, "protected" villages were militarily guarded compounds for which residents were issued passes. The system of "protected" and "consolidated" villages was part of the government strategy to deprive the guerrillas of access to food supplies and shelter from the African populations.)

A guerrilla, Albert Ncube, who had confessed to the murder of seven civilians, including three Roman Catholic missionaries, escaped from Rhodesian custody Jan. 9.

Father Paul Egli, a Swiss-born Roman Catholic missionary, Jan. 12 was sentenced to five years in prison after pleading guilty to charges of failing to report nationalist guerrillas in the vicinity of his mission. He was released on bail pending appeal, and his sentence was reduced April 6 to three years.

A Jan. 12 Rhodesian security forces communique reported the downing of a Rhodesian warplane by Mozambique gunfire. The border-patrol plane crashed in Mozambique territory, and three crewmen were later reported dead. It was the first time the government had acknowledged that a warplane had been shot down.

A Jan. 27 military communique said one white farmer, two police reservists and 25 guerrillas had been killed since Jan. 25. A Jan. 13 communique said eight nationalist guerrillas had been killed since Jan. 10.

Clashes along the Mozambique border were reported Jan. 31, Feb. 3, 6 and 15–16. Rhodesia was reported to be mounting attacks well within Mozambique territory, destroying bridges and roads and severing the country's main communication links.

Rhodesian soldiers desert. The Rhodesian Defense Ministry Jan. 7 confirmed the desertion of a U.S. soldier serving in the Rhodesian army. Private Lawrence Meyers had been absent without leave since Dec. 30, 1976, the ministry reported, and he and a Rhodesian-born soldier were reported to have fled to Botswana.

In an interview on Botswana radio, the two men said there had been 10 desertions from the Rhodesian Light Infantry since December 1976. The Defense Ministry called their allegation "grossly misleading," and one made "to raise funds and sympathy for a free trip home." Both men also estimated that 30% of the whites in the Rhodesian army were foreigners.

Three U.S. nationals Feb. 9 deserted from the Rhodesian army in a stolen plane. South African police in Johannesburg March 2 said they had arrested one of the men, Douglas Sherck, who faced robbery charges in Salisbury.

Another deserter, Michael Steven Becks, had eluded an airport cordon in Johannesburg and had flown to Brazil. The third, Dennis Robert Pearce, was reported to have flown to Zambia in the stolen plane, according to police.

Rhodesian terrorists hanged. Eight black nationalists convicted of urban terrorism and sabotage were hanged Jan. 17 in Salisbury. It was the first time an execution had been confirmed officially since a 1976 ban on such information.

The eight were members of the African National Council headed by Bishop Abel Muzorewa. Muzorewa Jan. 17 denounced the executions, calling them "another strong indication to confirm our serious doubts" about Prime Minister Ian Smith's commitment to majority rule.

Bomb kills Nkomo aide. Jason Moyo, a chief aide to Joshua Nkomo, was killed Jan. 22 by a parcel bomb. Moyo had been Nkomo's liaison with members of Nkomo's Zimbabwe African People's Union (ZAPU) based outside Rhodesia and had been the organizer of ZAPU's guerrilla army. ZAPU blamed the killing on the Rhodesian army, but nationalist sources cited Jan. 24 said the package had been sent from Botswana, indicating that internal disputes among black nationalists may have been responsible.

The headquarters of the Zimbabwe African People's Union in Lusaka, Zambia was wrecked by two bombs July 31, according to a Zambian report Aug. 1.

Rhodesia call-ups increase. Rhodesia announced Jan. 27 that military call-ups would be extended to eligibles aged 38–50. Affected were all white, Asian and Colored (mixed race) males. (Blacks, who comprised 66% of the army and 75% of the police, were all volunteers.) Defense Minister Reginald Cowper said all deferments for men aged 18–38 would be cancelled.

It was feared the increased call-up would deal the final blow to Rhodesia's seriously troubled economy. Extended military service and increased white emigration had strained the country's limited white manpower reserves and had resulted in serious losses to businesses.

Rowan Cronje, new manpower chief, Feb. 28 said the government planned to recruit an additional 12,000 men aged 38-50 into the Rhodesian security forces. He said men in that age category would serve three months in the field. Cronje had replaced defense minister Reginald Cowper, who had resigned because of his opposition to increasing the draft.

Cowper had said Feb. 11 that he was resigning "to make way for someone else who might be able to provide the panacea now being sought" for Rhodesia's manpower problem. The increased demand for troops had put a strain on Rhodesia's white work force and businessmen had complained the added call-ups would wreck the economy.

Prime Minister Smith Feb. 15 had then announced the creation of a National Manpower Board, headed by Cronje, who was named lands and natural resources minister of labor, health and social welfare, to handle military manpower requirements.

(Lands & Natural Resources Minister Mark Partridge was named defense minister March 10 to replace Cowper.

(Education Minister Philip Smith was named lands and natural resources minister to replace Partridge, and Wilfrid Waller replaced Smith. Archie Wilson was named minister of transport, power and and roads to replace Roger Hawkins, who March 7 had been named minister of combined operations, a special new post coordinating defense-related activities of various ministries and the civilian and military sectors.)

400 students taken by ZAPU. A Jan. 31 Rhodesian military statement said 400 black students at a Lutheran mission school near the Botswana border had been taken from the school at gunpoint Jan. 30 by nationalist guerrillas and forced to march to Botswana. The statement said 230 male and 170 female students, aged 12-20, had been taken from the Manama Lutheran Mission secondary school 15 miles from Botswana. Five teachers, two nurses and a clerk were taken with the students. The guerrillas also stole

$20,000, representing students' tuition fees, from the institution.

The headmaster reported that the guerrillas had told the students they had to join the army of Nkomo's Zimbabwe African People's Union (ZAPU). ZAPU had been reported undertaking a mass kidnap campaign to strengthen its guerrilla forces, which were smaller than Mugabe's Zimbabwe African National Union.

Five of the students and two teachers reportedly escaped from the group and returned to the mission school that night. The Botswana government Jan. 31 confirmed that the group had arrived in two border villages. That day, Rhodesian Foreign Minister Pieter van der Byl said the raid was "complicating our relations with Botswana." He added that Botswana had rejected recent Rhodesian charges that Botswana was allowing Rhodesian guerrillas to operate from within its borders.

Botswana Feb. 1 denied that the students had been kidnapped, saying they "were fleeing from harassment by Rhodesian forces" who had been ordered to shoot "innocent" people to maintain a casualty rate of 10 blacks killed for every Rhodesian soldier killed. That day, Rhodesia said it had asked the International Red Cross to investigate the case, but a Red Cross spokesman in Geneva declined to say if any action would be taken.

Most of the students taken from the mission school chose to stay with nationalist guerrillas in Botswana, it was announced Feb. 6. After visiting with their parents that day only 51 students decided to return home.

The meeting with the parents was supervised by three International Red Cross officials, two Rhodesian Catholic priests, a British diplomat and a representative of Botswana President Seretse Khama. Parents reported their children feared reprisals by nationalist guerrillas if they returned to Rhodesia. The two priests who had accompanied the group said Feb. 7 the children had been influenced to stay by "indoctrination, threats and promises."

(One of the mission nuns Feb. 2 said 10 children and two teachers had escaped from Botswana Jan. 30. Two more children were reported to have left Botswana Feb. 5.)

More than 100 of the 331 children in Botswana left Feb. 8 for guerrilla training in Mozambique.

In a related development, three Rhodesian television reporters were sentenced in Botswana Feb. 8 to six months in jail for illegal entry and possession of a firearm. They had been arrested Feb. 5 by Botswana police while trying to film the arrival of the parents of the abducted schoolchildren.

Earlier in January ZAPU had been accused of a mass kidnap campaign to gather recruits for its guerrilla army, the London Times reported Jan. 21. Africans who had been kidnapped to Botswana and had escaped said armed terrorists had invaded their village and forced 124 men to march at gunpoint over the border. Government officials estimated that about 1,000 Africans had been abducted since November 1976 from Matabeleland in the southwest, compared with 600 during the previous 15 months.

In a previous dispute, Botswana Jan. 12 had presented a complaint against Rhodesia in the United Nations Security Council, charging Rhodesian military forces with border violations. Van der Byl Jan. 13 said Rhodesia would ask to take part in the debate on the complaint under a rule providing for participation on Security Council debates by non-member states. The Rhodesian request was in response to Botswana rejections of direct talks over the problem.

Rhodesia Feb. 16 announced it had established for the first time a restricted area along its Botswana frontier. A 19-mile strip along the border had been cleared of homes and underbrush and troops had been ordered to fire on any unauthorized person in the area.

A security-force communique Feb. 19 said a white police officer had been killed the night before in a raid into Botswana. It was the first Rhodesian admission of military operations in Botswana. The Rhodesian government said security forces had been hunting nationalist guerrillas operating from across the border, and the officer had been killed by nationalists. Botswana, however, said the man had been killed by a Botswana police unit. The attack had taken place as a United Nations mission was investigating Botswana's charges of Rhodesian border violations.

Guerrillas kill white clerics. Seven white Roman Catholic missionaries were killed by Rhodesian nationalist guerrillas Feb. 6 at the St. Paul's Mission at Musami, 37 miles north of Salisbury. The dead included two priests, a lay brother and four nuns from Britain, Ireland, Kenya and West Germany.

Rev. Dunstan Myerscough, who survived the massacre, said about 12 guerrillas entered the mission late at night, rounded up the missionaries, herded the group outside the mission, and shot them. Myerscough said he was able to survive by dropping to the ground as soon as he heard the shots.

Patrick Chakaipa, the first black Catholic archbishop of Salisbury, Feb. 7 issued a statement calling the slain clerics "friends and servants of the African people." At a requiem mass later that day, Chakaipa said: "Whoever did this makes a mockery of the ideals they claim to serve." Chakaipa said he had received a telegram from Pope Paul VI expressing sorrow and outrage over the attack.

The police said evidence indicated the guerrillas were members of the Zimbabwe African National Union, a group headed by Robert Mugabe. Police Superintendent John Potter Feb. 7 expressed doubt the killings had been ordered by Mugabe, however, saying guerrilla groups "seem to do their own thing."

The Patriotic Front, a union of Mugabe's forces and the Zimbabwe African People's Union of Joshua Nkomo, Feb. 7 accused a unit of the Rhodesian army called the Selous Scouts of the killings.

Information Minister Elias Broomberg Feb. 8 criticized Western nations for failing to support Rhodesia in its anti-guerrilla campaign. In the government's first official reaction to the killings, Broomberg called it "an infamous act."

Security forces Feb. 8 said a second mission had been attacked and burned by guerrillas. The Nyashanu Mission, 125 miles southeast of Salisbury near Mozambique, was robbed of about $5,400 and a workshop and office were burned. No casualties were reported.

The body of a priest, Jose Manuel Rubio Diaz, was found March 1 near the Bangala Mission station, 80 miles from the Mozambique border in southeastern Rhodesia. He apparently had been killed by nationalist guerrillas.

According to an estimate made April 3 by a Roman Catholic cleric, at least 33 missionaries had left Rhodesia because they feared guerrilla attacks on their missions. Father Mel Hill said more would leave because "the Catholic Church goes along with the advocates of turning a blind eye" to guerrilla activities.

Two white missionaries were killed by nationalist guerrillas Aug. 9 at the St. Paul's Roman Catholic Mission in the Lupane area 220 miles west of Salisbury. A government spokesman said Aug. 10 that a woman doctor and a nun had been killed by guerrillas who had invaded the mission looking for money.

Rudi Kogler, a building contractor, was killed Aug. 6 in a shootout with nationalist guerrillas who had invaded the Regina Mundi Mission in the Lupane area. According to a military communique Aug. 7, the guerrillas had attacked the mission in a robbery attempt, and Kogler had shot and killed one of them.

Dr. Selwyn Spray, a missionary doctor of the United Church of Christ, June 22 said the nationalist guerrillas had the overwhelming support of Rhodesia's black population. He said that in three years of treating about 1,000 black patients a month, he had not met anyone who opposed the guerrilla movement. Spray had been deported from Rhodesia June 21 after admitting that he had given food and shelter to guerrillas.

Deaths pass 4,000. According to official statistics released March 24, 1976, a total of 4,044 people had been killed in the fighting since the guerrilla war had begun in December 1972. Included in the total were civilian fatalities of 79 whites and 1,394 blacks.

In the latest action, a military communique March 31 said 24 persons had been killed the previous two days. They included 10 guerrillas, two black members

of a paramilitary unit and 12 black civilians. The communique also said 29 troops had been killed in fighting during March, the highest monthly total since the fighting began.

A clash between Rhodesian security forces and black guerrillas May 6 left more than 30 black civilians dead. The civilians had been caught in cross-fire in the engagement in a tribal trust area southeast of Salisbury near the Mozambique border.

Rhodesian security forces May 9 reported that 18 guerrillas and one member of the security forces had been killed since May 1 when the government's annual dry-season anti-guerrilla offensive had begun.

A Rhodesian military communique July 1 said 20 guerillas and suspected sympathizers had been killed since June 29. According to military communiques released during June, more than 50 guerrillas and five security-force members had been killed.

Police rounded up a number of officials of nationalist organizations June 30 in a nationwide wave of arrests. Josiah Chinamano, acting president of the African National Council, said more than 100 ANC officials had been arrested. Police disputed his figures but did not release a total of their own.

Guerrillas June 5 blew up a Salisbury-Johannesburg railway bridge, forcing a halt of seven to nine hours in service. A communique said the explosion had occurred 100 miles southwest of Salisbury and added that no trains were damaged and there were no injuries. In a similar incident May 3, a black workman had been killed when guerrillas derailed a train near the Botswana border.

A section of railway line outside Salisbury was blown up Aug. 8 by guerrillas. The line was out for 12 hours, but there were no casualties or damages to rolling stock.

Both sides accused of civilian killings. The World Council of Churches in Geneva charged that Rhodesian security forces disguised as guerrillas were killing civilians in order to discredit the nationalist movement. In the July issue of its publication One World, cited in the Times of London July 8, the WCC said that after "exhaustive" interviews with Rhodesian army deserters it had concluded that the operations were carried out by the Selous Scouts, an elite multiracial unit. The Selous Scouts previously had been accused of atrocities by black nationalist leaders.

Brian Barron, TV reporter for British Broadcasting Corp., left Salisbury Aug. 2 after Rhodesian authorities refused to renew his temporary work permit. The permit had been withdrawn as a result of a story he had broadcast about the massacre of a black Rhodesian family.

In his report, Barron had noted that the Rhodesian security forces were the only source of the allegation that the massacre had been carried out by nationalist guerrillas. He had added that nationalist fighters usually had denied such charges and had blamed atrocities on Rhodesian security forces. The government said Barron's report had given the impression that Rhodesian forces were responsible for the massacre.

According to a military communique, an African man, his nine wives and 13 of his 36 children had been massacred July 15 at their home 15 miles from the Mozambique border. A military spokesman July 22 reported that subsequent investigation had determined that a total of 17 children had been killed.

Salisbury store bombed; 11 die. An explosion shortly after noon Aug. 6 in a crowded department store in Salisbury killed 11 people and injured 76. According to police, it was the worst act of urban terrorism since the start of the five-year-old guerrilla war.

Eight of the dead were black and three were white. The store was on the edge of the Rhodesian capital's business district in an area of Asian-owned shops frequented largely by blacks. The explosion was caused by 75 pounds of TNT that had been placed in an area of the store where incoming customers left packages before shopping.

Prime Minister Ian Smith denounced the bombing, saying: "Those who have perpetrated this barbarous outrage can hardly be described as human." Bishop Abel Muzorewa, the most popular nationalist figure among Rhodesian blacks, Aug. 7 called it a "senseless act" and blamed it on Joshua Nkomo's nationalist faction, the Zimbabwe African People's Union. A ZAPU spokesman that day called the incident "regrettable." He added that it was inappropriate at the time to blame anyone.

Neighboring States Involved

'Front-line' states back Patriotic Front. At the end of a two-day meeting in Lusaka, Zambia, Jan. 9, 1977, delegates of the five "front-line" black African nations (near or bordering Rhodesia) declared their support for the Patriotic Front of Joshua Nkomo and Robert Mugabe in Rhodesia.

The Patriotic Front, a coalition of Nkomo's Zimbabwe African People's Union and Mugabe's Zimbabwe African National Union, had been formed as a negotiating team at the adjourned Geneva conference on Rhodesian majority rule. As a result of the endorsement, it appeared likely that the initial informal union of the two rival factions of the African National Council (ANC) had strengthened their bid for political power in a future transitional government.

Since the front-line states previously had refrained from expressing official support for any of the nationalist factions at Geneva, their move was seen as a setback for Bishop Abel Muzorewa, ANC president. A spokesman for Muzorewa that evening denounced the decision, saying: "The [front-line] presidents do not live in Rhodesia and have no right to tell the seven million people of Zimbabwe what they should do or feel."

The meeting, which began Jan. 8, was attended by: Tanzanian President Julius Nyerere, chairman of the front-line states, Zambian President Kenneth Kaunda, Mozambique President Samora Machel, Botswana Vice President Quet Masire and Angolan roving Ambassador Pascal Luvualu.

Van der Byl warns of separate settlement—Rhodesian Foreign Minister Pieter van der Byl Jan. 12 said the endorsement of the Patriotic Front by the front-line nations left the Rhodesian government with no alternative but to negotiate a separate settlement with other black groups and hope that Western countries would accept the result.

While van der Byl did not specify which groups his government would meet with, it was believed the Rhodesian government favored Muzorewa as the most moderate of the nationalist leaders. However, later that day, Muzorewa ruled out negotiations with the Rhodesian government unless Britain were included. (The Rhodesian government opposed a British role in the transition to majority rule.)

OAU backs 'front-line' decision—The Liberation Committee of the Organization of African Unity (OAU) Feb. 4 announced its support for the Patriotic Front of Robert Mugabe and Joshua Nkomo in the struggle for majority rule in Rhodesia. After a one-week meeting in Lusaka, Zambia, the 22-nation committee endorsed the decision of the "front-line" states "to give full political, material and diplomatic support" to the front.

The Liberation Committee rejected a Nigerian proposal to withdraw recognition from the Patriotic Front's rival nationalist groups, led by Bishop Abel Muzorewa and Rev. Ndabaningi Sithole. The OAU resolution said, "The door should remain open to all groups of Zimbabwe nationalists . . . to join the Patriotic Front."

Heads of state and cabinet ministers of 48 OAU nations, at the group's annual summit meeting, held in Libreville, Gabon July 2–5, approved a vaguely worded resolution supporting the Patriotic Front.

Front-line states urge nationalist unity—Representatives of the five front-line states July 25 urged the Rhodesian guerrillas to unite their forces. After a brief meeting in Lusaka, Zambia, the front-line states called for "one army to maintain the internal security and national integrity" of black majority rule in Rhodesia.

Their statement reflected the fears of African leaders that the nationalist movement was united only by its opposition to white minority rule.

Zambia declares war on Rhodesia. President Kenneth Kaunda of Zambia said May 16, 1977 that Zambia was in a "state of war" with Rhodesia and that his 10,000-man army had been ordered to shoot on sight any Rhodesian planes straying into Zambian airspace.

At a press conference announcing the action, Kaunda said his decision had been taken in response to a Rhodesian warning that its troops might attack guerrilla camps inside Zambia. The warning had been expressed in a May 11 letter from Rhodesian Prime Minister Ian Smith to British Foreign Secretary David Owen. Rhodesian officials May 16 denied that a direct threat to Zambia had been implied in the note.

(Zambian and Rhodesian troops exchanged fire May 18 at Victoria Falls, but no damage or casualties were reported.)

The Bank of Zambia had suspended all payments to Rhodesia because of the state of war, the Journal of Commerce reported May 24. According to a bank spokesman, no currency could be transported across the border, whether for personal or business reasons.

The Rhodesian resort town of Kariba was shelled June 4 from Zambia, according to a communique the next day. One man was slightly wounded in the half-hour attack, which caused only minor damage. Rhodesia June 7 indicated it might cut off Zambia's electric power from the Kariba Dam in retaliation, but withdrew the threat the next day.

A report in the Johannesburg's Rand Daily Mail July 7 said black refugees in Botswana were being flown to Zambia for military training. The report said a regular air shuttle service for transporting recruits existed between the two countries. A Botswana government spokesman was reported to have confirmed that 600 refugees were flown to Zambia each week. Most of the refugees had come from Rhodesia, but a steady flow of blacks from South Africa also was reported.

During a conference of Commonwealth heads of government in London, Kenneth

Kaunda June 9 called for a seven-point program to topple the Rhodesian regime. He also said that a widened war in the area was inevitable if the Rhodesian regime continued in power. His statement was considered particularly significant because of his reputation as the most moderate of the black leaders whose nations surrounded Rhodesia.

President Kaunda announced July 8 that he had accepted in principle offers of military aid from Cuba and Somalia to defend Zambia against Rhodesian attacks. He said such aid would be requested only if Zambia were in serious need of help.

The Zambian army July 11 reported that five Zambians had been killed since July 6 in border incidents with Rhodesia and with South African troops in Namibia (South-West Africa).

Nationalist guerrillas launched a brief attack July 31 on a motel at Victoria Falls on the Rhodesia-Zambia border near Namibia (South-West Africa). No casualties were reported but two rooms were destroyed. That night, government troops intercepted a group of guerrillas escorting nationalist recruits over the Botswana border and killed 13 and captured 17, according to a military communique Aug. 1

Rhodesia Aug. 5 accused Zambia of mounting a mortar attack across the Zambesi River. The government also said 14 people, including 12 guerrillas and a white farmer, had been killed since the previous day.

Rhodesia raids in Mozambique. Rhodesian troops were reported June 2, 1977 to be withdrawing from Mozambique territory after completing a five-day raid on guerrilla bases that had included the brief capture of Mapai, a village 60 miles inside the country. The raid was the third major Rhodesian incursion into Mozambique in a campaign to destroy guerrilla bases near the border.

According to a military communique, Rhodesian forces had crossed the border early May 29 from an outpost 300 miles south of Salisbury, destroying a guerrilla base and killing more than 20 guerrillas.

Two more bases were reported destroyed the next day, with the loss of another 20 guerrillas, as the troops struck deeper into Mozambique. One of the bases reportedly was "the controlling center for all incursions into southeastern Rhodesia," according to a military communique. About 700 Rhodesian soldiers and airmen were reported taking part in the operation.

Mapai was captured May 31, and Rhodesia announced it would hold the town until the area had been cleared of all guerrillas. Gen. Peter Walls, commander of the operation, acknowledged that day that the troops had found fewer guerrillas than intelligence reports had led them to expect. He said there had been no contact with Mozambique forces, adding that the objective was to hit guerrillas only.

According to his report, Rhodesian troops had suffered only minor injuries, and large amounts of ammunition, weapons and other equipment had been captured or destroyed. Walls said that the guerrilla forces were members of the Zimbabwe African National Liberation Army, the military wing of the Zimbabwe African National Union headed by Robert Mugabe.

The raid was condemned by the British Foreign Office June 1 as a threat to the British-U.S. attempt to achieve a peaceful transition to majority rule. The same day, the U.S. State Department said it considered the raid a major international problem and warned that it might support moves by the United Nations against Rhodesia as a result.

The Rhodesian government June 2 defended the incursion into Mozambique as "a necessary part of self-defense."

Foreign Minister Pieter van der Byl, replying to international criticism, denied that Rhodesia had invaded Mozambique, saying its forces "were led in there by the terrorists" and had taken "a great deal of trouble" to avoid contact with Mozambique soldiers.

Rhodesian troops were reported to have completed their withdrawal from Mozambique territory June 4. According to final reports on the operation, 32 guerrillas had been killed. Rhodesian casualties were given as one helicopter pilot killed.

The quantity of captured arms displayed after the raid was much smaller than the amounts displayed after previous raids. According to military reports, two of the four guerrilla bases attacked had been deserted by the rebels before Rhodesian troops had arrived.

A military communique June 10 said Rhodesian troops had staged a second raid into Mozambique earlier in the week. It said the objective had been a guerrilla base located through information obtained from the May 29 raid. The guerrillas had fled the camp, according to the report, but had left behind a large quantity of equipment and weapons including about 90,000 rounds of ammunition. The communique said one Rhodesian soldier had been killed in the attack.

Six refugees from Mozambique said the Rhodesian troops had been welcomed by the local population as liberators from the country's Marxist government. At a Salisbury news conference reported June 9 in the New York Times, the refugees said they had welcomed the rule of the Front for the Liberation of Mozambique (Frelimo) in 1975 but subsequent repression and food shortages had forced them to flee to Rhodesia the previous week.

(Foreign journalists who had visited Mozambique had found general satisfaction with Frelimo, according to the Times. However, the newspaper noted that their visits had been closely escorted and they had not been able to make contact with dissidents.)

Mozambique June 17 said Rhodesian troops had launched a major attack on a village about 400 miles north of Maputo. Salisbury the next day denied the charge.

The U.N. Security Council June 30 unanimously adopted a resolution calling on member countries to help Mozambique defend itself against Rhodesian attacks. After a three-day debate, the world body called for "material" assistance to Mozambique, a statement that permitted U.N. members to send either weapons or humanitarian aid. Mozambique had charged that Rhodesia had mounted 150 raids causing a total of 1,432 deaths and $13 million worth of property damage.

(Commenting on the Security Council deliberations June 29, the Rhodesian government called the Mozambique charges "ridiculous" and added that

Mozambique soldiers had crossed the border 102 times in robbing and looting incidents.)

Settlement Efforts

Richard begins Rhodesia shuttle. Ivor Richard, British chairman of the adjourned Geneva conference on Rhodesian majority rule, met Jan. 1, 1977 with Prime Minister Ian Smith in the second of a series of meetings with southern African leaders to discuss Britain's new proposals for the transitional government.

Richard, who had arrived in Salisbury Dec. 30, 1976 after seeing Zambian President Kenneth Kaunda in Lusaka, said that his meeting with Smith was "a longish, frank, vigorous exchange of views," but he indicated little progress had been achieved.

During his meeting with Kaunda, Richard had suggested that all Rhodesian blacks and whites swear allegiance to the British crown to ensure a peaceful transition to black rule. He indicated that a British role in the transition would involve appointment of an "interim commissioner or resident commissioner," an idea that was rejected by Smith.

Richard left for South Africa Jan. 2 and consulted with Prime Minister John Vorster Jan. 3. He described his talks with Vorster as "useful, helpful and constructive." Richard said he was finding that African leaders shared "a desire to end the war, to have a peaceful transition to majority government . . ."

In Botswana Jan. 4, Richard said his trip was giving him clearer ideas for the role Britain would play in an interim government leading to majority rule. He met with President Seretse Khama Jan. 5 and reported that "the president believed the idea of a resident commission would be quite a reasonable idea, worth pursuing."

Richard next saw Mozambique President Samora Machel Jan. 6. In Tanzania later that day, Richard described the talks as "extremely helpful, in which there was a great deal of common ground between the two of us." He received Julius Nyerere's support for Britain's role in the transition to majority rule Jan. 7 and a promise from the Tanzanian president that "once the majority government—truly representing the people of Zimbabwe—has been established, the armed struggle will be halted." Tanzania was a major training and supply base for guerrilla forces fighting the white Rhodesian government.

Richard met with ZAPU leader Joshua Nkomo and ZANU leader Robert Mugabe in Zambia Jan. 10 but failed to win their support for the British proposals for the interim Rhodesian government. The two nationalist leaders rejected British plans for a resident British commissioner to supervise the transition and a British role in the areas of national defense and security, insisting on a limited British role and nationalist responsibility for internal security and defense.

Later that day, Richard said President Kaunda had assured him during their Jan. 10 evening meeting of the front-line nations' commitment to end the guerrilla war once majority rule had been established.

Richard flew to Tanzania Jan. 11 to discuss with President Nyerere the results of the front-line meeting. He termed the governments' decision to support the Patriotic Front "a statement of opinion" and said it was too early to tell what effect the decision would have on the future of a peaceful settlement. However, he postponed the reopening of the Geneva conference, scheduled for Jan. 17, saying he wanted time for "reflection and thought" and would continue his rounds of talks.

In Nairobi, Kenya Jan. 12 Richard briefed Foreign Minister Munyua Waiyaki on his latest talks with African leaders. Richard had seen Waiyaki Jan. 8 and reported "a reasonable identity" between their views on Rhodesia.

Richard Jan. 19 met again with South African Prime Minister Vorster. Neither of the two men commented at length upon the private meeting, but it was thought Vorster would accept a settlement that departed from the proposals set forth by U.S. Secretary of State Kissinger. Vorster previously had backed Ian Smith's position that the proposals were not negotiable, but it appeared he might change his mind if the Rhodesian nationalists continued to reject the Kissinger plan, according to the New York Times Jan. 20.

Sources cited in the Jan. 20 Washington Post said both Kissinger and Secretary of State-designate Cyrus Vance had urged Vorster to use his influence with Smith to continue peaceful efforts to establish majority rule. South Africa was Rhodesia's only outlet to the ocean and its only supplier of arms.

(South Africa informed Britain it would consider sending troops to Rhodesia if the guerrilla war intensified, according to a Jan. 16 Johannesburg Sunday Express report. Previously, the South African government had rejected military involvement in Rhodesia, but Vorster was reported to have told Richard during their Jan. 3 meeting of South Africa's refusal to tolerate guerrilla activity which might threaten South African security.)

Meanwhile, Smith Jan. 14 said Richard's round of talks with southern African leaders "is a dead duck, at the moment." In a New York Times interview, he said the U.S. should support his efforts to negotiate a separate settlement with moderate black groups in Rhodesia.

U.S. mission to Rhodesia urged. A staff study for the U.S. Senate Foreign Relations Committee had recommended a special, temporary mission be sent to Salisbury if the Rhodesian government accepted proposals to end racial discrimination, the New York Times reported Jan. 10.

The report favored a more active U.S. role in bringing about the transition to black majority rule. It termed a U.S. presence more helpful to U.S. aims than an "attempt to carry forward [U.S.] efforts at long distance or through proxies such as the government of South Africa. . . ."

The report noted the political risk involved and suggested the sending of the mission be made conditional upon Rhodesian government acceptance of the Quenet Commission's proposals on ending racial discrimination.

Sen. Dick Clark (D, Iowa), chairman of the Foreign Relations Committee's subcommittee on Africa, warned, however, that the dispatch of such a mission to Rhodesia would give the white Rhodesians hope that they could hold out against black majority rule.

Smith bars British plan. Ian Smith Jan. 24 rejected a British proposal to reconvene the Geneva conference and move toward black majority rule in Rhodesia. The proposal had been presented to him Jan. 21 by Ivor Richard.

The plan would have established a resident British commissioner with extensive executive powers to insure an orderly transition to black majority rule in the former British colony. A council of ministers would have been established with a two-thirds black majority, with responsibility for defense and internal security reserved for a separate National Security Council. The security council would have had a two-thirds black majority as well, and the white representation would have included members of white opposition groups. The British plan differed from the proposal sponsored by Kissinger and accepted by Smith in September 1976. Kissinger's plan had called for a two-tiered government composed of a council of state equally divided between blacks and whites and an executive council of ministers with a black majority, a white chairman and white ministers of defense and internal security. There was no provision for direct British participation.

In rejecting Richard's plan, Smith charged that "immediate black rule . . . would be imposed from outside and would in no way represent the views of the majority of black Rhodesians." (In contrast, the Kissinger plan had outlined a transition period of two years.)

Smith added, "The British government wishes to impose upon us an interim government recommended to it by the front-line presidents [of Angola, Botswana, Mozambique, Tanzania and Zambia] in

collusion with the terrorist-oriented Patriotic Front [of Joshua Nkomo and Robert Mugabe]. "If we were to give way now," he continued, "it would not be to majority rule. It would be to a Marxist-indoctrinated minority."

Smith denied closing the door to further negotiations. He stressed his willingness to search for a settlement on the basis of the Kissinger proposals. He said he had "issued invitations to the black leaders to join me," but he did not specify which leaders he meant.

Richard Jan. 24 rebuked Smith for his stand. "Mr. Smith alone has rejected our proposals as even a basis for further discussion," he said. "He bears, as we see it, a heavy responsibility for what may now follow." Richard added that he saw no use in reconvening the Geneva negotiations, adjourned since December 1976.

In a Jan. 23 speech on Rhodesian television, Richard had warned Smith against a separate settlement with moderate and conservative blacks. He said Britain could not endorse such a settlement, saying it would end neither the world trade sanctions against Rhodesia nor the guerrilla war

The U.S. State Department also rejected support for separate negotiations between Smith and other black groups. A spokesman Jan. 26 said, "Negotiations which exclude leaders of nationalist movements will not produce a settlement." The State Department Jan. 24 had indicated that the U.S. would still press for a peaceful solution in spite of the apparent breakdown in negotiations.

British Foreign Minister Anthony Crosland Jan. 25 expressed fear of armed intervention in Rhodesia from outside Africa. Speaking in the House of Commons, he said the possibility of Soviet and Cuban intervention was a dominant factor. Crosland had appealed to Smith before Smith had made his Jan. 24 announcement "not to close the door irrevocably to any further discussion" and warned of "calamitous consequences for southern Africa" as a result of Smith's position.

The African states and nationalist groups called Smith's rejection a signal for total guerrilla warfare against the white minority government. William Eteki Mboumoua, secretary general of the Organization of African Unity, Jan. 25 said, "Africa is now obliged to consider seriously the strengthening of the liberation struggle." Zambian Foreign Minister Siteke Mwale that day called upon the white opposition "to revolt against the Smith regime." He also called for an intensification of the guerrilla struggle.

Britain's Rhodesia mission ends. Ivor Richard, British chairman of the suspended Geneva talks on Rhodesian majority rule, Jan. 31 ended his southern African shuttle, apparently conceding defeat in his efforts to solve the Geneva impasse.

Richard's mission was criticized by African leaders and Rhodesian nationalists Johshua Nkomo and Robert Mugabe of the Patriotic Front. Addressing the Liberation Committee of the Organization of African Unity (OAU) Jan. 29, Zambian President Kenneth Kaunda charged Richard with calling off the Geneva negotiations without consulting Rhodesian nationalists.

The Patriotic Front Jan. 30 refused to meet Richard in Lusaka, Zambia because of Kaunda's charge. They said Richard's action had left the nationalists with no choice but guerrilla warfare to defeat the white-minority government. They rejected future consultations with Britain until "Britain is prepared to adopt a positive, unequivocal and more determined stand to effect the transfer of power. . . ."

The OAU Liberation Committee, which coordinated assistance to liberation groups, Jan. 29 had opened a meeting in Lusaka to draw up a common policy toward the various nationalist factions fighting for black rule in Rhodesia. Many delegates expressed support for the Patriotic Front because it was backed by guerrilla forces in Rhodesia's neighboring states. They urged a common stand on backing the Patriotic Front to avoid a repetition of the situation in Angola, where an OAU split contributed to the civil war between pro-West and pro-Communist factions.

The collapse of Britain's effort to reach a compromise appeared to increase the desire of all sides for a more direct U.S. role in southern Africa, the Jan. 26 New York Times reported. It was believed by both blacks and whites in southern Africa that the U.S. would have a more decisive effect on the majority-rule struggle in Rhodesia and South Africa.

In a Jan. 31 news conference, U.S. Secretary of State Cyrus Vance condemned the Rhodesian government and said "under no circumstances can they count on any form of American assistance." Vance criticized Rhodesian Prime Minister Ian Smith's decision to seek a separate settlement with moderate Rhodesian blacks, saying it "will not produce a peaceful settlement and therefore will not have the support of the U.S."

Vance said the U.S. Administration would lobby actively for the repeal of the Byrd Amendment, named after U.S. Sen. Harry F. Byrd Jr. (Ind, Va.), which allowed the U.S. to import Rhodesian chrome in defiance of world trade sanctions.

(U.S. Representative to the United Nations Andrew Young left Feb. 1 on a round of consultations with southern African leaders.)

Vorster rules out pressure—In a Jan. 28 speech to Parliament, South African Prime Minister John Vorster asserted that South Africa would not exert pressure on Rhodesia to change Smith's policy toward majority rule. Vorster did not comment on the breakdown of the Geneva negotiations but his speech contradicted speculation that South Africa might help effect a peaceful transition to back rule in Rhodesia.

Vorster said he was willing to cooperate in finding a peaceful solution to the impasse, but said it would be "wrong in principle to exert pressure" on Smith, especially since Smith already had accepted Kissinger's proposals for majority rule in September 1976. "I am not prepared to do anything dishonorable," Vorster said. He noted that Smith had had to persuade his Cabinet to accept Kissinger's plan while "Nkomo and Mugabe are not responsible to anybody and they can change their stance all the time."

Smith sees Vorster. Rhodesian Prime Minister Ian Smith met with South African Prime Minister John Vorster Feb. 9–10 for the first time since September 1976 in an apparent attempt to gain South African support for an internal settlement for Rhodesian majority rule.

Before leaving the Cape Town meeting Feb. 10, Smith said his talks had been "very congenial." He added that he was willing to accept new proposals from countries offering "constructive suggestions" for transferring power to Rhodesia's black majority. It was the first indication Smith had given since the breakdown of British-sponsored talks with black African leaders that he was still receptive to proposals for a political settlement from outside Rhodesia.

In a television interview Feb. 4, Smith had repeated his intention to achieve a political settlement by means of negotiations with black leaders inside Rhodesia.

Hilgard Muller, South African foreign minister, had said Feb. 2 that Smith's plans for an internal settlement would not work because they would exclude Robert Mugabe and Joshua Nkomo.

Smith's authority reaffirmed—The ruling Rhodesia Front April 18 gave Smith full power to negotiate a settlement for black majority rule. In a special congress, more than two-thirds of the 800 party delegates voted a resolution which "authorizes the government to negotiate a settlement in the best interests of Rhodesia and urges that in so doing it shall strive to abide by the principles and policies of the party." Another resolution passed by the congress accepted "the need for a settlement" but called upon the government "to insure that the rights of all communities are meaningfully guaranteed." The resolutions gave Smith broad negotiating powers and strengthened his position against opposition from the right.

Three white opposition groups, the Rhodesia Party, the Center Party and the National Pledge Association, a group formed in 1976 to oppose racial discrimination, had announced Jan. 10 formation of a united pressure group to press for a voice in the talks on a Rhodesian majority-rule constitution.

Carter Regime Joins in International Discussions

The U.S. administration, under the recently inaugurated President Jimmy Carter, began again in February 1977 to take a hand in the Rhodesian settlement negotiations. Major U.S. officials, including the Vice President, the Secretary of State, the ambassador to the U.N.—and ultimately the President himself—became actively involved in the problem as a major facet of the U.S.' overall policy toward Africa.

Young visits Africa for Carter. Andrew Young, U.S. representative to the United Nations, visited Africa as an ambassador from the new Carter Administration Feb. 3–10. The visit was marked by a series of policy observations that seemed to be at variance with Administration positions.

Young stopped off in London before and after his African trip for discussions on the Rhodesian situation. He met both times with Ivor Richard, British chairman of the Geneva talks on Rhodesia. On his first visit to London Feb. 2, the discussions were joined by British Foreign Secretary Anthony Crosland.

As a consequence of the first talks, Young said his optimism for a quick settlement in Rhodesia had "waned." On his second visit Feb. 11, he said he thought a shooting war to obtain black rule would be "a last resort—out of desperation."

In Africa, Young spent most of his time in Tanzania and Nigeria, with a stopover Feb. 7 in Nairobi, Kenya. In Tanzania Feb. 3–6, Young met with Tanzanian President Julius Nyerere and four other African presidents who were attending a celebration of the launching of a unified political party for the Tanzanian mainland and the island of Zanzibar.

Young conferred on Zanzibar Feb. 4 with Nyerere and President Juvenal Habyalimana of Rwanda and Feb. 5 with Presidents Kenneth Kaunda of Zambia, Siad Barre of Somalia and Jean-Baptiste Bagaza of Burundi. Young met again with Nyerere in Dar es Salaam Feb. 6.

Young arrived in Nigeria Feb. 7.

Among the leaders he conferred with in Lagos were Lt. Gen. Olusegun Obasanjo, the Nigerian head of state, and President Agostinho Neto of Angola. The meeting with Neto, in Neto's hotel room Feb. 8, was the first high-level contact between the U.S. and the Neto government.

Some observations by Young that appeared to cause problems for U.S. diplomatic efforts concerned the Rhodesian situation. Young spoke Feb. 10 of recommending a conference among the U.S., Britain, black African states and the Rhodesian black nationalists. The purpose of the conference, he said, would be to solidify proposals for black majority rule for presentation to the white minority government. The official U.S. position had been to support the British attempt to involve the Rhodesian government and the black nationalists in direct negotiations.

The official U.S. stance was more or less endorsed by Nyerere, who told reporters after his meeting with Young Feb. 6 that Britain should keep playing the lead role, with the U.S. lending support in the background. Nyerere urged the U.S. to use its economic leverage on Rhodesia to help move the government toward transition to black rule. He said he did not think the current mediation should be given up because of the rejection of the British plan by the Rhodesian government. He favored continuing talks between the British and the black nationalists.

Zambia's Kaunda, however, told reporters, after his meeting with Young Feb. 5, that "the Carter Administration should take the lead" in trying to solve the problems of southern Africa.

In Nigeria, after his meeting with Obasanjo Feb. 10, Young said he had been struck by the "unmilitant" tone of the conversation. "The valuable thing was," he said, "it seemed to indicate that Nigeria's weight was firmly to be thrown behind a negotiated settlement [in Rhodesia] and a unified nationalist movement."

Participating in a joint news conference, Obasanjo spoke of "achieving objectives without creating a state that would be destroyed completely in battle." He said "America has to be heavily involved" in the negotiations on Rhodesia for them to be successful.

Young said that the common theme of his talks with about 20 African leaders during his trip was that "they want the United States involved" in southern Africa.

Winding up his trip in London Feb. 12, Young remarked to newsmen that "in a way the United States was rather unfair to Britain." Former Secretary of State Henry Kissinger had "put a burden on the back of the British and then abandoned them," he said.

"Of course, I don't say that he did that deliberately," Young continued. "I think he actually thought he was going to win the election, in which case he probably would have been involved."

President Carter assured reporters Feb. 13 that he did not think Young had meant to criticize the preceding Republican Administration. Young's remarks had been "taken out of context" in some news reports, he said.

Because of the 1976 presidential campaign, Carter said, former President Ford and Kissinger "could not proceed as vigorously" with U.S. policy in Africa as they might have desired. Some "trouble spots went into limbo" during the election and pre-inaugural period, Carter said, and the situation was "no reflection" on Kissinger or Ford.

Nkomo group backs Geneva talks. The Zimbabwe African People's Union (ZAPU), the nationalist group headed by Joshua Nkomo, Feb. 22 called for the resumption of the Geneva conference on Rhodesian majority rule. ZAPU, which formed the Patriotic Front with the Zimbabwe African National Union, urged talks among Ian Smith and the leaders of the Patriotic Front, Nkomo and Robert Mugabe. ZAPU made no mention of the other nationalist groups led by Bishop Abel Muzorewa and Rev. Ndabaningi Sithole.

Britain seeks new Rhodesia parley. British Foreign Secretary David Owen toured southern Africa April 11–17 in an effort to renew British-U.S. efforts to establish a peaceful transfer of power to Rhodesia's black majority.

Owen visited Tanzania April 11, Mozambique April 12, South Africa April 13, Botswana April 14, Zambia April 14–15, Rhodesia April 15–17 and Angola April 17. He met with leaders of Rhodesian and South African nationalist groups as well as with heads of state.

Owen met first with Rhodesian black nationalist leader Robert Mugabe upon arrival in Dar es Salaam, Tanzania April 11. Owen said at a subsequent press conference that Mugabe had insisted on direct negotiations only between the Patriotic Front and Britain on Rhodesia's future. Mugabe opposed any conference role for Prime Minister Ian Smith and the other black nationalist figures—Bishop Abel Muzorewa of the African National Council and Rev. Ndabaningi Sithole, a rival for leadership of Mugabe's faction of the Patriotic Front, the Zimbabwe African National Union.

Owen rejected Mugabe's stand and insisted that all nationalist groups be represented at any conference concerning Rhodesia's future government. The foreign secretary proposed convening a constitutional parley to replace the unsuccessful Geneva conference. The new conference would seek to draft a Rhodesian constitution and leave aside the mechanism of transferring power to Rhodesia's six million blacks from its 270,000 ruling whites. (The Geneva conference had concentrated on the question of transferring power first before setting up a constitutional convention for the new government.)

At his press conference, Owen said his talks with Tanzanian President Julius Nyerere April 11 had gone "very well." There was no official comment from Nyerere, but sources quoted in the London Times April 13 said Nyerere had indicated he would accept the inclusion of other black nationalists besides the Patriotic Front leaders at a constitutional conference.

Owen said after meeting Mozambique President Samora Machel April 12 that the president had agreed to the inclusion of all Rhodesian nationalist figures in the proposed constitutional conference. (Machel was considered the most militant of the five leaders of the so-called front-line African states [Angola, Botswana, Mozambique, Tanzania, Zambia] opposing white minority rule in southern Africa. The front-line states earlier in the year had decided to give sole support to the Patriotic Front.)

Owen said Machel had agreed with him on the need for greater U.S. involvement in insuring the successful implementation of a Rhodesian constitution.

Owen conferred in Capetown, South Africa April 13 with Prime Minister John Vorster and Rhodesian Prime Minister Smith who was vacationing in South Africa. He said both leaders had agreed on the need for a direct U.S. role in talks between the Rhodesian government and black nationalists. (The U.S. had sent only an observer delegation to the majority-rule talks in Geneva.)

The U.S. in a policy reversal April 14 announced it was willing to serve as co-sponsor with Britain of a new Rhodesia conference. "If Owen could report that all sides wanted a new meeting, then the U.S. is willing to serve as a co-convener or co-sponsor of that new conference," a State Department spokesman said. Previously, the U.S. position had been that Britain, since it legally was still the colonial ruler of Rhodesia, was responsible for the negotiations for majority rule.

After talks with President Seretse Khama of Botswana April 14, Owen said he was opposed to proposals for a referendum among Rhodesia's blacks to choose a leader before a constitution was written. Smith favored a referendum to choose a nationalist figure who would then negotiate with the Rhodesian government on the transfer of power. Muzorewa, considered the most popular figure among Rhodesian blacks, also favored such a referendum, but insisted the white government immediately turn over power to the winner.

In Zambia April 15 Owen met President Kenneth Kaunda, who repeated his desire for peace but expressed "deep skepticism" over the chances of a peace settlement, according to Owen.

Owen's arrival in Salisbury, Rhodesia

later April 15 marked the first visit by a top-level British government official since the 1971 visit of former Foreign Secretary Alec Douglas-Home. Owen had not announced his intention to visit the breakaway colony until April 13.

At the end of his stay, Owen said he and Smith had made progress toward convening another conference. Owen had told reporters upon arrival that he believed chances for ending the guerrilla war were "not tremendously high."

Front-line states warn on use of force— A two-day meeting of the "front-line" presidents took place in Luanda April 17–18. After the conclusion of their talks April 18, they reaffirmed their commitment to the overthrow of the white minority regimes in Rhodesia, South Africa and Namibia, by force if necessary. Also present at the meeting were Robert Mugabe, Joshua Nkomo, Sam Nujoma of SWAPO and Oliver Tambo of the African National Congress, a South African nationalist group. At the opening of the talks, Mugabe had repeated his demand that only the Patriotic Front represent Rhodesia's blacks in talks on majority rule and warned "settlement in Rhodesia will come through a bazooka."

Young again in Africa. Andrew Young again toured Africa May 10–24 to stress increased U.S. interest in Africa and U.S. determination to effect changes in southern Africa.

Young's first stop was Abidjan, capital of the Ivory Coast, where he attended a four-day meeting of more than 30 U.S. ambassadors to various African countries. The meeting, which had begun May 9, was the first comprehensive conference on U.S. Africa policy in recent years to include diplomats. It reflected the Carter Administration's desire for both a cohesive U.S. policy and for closer consultations with U.S. diplomats. Young explained upon arrival that "the State Department felt it was important for the policy not only to come from Washington but to come from Africa itself."

After conferring with Ivory Coast President Felix Houphouet-Boigny May 12, Young defended U.S. caution on the recent invasion of Zaire, saying: "It's better for Africans to deal with African problems. . . . "

From the Ivory Coast, Young traveled to Ghana May 12 for a short visit that was designed to improve U.S. relations with that West African country. Young May 13 met with Rev. Ndabaningi Sithole, a Rhodesian nationalist leader, in Accra, the Ghanaian capital. Young stressed the importance of solving differences among the rival Rhodesian nationalists to insure a "rational transition" to majority rule in the breakaway British colony.

From Ghana, Young flew to Liberia May 13 where he met with President William Tolbert.

Young at U.N. parley—Young arrived in Maputo, Mozambique May 16 for a U.N. conference to back the people of Zimbabwe and Namibia. The session, attended by representatives of 87 nations, black nationalist movements and international organizations, was seen as a major effort to rally world support for the establishment of black majority rule in southern Africa.

Addressing the opening of the meeting, U.N. Secretary General Kurt Waldheim said failure to find a peaceful solution to problems in southern Africa would result in "a disaster of grave dimensions" for Africa and the rest of the world.

In contrast to previous international meetings on southern Africa (particularly of black African states surrounding South Africa and Rhodesia), the Maputo conference struck a moderate tone. Mozambique President Samora Machel, in his opening speech, termed the new British effort for a Rhodesia conference a "positive factor so long as it has as a sincere objective the complete independence of the country."

After talks with Young the next day, Machel indicated greater approval of the U.S. role: "I am not saying the U.S. has a solution, but it has a great contribution to make." Machel previously had denied the U.S. had any role to play in solving southern African problems.

Leaders of African nationalist movements appeared to disagree with Machel.

Robert Mugabe of the Patriotic Front, the major group fighting in Rhodesia, May 16 rejected U.S. participation in a conference on Rhodesian majority rule.

Young seemed to have achieved a substantial measure of success in private talks with African leaders. He met May 18 with William Eteki Mboumoua, secretary general of the Organization of African Unity, who endorsed the change in U.S. policy toward Africa, although he observed the U.S. "can do even more about mounting pressure on racist regimes."

After meeting with Eteki, Young said the U.S. "will not be drawn into the [Rhodesian] conflict under any circumstances." He was referring to an incursion into Botswana May 16 by 50 Rhodesian soldiers engaged in a hot-pursuit action against guerrillas. Young said the one-hour operation had been meant to "get the liberation movements to bring in Cuban troops" and strengthen Salisbury's appeal for Western help.

In spite of the generally warm reception Young received from African leaders, his speech to the conference May 19 calling for peaceful change was strongly criticized. Young compared the situation in southern Africa with conditions in the American South before the civil rights movement, saying the Carter Administration's change of policy on Africa was the result of "a silent and nonviolent revolution" that had changed American attitudes toward race. In support of peaceful change, Young observed: "The majority of nations of Africa achieved their independence through negotiated settlements, and where there was a possibility of settlements those countries moved much more rapidly in their development." He urged the assembled nations to oppose white regimes with "economic force" but cautioned against "blanket sanctions" that most of the delegates favored. A "combination of pressure and incentives can be more effective," he said.

Delegates were disappointed by Young's call for nonviolent change and complained the speech had style but no substance. They also expressed irritation at Young's concentration on the U.S. experience. Leslie O. Harriman, Nigerian

delegate to the U.N. and chairman of the U.N. Special Committee on Apartheid, said: "We are not talking about how to improve the lot of Africans; we are talking about liberation and majority rule."

At the end of the conference May 21, the delegates adopted a declaration calling for international compliance with U.N. sanctions against South Africa and Rhodesia and for moral and material support for the nationalist groups. The European, U.S. and Canadian representatives dissociated themselves from parts of the document calling for a complete arms embargo of South Africa and the severing of postal and telecommunications links with Rhodesia. They agreed to all the other provisions of the declaration, but said efforts to negotiate settlements in southern Africa would be hampered by breaking all economic and communications links.

Young in South Africa & other states—
Young visited South Africa May 21–22 at the invitation of Harry Oppenheimer, the nation's leading businessman and a supporter of race reform.

Young told a group of 200 South African business leaders May 21 that "you have no real alternative" to sharing power with blacks, Coloreds (persons of mixed race) and Asians.

The next day Young spoke to white university students and to black and white community leaders at a U.S. government office in Johannesburg. He suggested that blacks use economic boycotts to effect changes in racial policy.

Young's visit to South Africa had been in doubt until May 11, when the U.N. envoy was already in the Ivory Coast. The South African government May 6 had indicated that a visit by Young would "not be convenient" because of Young's stated intention to talk to black leaders and not government representatives, and because Young had not formally asked approval from Pretoria before his intended visit had been announced in the U.S. press. (The South African government the next day said it had received a request from the U.S. for Young's visit.)

South Africa said May 23, after Young's departure, that the U.S. envoy had broken his promise to refrain from making controversial statements.

Young traveled to Zambia May 22. He met the next day with President Kenneth Kaunda, who reportedly asked him to urge President Carter to force U.S. oil companies to cut off deliveries to Rhodesia. Kaunda praised Carter, saying: "We should not dismiss him as just another Westerner; we should give him a chance."

Mondale sees Vorster on European tour. U.S. Vice President Walter Mondale met with South African Prime Minister John Vorster in Vienna May 18–20. The U.S.-South Africa contact was on the highest level since Vorster's National Party had taken power in 1948.

Mondale's meeting with Vorster came during the course of a tour of Europe.

After two closed sessions May 18–19, Vorster and Mondale held separate press conferences May 20. Mondale told reporters that no progress had been made in resolving "fundamental and profound disagreement" over apartheid.

In his news conference, Vorster countered Mondale's comments by confirming his refusal to make any major reforms in South Africa's social structure.

Both men indicated agreement on several issues that reflected no departure from earlier policies. Mondale agreed with a statement by Vorster urging an end to the guerrilla violence in Rhodesia. Mondale said Vorster had agreed to support a new effort by the U.S. and Great Britain to reopen negotiations on Rhodesian majority rule, a stand Vorster previously had taken in talks with British officials.

In London May 22, Mondale conferred with Prime Minister James Callaghan and Foreign Secretary David Owen on the results of his meetings with Vorster. At a news conference earlier in the day, Mondale had said "significant progress" might have been made on Rhodesian majority rule because of Vorster's support for the U.S.-British initiative.

U.K.-U.S. team tours region. A joint team of British and U.S. diplomats toured southern Africa May 17–June 1 to assess the chances of reopening negotiations on Rhodesian majority rule. The visit was a follow-up to an earlier tour by British Foreign Secretary David Owen.

The four-member team was headed by John Graham, British Foreign Office deputy undersecretary for African affairs, and Steven Low, U.S. ambassador to Zambia. They met with government and nationalist representatives in Zambia, Botswana, Tanzania, Mozambique and Rhodesia.

In Rhodesia May 27–29, Low and Graham were told that the government would not accept a majority-rule settlement that called for universal suffrage. According to reports, the Rhodesians favored extending the black franchise somewhat but feared that universal voting rights would jeopardize the position of the white minority.

In Mozambique, Graham conferred May 30 with Robert Mugabe, a leader of the Patriotic Front, the principal Rhodesian nationalist group. Low did not attend because Mugabe was opposed to U.S. involvement in a Rhodesian settlement.

Graham and Low met in Zambia May 31 with Joshua Nkomo, the other Patriotic Front leader. Nkomo reportedly told the two that he was not interested in reopening a conference on Rhodesian majority rule because he saw little chance of success. However, he reportedly agreed to attend such a conference if Britain convened it.

In a second round of talks in Africa by the same team, Graham and Low met with representatives of both sides in Lusaka and Salisbury July 5–10.

The talks produced no new suggestions for a Rhodesian constitutional conference. Nkomo July 7 called the talks unsuccessful. He said the Patriotic Front refused to hold constitutional talks until Britain committed itself to handing over power in Rhodesia to the front. He said the front had agreed orally to constitutional guarantees of human rights, free elections, universal suffrage and an independent judiciary for the future government of an independent Rhodesia.

In Salisbury July 8–10, Graham and Low presented Britain's proposals for an interim British administration of Rhodesia to supervise the transition to majority rule. Both sides, however, ruled out such a compromise. In separate news conferences July 12, Nkomo repeated his position that Britain must transfer power directly to the front, while Rhodesian Prime Minister Ian Smith said any British control of Rhodesia was unacceptable.

Sithole returns to Rhodesia. Rev. Ndabaningi Sithole, one of the rivals for leadership of the Rhodesian nationalist movement, returned to Rhodesia July 10 after two years of self-imposed exile. Prime Minister Ian Smith reportedly had said Sithole would be permitted to return if he renounced terrorist tactics for achieving majority rule. On his arrival in Salisbury, Sithole endorsed the U.S.-British effort to find a peaceful solution to Rhodesian majority rule and denounced the decision of the Organization of African Unity to support the Patriotic Front. (Sithole had fled Rhodesia in 1975 while under detention.)

Smith dissolves Parliament, says Anglo-U.S. effort failed. In a new move, Prime Minister Smith July 18, 1977 dissolved Parliament and set new elections for August 31. He said the decision had been taken in the light of what he termed the failure of the British-U.S. team to present a workable proposal for black majority rule.

Smith said his government was seeking a popular mandate to draw up a Constitution and negotiate with moderate blacks for a multiracial government. He said the negotiations carried on by the British and U.S. representatives had achieved nothing because of their insistence on one-man-one-vote representation for a future Rhodesian government and their refusal to provide guarantees of the status of the country's white minority.

Britain July 19 condemned Smith's decision. Prime Minister James Callaghan said the move was "largely irrelevant," since only a minority of Rhodesians could vote. (About 85,400 whites out of a white population of 270,000 and 10,000 blacks out of a black population of six million were permitted to vote.)

Foreign Secretary David Owen said Smith's action would delay but not end the U.S.-British peace efforts.

Bishop Abel Muzorewa and Rev. Ndabaningi Sithole, the two principal black leaders inside Rhodesia, July 19 said that Smith's plan to negotiate an internal settlement would achieve little unless the Rhodesian prime minister agreed to establish universal suffrage.

Muzorewa had returned to Salisbury July 17 after a six-month foreign tour to enlist support for his bid to lead Rhodesia's blacks in a majority-rule settlement. Muzorewa had demanded "immediate settlement" between himself and Smith to transfer power to the black majority. He also had denounced the Patriotic Front, the guerrilla group led by Joshua Nkomo and Robert Mugabe, as having "already started a civil war" against Muzorewa's organization, the United African National Council (formerly the African National Council).

Muzorewa for majority rule in 1978— Muzorewa July 24 proposed a plan to establish majority rule by March 1978. He called for the immediate convening of a constitutional committee consisting of his United African National Council and representatives of Britain and the Rhodesian government. The committee, according to Muzorewa's plan, would prepare a constitution by January 1978 and general elections would be held the following March. He said he was "ready, here and now, to negotiate on the basis of one man, one vote," a proposal Prime Minister Ian Smith rejected. Muzorewa criticized the British government for "suffering from debilitating indecision. . . ."

U.S., Britain endorse majority rule. After meeting with U.S. Secretary of State Cyrus Vance July 23, British Foreign Secretary David Owen said the U.S. and Britain would "put forward our firm proposals" for majority rule in Rhodesia. The one-day round of talks in Washington was held in reaction to the decision by Rhodesian Prime Minister Ian Smith formally to abandon the U.S.-British initiative on a peaceful Rhodesian settlement.

Owen briefly met with President Carter. He said Smith's decision to dissolve the Rhodesian Parliament was not a "major new factor" and would not affect the British-U.S. mission to work out a peaceful transfer of power to the country's black majority.

South Africa backs Smith. South African Foreign Minister Roelof Botha Aug. 4 pledged his government's full support for Rhodesian Prime Minister Ian Smith's effort to reach a political settlement with Rhodesia's black majority. Indirectly criticizing the U.S.-British negotiating team, Botha said outsiders should not be allowed to dictate solutions to Rhodesia.

In an interview published July 28 in the Times of London, Botha said Britain was "trying to lean over backwards to please the men with the guns," referring to the Patriotic Front, the principal guerrilla group fighting the white minority government. Botha said Rhodesia's blacks should elect a leader to negotiate with the white government on a new constitution, or Britain should draw up a constitution and impose it upon the country. He said the biggest obstacle to a settlement was the lack of a party commanding universal Rhodesian black support.

Vorster assails U.S. policy—South African Prime Minister John Vorster Aug. 5 denounced U.S. policy toward his white minority government and appealed to the American public to reject President Carter's approach to southern Africa. Vorster's speech to the South African Foreign Affairs Association appeared to confirm the deterioration of Pretoria-Washington ties in recent months.

South African support for U.S. policy had been considered crucial in solving the Rhodesian and Namibian crises. It had appeared that the U.S. had been making progress in enlisting Pretoria's aid, but in recent months the South African government had adopted an increasingly hard-line stance on Rhodesian majority rule.

Nyerere visits Carter. Tanzanian President Julius Nyerere conferred with U.S. President Carter Aug. 4-5 in the course of a 10-day round of consultations with foreign dignitaries on Rhodesian majority rule. It was the first visit to the U.S. by a black African leader since Carter had taken office.

The Carter Administration was seeking Nyerere's support for the joint Anglo-American effort to effect a peaceful transition to majority rule in Rhodesia. Nyerere was considered to be the most influential of the leaders of the five black African nations involved in the Rhodesian crisis.

After conferring with Carter Aug. 5, Nyerere expressed pessimism over the prospects of a peaceful solution, but he gave qualified encouragement to the Anglo-American effort. After Nyerere's departure from the White House, Carter said he and the African leader were in "almost complete agreement" on a course of action to end white minority rule.

After seeing Carter, Nyerere spent five days touring the U.S. In a television interview Aug. 7 he said Carter "is not making a show about" ending minority rule, adding that the President was willing to use any pressure necessary to end white rule in southern Africa. In a speech the night before, Nyerere had called for an escalation of the five-year-old guerrilla war against Rhodesia and for a U.S. arms embargo of South Africa. He had said the war and pressures from the U.S. would force the white Rhodesian government to come to terms with Rhodesia's black majority.

Nyerere met with U.S. Secretary of State Cyrus Vance Aug. 13 in London. Both men said they were encouraged by the talks, and Nyerere indicated that he might be willing to accept an Anglo-American proposal for majority rule. His expression of support appeared to be more definite than it had been with President Carter.

Nkomo rejects U.K.-U.S. strategy. Joshua Nkomo, one of the principal Rhodesian black nationalist leaders, Aug. 15 rejected the approach taken by the U.S. and Great Britain in working out a formula for Rhodesian majority rule. After meeting with U.S. Secretary of

State Cyrus Vance, Nkomo refused to endorse a proposed Rhodesian constitution before the guerrilla war against the white government was ended. "The war has got to be taken as a basis for settlement of the problem," he said.

According to a statement Aug. 12, one of the conditions Nkomo demanded for ending the war was the removal from office of Rhodesian Prime Minister Ian Smith. Nkomo rejected the possibility of joint U.S.-British sponsorship of a conference on Rhodesian majority rule, saying Rhodesia was Britain's responsibility alone. Nevertheless, he said, he approved of U.S. consultations with Britain. Other proposals he rejected were: the introduction of foreign peacekeeping troops into Rhodesia during the transfer of power and the use of foreign troops by the Rhodesian nationalist guerrillas.

Owen, Young seek support for new plan. David Owen, British foreign secretary, and Andrew Young, U.S. ambassador to the United Nations, began a joint tour of southern Africa Aug. 26 to seek support for a new set of proposals to achieve majority rule in Rhodesia. The proposals had been worked out Aug. 12 at a meeting between Owen and U.S. Secretary of State Cyrus Vance in Washington.

Details of the plan were leaked Aug. 24 after Young met with Lt. Gen. Olusegun Obasanjo, Nigeria's head of state, in Lagos. Young was in Lagos for a U.N.-sponsored conference on South African apartheid.

The plan called for the dismissal of Rhodesian Prime Minister Ian Smith from office and the appointment of an interim British administrator during the transition to majority rule. The British administrator would supervise negotiations by all sides in the Rhodesian dispute on a constitution providing free elections and universal suffrage. The Rhodesian security forces would be dissolved and replaced by an international peacekeeping force under U.N. supervision. The U.N. force would create a new Rhodesian army incorporating units of the government army and the guerrilla forces currently fighting the white minority government.

In Lusaka, Zambia Aug. 27, Young and Owen met with representatives of the front-line African states (Angola, Botswana, Mozambique, Tanzania, Zambia) involved in the Rhodesian crisis. The front-line states made it clear that there could be no compromise over Smith's removal from office and the dismantling of the Rhodesian army. The representatives said they would not make a formal reply to the proposals until they had been made public after being presented to Smith.

Owen and Young Aug. 28 met with Robert Mugabe and Joshua Nkomo, joint leaders of the Patriotic Front, the principal guerrilla organization in the Rhodesian struggle. Mugabe and Nkomo rejected the proposal to introduce a U.N. peacekeeping force in Rhodesia, saying the Patriotic Front forces were the only forces entitled to supervise the transition to majority rule. Like the front-line states, they refrained from making a formal statement on the entire set of proposals until it was officially made public.

Owen and Young traveled to South Africa for talks with Prime Minister John Vorster Aug. 29. Vorster reportedly expressed strong objections to the establishment of a neutral peacekeeping force and the dismantling of the Rhodesian army.

The two envoys made an unexpected stop in Dar es Salaam, Tanzania Aug. 30 for additional consultations with Tanzanian President Julius Nyerere. They then flew to Nairobi, Kenya to await the results of the Rhodesian parliamentary elections before conferring with Prime Minister Smith.

Post-Election Maneuvers

Ian Smith's hand was strengthened by an overwhelming victory in general elections held at the end of August 1977. Although at first it appeared that his election triumph would reinforce his intransigence, Smith continued to try to negotiate with representatives of Rhodesia's black majority. But some observers suggested later that the Smith regime seemed somewhat more amenable to compromise after its electoral achievement than it had been previously.

Smith's party sweeps Rhodesian vote. Prime Minister Ian Smith's ruling Rhodesian Front party scored an overwhelming victory in elections Aug. 31, gaining all 50 white seats in the 66-seat Parliament. The vote gave Smith an unequivocal mandate to negotiate a settlement with black leaders inside Rhodesia on greater political representation for the country's six million blacks.

With a voter turnout estimated at 80% of the 85,000-member white electorate, Smith's party won 83% of the popular vote. The newly formed Rhodesian Action Party, which consisted of right-wing defectors from Smith's party, won 9% of the vote. The National Unifying Force, a liberal group that supported efforts by the U.S. and Great Britain to achieve majority rule in Rhodesia, won 6% of the vote.

Blacks boycotted the election, and only three of the eight elected black seats in Parliament were contested. The other eight seats reserved for blacks were filled by tribal chiefs elected by tribal councils.

The election results appeared to complicate the task of the U.S. and British representatives who were trying to work out a peaceful transition to black majority rule in Rhodesia. In a victory speech, Smith expressed doubt that the latest set of Anglo-American proposals would bring both sides nearer to a solution. He pledged intensified efforts to achieve an internal settlement independent of the British-U.S. efforts and barring negotiations with the Patriotic Front, the principal nationalist guerrilla group fighting the white minority government.

Minor changes made in Cabinet posts— Ian Smith made several minor Cabinet changes Sept. 18 to replace ministers who had not run in the parliamentary elections. The Defense Ministry was taken over by the Ministry of Combined Operations, which was headed by Roger Hawkins.

Mark Partridge, the former defense minister, was named agriculture minister. Foreign Minister Pieter van der Byl was given the portfolio of information, immigration and tourism, replacing Elly Broomburg.

Smith derides Anglo-U.S. plan. Smith Sept. 2 scoffed at the Anglo-American plan for majority rule as "crazy" and "insane" but did not formally reject it. Smith had formally received the proposal Sept. 1 at a meeting with British Foreign Secretary David Owen and U.S. Ambassador to the United Nations Andrew Young in Rhodesia. Smith said he would give the plan careful consideration before making a formal reply.

(It was generally believed that Smith was holding back on formal comment in expectation that the Patriotic Front, the principal black nationalist group, would reject the plan. If the Front rejected the plan first, Smith could accuse the black nationalists of defeating the latest British-U.S. initiative, according to observers.)

Smith's only specific comment was a strong objection to the proposal to disband the Rhodesian army and replace it with a U.N. peacekeeping force during the transition to majority rule.

Defense Minister Mark Partridge Sept. 8 issued an outright rejection of the plan because of the provision concerning the army. He also criticized the proposal to institute universal suffrage "despite the obvious ill results that have followed upon its introduction elsewhere in Africa." His statement was the first official comment on the plan by a member of the white minority government.

Three key black moderates in Rhodesia Sept. 2 had generally favored the U.S.-British proposal. Bishop Abel Muzorewa, the Rev. Ndabaningi Sithole and Chief Jeremiah Chirau especially welcomed the provision for elections based on universal suffrage.

Chikerema returns, backs Smith. James Chikerema, one of Rhodesia's first black nationalist leaders, returned to Salisbury Sept. 18 after 13 years of self-exile and announced the next day that he supported Prime Minister Ian Smith on two major points concerning majority rule. He asserted that the army and police forces should remain under white control during the transition period and that whites should have a measure of parliamentary power under the future black government.

Long regarded as a militant opponent of the white regime, Chikerema said whites should be given "effective guarantees of individual and group security. . . such as a blocking mechanism in Parliament" against discriminatory legislation. He added that white control of the armed forces was "the best reassurance to anyone genuinely concerned for the future and peace and welfare of our country, as opposed to those concerned only with their own particular power irrespective of the cost to the state."

Chikerema denied having made any deals with the Smith government for being allowed to return without facing arrest. He said he had not abandoned the guerrilla movement and warned that "the armed struggle will go on" until majority rule was achieved.

Front-line states back U.K.-U.S. plan. The five black African front-line nations Sept. 24 gave qualified but formal support to the Anglo-American plan to bring majority rule to Rhodesia. After a two-day meeting in Maputo, Mozambique, representatives from Angola, Botswana, Mozambique, Tanzania and Zambia said the plan would serve as a "basis for further negotiations" despite "a lot of negative points."

One of their chief reservations, according to a spokesman for Zambian President Kenneth Kaunda, was that the plan had no provision for removing Rhodesian Prime Minister Ian Smith from office if he refused to go. However, the spokesman said, the front-line leaders were encouraged by the plan to involve the United Nations in the transition to majority rule. He added that the presidents stressed the positive aspects of the plan in their endorsement and expected that "the negative elements . . . will become positive and answered as negotiations proceed."

The support of the front-line nations was considered a major triumph for the U.K.-U.S. plan because it was expected that they would persuade the guerrilla groups, chiefly the Patriotic Front, to accept the plan. Mozambique, Zambia and Botswana served as havens for guerrilla bands and bases for raids into Rhodesia, and Mozambique and Tanzania were the rebels' chief sources of weapons and training facilities. In addition, it was felt that front-line support in the U.N. would assure backing for the plan in the world body.

Robert Mugabe and Joshua Nkomo, co-leaders of the Patriotic Front, Sept. 14 had rejected key parts of the plan. In a joint statement, they criticized four points: the appointment of a British administrator with broad powers to oversee and enforce the transition to majority rule, the placing of the U.N. peace-keeping force under the administrator's control, the retention of the Rhodesian police and judicial systems and the creation of a new Rhodesian army from both the guerrilla forces and the government security forces.

Smith vs. army plan—Prime Minister Smith also opposed the formula for a new Rhodesian army. He charged Sept. 21 that the details dealing with the army had been misrepresented to him by British Foreign Secretary David Owen and U.S. Ambassador to the U.N. Andrew Young. Smith said Owen and Young had told him that the Rhodesian army would "absorb certain of the terrorists," but, he said, they later had told the press that the Rhodesian army would be disbanded and "future security forces . . . would be based on the terrorist forces" with "certain selected members of the Rhodesian security forces." Smith called such a plan "incomprehensible."

Nevertheless, Smith said, his government was "reconciled" to establishing majority rule on the basis of the Anglo-American plan. He acknowledged that "we've got to get away from discrimination based on color" and that he was ready for compromise if some of the proposals were modified.

Smith added that he had put aside for

the time being his plan to reach a political settlement with moderate blacks inside Rhodesia as a result of "a request from the other people with whom I am in contact." He apparently was referring to the South African government, with which he had been in constant contact during the negotiations with the U.S. and Great Britain.

Smith, Kaunda meet secretly. Rhodesian Prime Minister Ian Smith and Zambian President Kenneth Kaunda met secretly in Lusaka, Zambia Sept. 25. The meeting was the first official contact between the Rhodesian and Zambian governments since 1975.

No details were released about their discussions when they were publicized Oct. 1 by the Rhodesian government. A spokesman said Smith and Kaunda had held talks in a "cordial atmosphere" and Smith had been accompanied by Foreign Minister Pieter van der Byl and other top aides.

A Zambian spokesman Oct. 1 confirmed that the meeting had taken place but added that "nothing of great significance" had been achieved.

Smith's aim in seeing Kaunda was not known, but initially it was believed that the discussions had centered on Joshua Nkomo, a leader of the Patriotic Front, the principal nationalist group fighting the white government. Nkomo's wing of the Patriotic Front, the Zimbabwe African People's Union, had its headquarters and guerrilla bases in Zambia. (Robert Mugabe, the other Patriotic Front leader, based his Zimbabwe African National Union in Mozambique.)

Kaunda said Oct. 26 that he was willing to meet Smith again if the meeting could serve the interests of majority rule in Rhodesia. He said Smith had given him assurances that he would accept majority rule but had refused to accept the appointment of a British resident commissioner. He said Smith had suggested handing the Rhodesian government to a non-British resident commissioner but had insisted upon keeping the Rhodesian army intact. Kaunda said Smith's suggestions had been unacceptable because they deviated from the Anglo-American plan.

Kaunda added that Smith had proposed as alternatives to the Anglo-American plan either a meeting with Nkomo or a conference with the Patriotic Front, the front-line African states, the Rhodesian government and other Rhodesian black nationalists in order to agree on a settlement plan for Rhodesia. Kaunda said that suggestion also was unacceptable to him.

Kaunda revealed that the meeting had been arranged by Roland W. Rowland, head of Lonrho Ltd., a British mining company with extensive interests in southern Africa. Kaunda called Rowland "one of six good capitalist friends" and said Rowland had told him Smith wanted to discuss the Anglo-American plan with him.

Kaunda drifts toward guerrilla stance— In an interview Oct. 21, Kaunda shifted his attitude toward a Rhodesian settlement to conform with the demands of the Patriotic Front. He said the U.S., Britain and Rhodesia "will have to accept the handing over of power to the Patriotic Front" to end the guerrilla war. He said political power should go to the Patriotic Front since the Anglo-American plan envisaged the guerrilla forces as the basis of a new Rhodesian army.

Kaunda acknowledged that Smith and black nationalist figures such as Rev. Ndabaningi Sithole, Bishop Abel Muzorewa and James Chikerema would be "anxious" about such an arrangement. He suggested preserving the Rhodesian police force or certain units of the Rhodesian army as a means of easing the fears of the whites and blacks who opposed the Patriotic Front.

Kaunda added that the subject of elections in Rhodesia was for the Patriotic Front to decide once it was in power. He acknowledged indirectly that the chances for an elected government would be slight if the Patriotic Front took control of Rhodesia. Since only the front was able to remove the white minority government, Kaunda said, "would anyone think they would be happy to serve other leaders? . . .To ask them to move out is to ask for civil war."

U.N. approves Rhodesia envoy. The United Nations Security Council Sept. 29

approved a motion by Britain to appoint a special U.N. representative to participate in the British-U.S. initiative to bring majority rule to Rhodesia. The plan had been suggested to the world body Sept. 26 as a means of implementing a cease-fire between the Rhodesian army and the black nationalist guerrillas. The cease-fire was the first step in the latest Anglo-American plan to transfer power to Rhodesia's black majority.

The appointment of the envoy was approved by 13 of the 15 Security Council members. The U.S.S.R. abstained, and China did not participate. Directly after the vote, U.N. Secretary General Kurt Waldheim proposed the nomination of Lt. Gen. Prem Chand of India to serve as the envoy, and his nomination was approved.

Prem Chand's appointment followed the naming of Field Marshal Lord Carver as Britain's choice for resident commissioner of Rhodesia, according to a report Sept. 2. According to the Anglo-American plan, Lord Carver was to administer the transition to majority rule once a cease-fire in the guerrilla war had been achieved.

Smith invites U.K., U.N. envoys—Prime Minister Smith Sept. 28 had invited the British and U.N. representatives to visit Rhodesia to discuss the creation of a U.N. peacekeeping force. The invitation was sent to Lord Carver and Waldheim and appeared to indicate that Smith was softening his opposition to a U.N. presence in Rhodesia to supervise the transition to majority rule. However, the Rhodesian government emphasized that the invitation did not mean total acceptance of the Anglo-American plan.

Smith issued a number of conflicting statements concerning his intentions toward the Anglo-American plan. In an interview reported Sept. 26, he gave qualified approval in principle to universal suffrage and indicated that he might be willing to consider the inclusion of black guerrillas in a new Rhodesian army under majority rule. He also indicated that he might consider disbanding the Selous Scouts, an elite Rhodesian army corps that had been accused by the nationalists of committing atrocities against civilians.

However, in an interview Oct. 17 Smith resumed his rigid stance toward the majority-rule plan. He urged the U.S. to dissociate itself from Britain's efforts, saying Washington had been "dragged along by Britain into imposing a preconceived solution on Rhodesia." He expressed no interest in universal suffrage unless, as he said, it would protect "individual rights" better than did the current limited Rhodesian franchise. On the subject of the Rhodesian army, he asserted that there was "no alternative to the status quo" of a Rhodesian force under white control excluding the guerrillas. He added that he had "not ruled out anything" in connection with the Anglo-American plan despite his objections.

Smith said the U.S. could not understand fully the Rhodesian situation as long as it played a secondary role to Britain. He called British Foreign Secretary David Owen "arrogant," and said he had achieved greater rapport with Andrew Young, U.S. ambassador to the U.N., during the joint visit of Young and Owen in September. He said Young "had been brainwashed by the British government" but had become "interested in the reasoning behind our ideas" after their discussions.

U.K., U.N. press Rhodesia solution. Field Marshal Lord Carver, Britain's choice to supervise a Rhodesian settlement, and Lt. Gen. Prem Chand, the United Nations' special representative, toured southern Africa Oct. 30–Nov. 9 to discuss the Anglo-American plan for Rhodesian majority rule. Their mission accomplished little except to confirm that the positions of the white Rhodesian government and the black nationalist guerrillas had hardened substantially.

Carver and Chand were in Tanzania Oct. 31–Nov. 1, in Rhodesia Nov. 2–6, in Botswana Nov. 7, in Zambia Nov. 7–8 and in Nigeria Nov. 9. The two men traveled separately, and Chand made an unscheduled visit to Mozambique Nov. 1 before joining Carver in Salisbury, Rhodesia.

In Tanzania, Carver and Chand met Oct. 31 with Joshua Nkomo and Robert Mugabe, co-leaders of the Patriotic Front, the principal guerrilla group fighting the white Rhodesian government. The meeting was brief, since the front already had announced that it would not accept the British plan of handing supreme power in Rhodesia to Carver during the transition phase to black rule.

(According to reports Oct. 30 from Lusaka, Zambia, there were indications of strain in the Patriotic Front's year-old alliance because of the secret talks between Rhodesian Prime Minister !an Smith and Zambian President Kenneth Kaunda in late September. Mugabe had charged that Kaunda favored Nkomo's nationalist faction and added that Nkomo himself had been at the meeting. Nkomo had denied the charges and criticized Mugabe for publicizing his accusation.)

Carver and Chand met with Rhodesian army and police officials in Salisbury Nov. 2. The next day the two men met with Rhodesian government officials, and on Nov. 4 they conferred with two moderate Rhodesian black nationalists, Bishop Abel Muzorewa and Rev. Ndabaningi Sithole.

Carver and Chand talked with Prime Minister Smith Nov. 6, but reported no progress. A statement from Smith afterwards said there had been "wide agreement" on the need for a cease-fire in the guerrilla war and a political settlement, but there had been "no measure of agreement" on "how this is to be achieved."

Upon leaving Salisbury Nov. 6, Carver held the first press conference of his tour. He said there had been basic agreement on several areas of the Anglo-American plan such as free elections for the new government, a transitional administration to supervise the elections and a cease-fire. However, he indicated that there had been no concessions by either side and no initiatives for putting the plan into action. He added that both sides remained deadlocked on the question of the composition of the security forces that would oversee the transfer of power.

After talks with Botswanan President Seretse Khama Nov. 7, Carver and Chand met with Zambian President Kenneth Kaunda that night. Little progress was reported after the meeting, and the next day Kaunda ruled out the Anglo-American plan for holding elections for a Rhodesian government. Kaunda, considered one of the more moderate of the front-line African leaders, had adopted the Patriotic Front's line that the guerrilla forces should play a prominent role in the transitional phase and in the new government.

On their way back from Africa, Carver and Chand stopped in Nigeria Nov. 9 to enlist support for the Anglo-American plan.

Nkomo, Mugabe delay unity talks. Joshua Nkomo and Robert Mugabe, co-leaders of the Patriotic Front, Oct. 3 postponed talks on a formal union of their two guerrilla factions. The leaders of Rhodesia's most powerful nationalist force had planned to discuss the military and political integration of their organizations, which had been violent rivals until the formation of the Patriotic Front coalition. The announcement said Mugabe had not been able to meet Nkomo in Lusaka, Zambia because of a heavy work load at his headquarters in Maputo, Mozambique.

Sanctions & Violations

Soviet bloc held violating trade sanctions. A report released Feb. 10 by the United Nations Secretariat accused the Soviet Union and four Eastern European nations of violating international trade sanctions against Rhodesia. The report was based on documents submitted to the U.N. Sanctions Committee by Britain in September and December 1976.

According to the report, the Soviet Union, Bulgaria, Czechoslovakia, East Germany and Rumania had imported tobacco from Rhodesia and had exported to Rhodesia "chemicals, metal and agricultural requirements." The report said the products had been traded through front corporations in Switzerland. The

U.S.S.R. and Rumania denied the charges.

U.S. bans Rhodesian chrome. President Carter March 18 signed a bill banning the U.S. import of Rhodesian chrome. The bill had cleared the House March 14, 250–146, and the Senate the following day, 66–26.

Enactment of the bill brought the U.S. into compliance with a United Nations embargo on Rhodesian chrome voted in 1966. The U.N. sanction had been voted in reaction to Rhodesia's white supremacist policies. Initially, the U.S. had complied with it, but in 1971 Sen. Harry F. Byrd Jr. (Ind., Va.) had succeeded in winning passage of legislation allowing chrome imports.

Carter had pressed hard for repeal of the so-called Byrd amendment, which had proved to be a thorny point in U.S. relations with black African nations.

The legislation allowed the President to lift the ban on Rhodesian chrome if he determined that such an action might be helpful in obtaining a negotiated settlement of the Rhodesian situation.

Opponents of the ban argued that imposing it would make the U.S. overly dependent on chrome imports from the Soviet Union. They also argued that it was inconsistent to ban Rhodesian chrome, when other countries the U.S. imported chrome from—such as the U.S.S.R., South Africa and Brazil—were also charged with violations of human rights.

However, supporters of the ban and Administration spokesmen argued that reimposing the ban would be seen as a friendly move by black African nations and would bring the U.S. once again into compliance with U.N. sanctions that the U.S. had originally voted for. They also maintained that the U.S. had adequate supplies of chrome without Rhodesian imports.

In recent years, Rhodesian imports had accounted for 5% to 10% of the chrome ore used in the U.S. The chrome was used chiefly in the making of stainless steel. The steel industry did not lobby in favor of retaining Rhodesian imports, because recent technological developments had permitted steelmakers to use cheaper grades of chrome obtained from other countries, instead of the high-grade Rhodesian ore.

In Senate debate on the issue March 15, Sen. Edward W. Brooke (R, Mass.) had summarized major arguments for the decision to repeal the Byrd Amendment:

"First, although choosing to respect the sanctions that have been imposed on Rhodesia would not give the United States a guarantee of success in promoting a solution to the conflict that minimizes violence and, hopefully, achieves a substantial amount of justice for the people in that country, we will have far less a chance of success in achieving these goals if we do not respect those sanctions. U.S. political capital in the minds of those who are determined and able to bring about change will be minimized if we fail to take this step to signify that further procrastination by the Smith regime is unacceptable to the United States.

"Second, there is no adequate economic justification for continued U.S. violation of the sanctions. The U.S. stainless steel industry has agreed that previous arguments for violating the sanctions no longer have validity. New technologies have made the utilization of lower grade chrome, found in many parts of the world, economically feasible. Moreover, in 1976 we imported only 5 percent of our metallurgical chrome needs from Rhodesia, the decrease largely due to our recognition of the basic unreliability of that source under prevailing military and political conditions in that country.

"Third, and related to the above, if the chrome located in Rhodesia is important to the United States, it is so in the long run rather than in the near term. If we are to have future access to that chrome on a just basis, then it is time to stop ignoring the inevitability of "revolutionary" changes in that country in the very near future. These changes will bring to power individuals who, at present, have serious reservations as to the desirability of good working relations with the United States. U.S. compliance with existing sanctions can begin to alter their perceptions, just as noncompliance can serve to deepen animosity without promising to limit the damage to our interests in the area.

"Moreover, it is important that we recognize that the whole question of the U.S. trading relationship with independent Africa can be affected by our decisions regarding Rhodesia. Many African States desire a mutually beneficial trading relationship with our country. They realize that we are, at least potentially, the most important market for many of their goods. They also realize that economic interdependence means that the United States has an interest in achieving and maintaining access to raw materials in Africa. Thus, the ingredients for a productive cooperative relationship exist. But U.S. policies in the past have reflected an inadequate appreciation of the depth of feeling Africans have regarding the vestiges of colonialism in southern Africa. Just as Americans feel deeply about their fundamental freedom from coercion provided for in the Constitution, so do Africans throughout the continent have a deep emotional commitment to doing what is necessary to be rid of the last tangible expressions of colonial coercion. And I am convinced that many in Africa are willing to pay a high price to do so, a price that could entail negative consequences for U.S. trading relationships with Africa if our policy choices are inept and irrelevant to evolving conditions.

"Fourth, a goal of U.S. efforts in southern Africa must be to minimize the possibility of the area becoming a focal point for competition between ourselves and the Soviet Union. Responsible African leaders certainly desire to avoid such a situation. The best way to do so, in my opinion, is to accelerate the changes needed to permit the Africans themselves to resist aggressive expansion of influence and control by any outside power. Having struggled for decades to achieve freedom from colonial control, the Africans do not want to be subject to the policy dictates of any power. U.S. policies in the past have not reflected an adequate appreciation of this fundamental truth. It is imperative that they do so now.

"We cannot nor should we attempt to dictate policies to any African state. What we can justifiably do is work with them to provide an environment where the United States and the African countries will have the necessary freedom of choice to work out their relationships unfettered by coercive influences from any source.

"Finally, U.S. compliance with these international sanctions has a very important moral dimension. There can be no question as to our obligation to do what we can to assist those who desire that changes in Rhodesia and the rest of southern Africa occur at the least possible loss of life and personal and societal freedom. Favorable action on S. 174 can place the United States in a better position to do so.

"Equally important is our obligation to advocate the principles we believe to be universally applicable to government. The manner by which we do so, of course, must be conditioned by the circumstances evident in any specific case if we are to avoid making conditions worse by well meant but inappropriate initiatives. This caveat explains why, at times, a great deal of ambiguity characterizes our Government's attempts to bring about greater respect for human rights in the world. But in the Rhodesia case, no such ambiguity exists. The present governmental structure cannot survive. It will be changed either through the carnage of escalating violence or, hopefully, through negotiations leading to the enfranchisement of those currently denied their rightful participation in the political and economic mainstreams of their country. Such enfranchisement is a fundamental right in our own society. And in keeping with our tradition, we desire it for the peoples of Rhodesia. . . ."

● Japan had reached agreement with the U.S. to test shipments of South African chrome to make sure they contained no Rhodesian chrome, according to a report Aug. 3 in the Wall Street Journal. The agreement was intended to insure compliance with U.S. regulations prohibiting the importation of Rhodesian chrome.

Under the terms of the agreement, the U.S. would reject shipments of chrome ore containing more than one part of chrome to 2.1 parts of ore. (Rhodesian chrome ore was known to be particularly rich in chrome.) Ferrochrome containing more than 60% chrome also would be prohibited from entering the U.S. from Japan. U.S. importers of ferrochrome and steel products that contained more than 3% chromium (the pure element) could request a certificate of origin from Japan stating that the shipments did not contain Rhodesian chrome.

(Japan had sent 32,000 tons of chrome to the U.S. in 1976. It was widely believed that Japan had been importing more than half of its chrome from

Rhodesia and the rest from South Africa. About 90% of the world's chrome ore came from South Africa, Rhodesia and the U.S.S.R)

U.N. charges U.S. imported chrome—The United Nations Security Council committee on Rhodesian sanctions July 25 reported that the U.S. had imported 45,-854 tons of minerals and other embargoed items from Rhodesia from October to December 31, 1976. The committee said the Mozambique port of Maputo was the port of origin for 4,899 tons of Rhodesian ferrochrome and 1,957 tons of chromite. It said South African ports were used for the rest of the shipments. The report did not mention that the shipments had been sent to the U.S. before Congress revoked a decision to permit the importation of Rhodesian metals.

Lonrho sues sanction breakers. Lonrho Ltd., a British mining company, May 31 brought suit in London against 29 oil companies for supplying fuel to Rhodesia in violation of United Nations sanctions. The suit named Mobil Oil Corp., Standard Oil Co. of California, Texaco Inc., Caltex Oil Co., Shell Oil Co., British Petroleum Co. and their subsidiaries in southern Africa.

Lonrho had closed its oil pipeline from Mozambique to Rhodesia when the U.N. voted a ban on trade with the breakaway colony in 1966. In the suit, Lonrho charged the corporations with breach of contract

and asked for an estimated $170 million in damages.

Information on sanction-breaking supplied by Lonrho had prompted British Foreign Secretary David Owen to set up an inquiry April 8 into allegations that the oil companies had set up a common system to circumvent the sanctions. An anti-apartheid organization had submitted a report to the Foreign Office April 25 alleging evidence of complicity by the oil companies in shipping oil to Rhodesia. Previously, the group had said that while oil was reaching Rhodesia from South Africa, it was uncertain whether the oil companies had been directly involved in the trade.

In a related development, the U.S. Treasury Department May 16 said it could not determine whether Mobil Oil Corp. had shipped petroleum products to Rhodesia. After an investigation, the department said that South Africa had denied it access to the files of Mobil's South African affiliate. The department said it had some information indicating that Mobil affiliates might have supplied Rhodesia with hexane, adding that it was turning the information over to the U.S. Commerce Department to determine whether export controls had been violated.

• The Zambian government Aug. 22 brought suit for more than $6 billion against 17 Western oil companies for allegedly supplying oil to Rhodesia in vio-

---

U.S. Imports of Metallurgical Grade Chromite for Domestic Consumption

[Percent by country; total imports by gross weight in thousands of short tons]

	1963	1964	1965	1966	1967	1968	1969	1970	1971	1972	1973	1974	1975	1976
Rhodesia	37	37	37	24	22				4	10	11	13	17	5
U.S.S.R.	49	42	27	33	45	59	57	58	41	59	53	51	50	44
Turkey	10	6	19	20	16	27	14	19	27	9	22	17	15	24
South Africa	5	5	13	20	14	13	27	14	21	16	9	18	12	26
Other	0	4	4	2	2	1	2	9	7	6	5	1	6	
Total imports	394	661	884	913	660	567	529	703	667	633	384	495	590	269

Note: January to November.
Source: Bureau of Mines Mineral Industry Surveys.

lation of U.N. sanctions. Among the companies named were Shell Oil Co., British Petroleum Co., Caltex Oil Co., Mobil Corp. and Compagnie Francaise des Petroles. The Zambian action reportedly was based on information supplied to the government by Lonrho Ltd.

Pretoria pressure on Rhodesia asked—A committee of the Commonwealth of Nations recommended Oct. 19 that South Africa be pressured into stopping supplies of oil from reaching Rhodesia. The Commonwealth Committee on Southern Africa, meeting in London, unanimously voted to urge its 35 member nations to warn South Africa that it would face a Commonwealth oil embargo if it did not guarantee a ban on oil shipments to Rhodesia.

U.N. asks more Rhodesian sanctions. The United Nations General Assembly's decolonization committee Aug. 8 unanimously approved a resolution calling for the extension of the boycott of Rhodesia to include communications cutoffs. A second resolution, also passed unanimously by the 24-nation committee, condemned the Rhodesian government for domestic repression and aggression against neighboring countries.

The U.N. Security Council May 27 had voted unanimously to approve a resolution to close Rhodesian government information offices outside Rhodesia. The move would affect one office in Australia and one in the U.S. The French government had closed a Rhodesian information office in Paris in February.

The U.S., however, decided not to close Rhodesia's government information office in Washington, according to a report Aug. 26. Despite the Security Council's passage of the resolution for its closure, the proposed move by the Carter Administration had been attacked by conservative and civil-rights groups in the U.S. as an infringement of the freedom of information.

Britain renews Rhodesia sanctions. Britain Nov. 11 renewed its sanctions against Rhodesia, for the twelfth consecutive year, by a vote of 77–26 in the House of Commons. The sanctions had been imposed in 1965 after Rhodesia unilaterally had declared its independence. Introducing the motion, Foreign Secretary David Owen emphasized that a Rhodesian defense force had to be created from both the guerrilla forces and the Rhodesian army. He had held two days of talks with Lord Carver Nov. 10–11 upon Carver's return from southern Africa.

Other Foreign Developments

Canada expels spy recruiters. Canada Jan. 10, 1977 ordered the ouster of five Cubans, including three members of the Cuban Consulate in Montreal, on charges of recruiting and training intelligence agents to be sent to Rhodesia.

According to an official in the External Affairs Department, the three consular staff members had been ordered "withdrawn" and the Department of Immigration had issued deportation orders against two more Cubans living in Canada on non-immigrant status. "On the basis of investigations," the official said, "it was determined that there was an intelligence operation being conducted in Canada involving the Cuban nationals in contravention of their status in Canada."

The Canadian government refused further comment on the case, but a report in the Jan. 10 Gazette, a Montreal newspaper, cited details first reported by the Sunday Mail of Salisbury, Rhodesia. According to the report, the existence of the Montreal operation was revealed by a U.S. citizen, David Bufkin, who said he had been recruited and trained by the Cubans. He was also reported to have spied on the Cubans for the U.S. Central Intelligence Agency. The Salisbury newspaper quoted Bufkin as saying he had been recruited in Mexico, trained in Montreal and sent to Rhodesia for "undercover activity," but had reported his mission to Rhodesian authorities upon his arrival in Salisbury.

Cuba on recruiting spies—The Cuban government Jan. 12 admitted using its Montreal consulate as a base for recruiting agents but denied "any actions . . . that would interfere with normal relations between Canada and Cuba."

The Cuban Foreign Ministry in Havana said it had recruited informants to operate against the National Front for the Liberation of Angola (FNLA), not against the Rhodesian government as had been suspected. Cuba accused the FNLA of attacking Cuban diplomats and said it was a "normal right" to gather intelligence on the group.

Four Cubans who had been ordered expelled from Canada in connection with the case left for Havana Jan. 12. They were: Montreal Consul General Jesus Rodriguez Verdes, Vice Consul Rene Valenzuela Acebal, consular employe Raul Hernandez Cuesta and Hector Arazoza Rodriguez, a lecturer at McGill University in Montreal. Fernando E. Rivero Milan, third secretary at the Cuban Embassy in Ottawa, was in Cuba on leave and was informed he would not be permitted to return to Canada.

Soviet President Podgorny tours region. Soviet President Nikolai V. Podgorny visited Tanzania, Zambia and Mozambique March 23–April 1, marking the first state visit of a top-ranking Soviet official to southern Africa.

Podgorny's tour was seen as a move to assert Soviet influence and to counter Western moves to settle racial conflicts in the area. Throughout his trip he stressed Soviet support for the guerrilla movements fighting white regimes in Rhodesia, South Africa and Namibia (South-West Africa).

In a speech welcoming the Soviet president March 23 in Dar es Salaam, Tanzanian President Julius K. Nyerere thanked the Soviet Union for its military assistance to the nationalist movements. (The Soviet Union was second to China in the amount of arms it supplied to Tanzania, which maintained training bases for guerrillas.)

A Soviet-Tanzanian communique issued on Podgorny's departure March 26 announced agreement on most major issues and endorsed the Patriotic Front of Zimbabwe, one of three Rhodesian nationalist groups competing for African and international recognition in white-ruled Rhodesia. The statement called the front an "important step" in unifying the Rhodesian nationalist movements.

Podgorny was received by Zambian President Kenneth Kaunda in Lusaka March 26, signaling a change in relations since Kaunda had opposed the Soviet-backed faction in the Angolan civil war.

(At a press conference March 25, Kaunda had described the Soviet Union as a "comrade and colleague in the struggle" against white minority rule. He had criticized the Western failure to effect a peaceful transfer of power to Rhodesia's black majority and warned that Africa's dependence on Soviet-bloc countries would grow since they were the only nations to supply arms to the nationalists. However, he affirmed his government's commitment to nonalignment and did not rule out the possibility of a peaceful Rhodesian solution.)

Podgorny March 28 met with Joshua Nkomo, a leader of the Patriotic Front, Oliver Tambo, acting president of the African National Congress of South Africa, and Sam Nujoma, leader of the South-West Africa People's Organization. (Rev. Ndabaningi Sithole, a rival Rhodesian nationalist figure, that day held a news conference to denounce Soviet support for the Patriotic Front. He also said the southern African states treated Rhodesia like a colony, because they backed the Patriotic Front without considering popular sentiment among Rhodesian blacks, who were believed to favor more moderate black nationalists.")

After the interview, Nkomo praised the Soviet Union and its allies for being "the only people who are prepared to work with the oppressed people."

The high point of Podgorny's tour was the signing of a treaty of friendship and cooperation with Mozambique March 31.

The terms of the treaty indicated the possibility of direct Soviet involvement in any conflict threatening Mozambique's security and pledged continuing military cooperation.

Soviet arms in Mozambique reported— The U.S.S.R. had sent Mozambique several shipments of antiaircraft missiles and artillery, according to a report April 24 in the New York Times. The report cited U.S. intelligence analysts who said that antiaircraft SAM-7 missiles, howitzers, rifles and tanks had reached Mozambique in past weeks. The amount of the shipments was not known, but analysts seemed certain that the Soviet Union intended to strengthen Mozambique's military position against Rhodesia. The return of "a few hundred" guerrillas to Mozambique from the Soviet Union and Cuba, where it was believed they had been trained, was also reported.

Development fund opposed. Rep. Don Bonker (D, Wash.), in the U.S. House of Representatives May 24, 1977, opposed the Anglo-U.S. proposal for a five-year Zimbabwe Development Fund to which some 20 countries would be asked to contribute about $1.5 billion (the U.S.' first-year share: $250 million) "to promote peaceful transfer to majority rule in Zimbabwe." Bonker provided these details and comments about the plan:

Virtually all of the testimony and documents submitted by the Administration to Congress in support of the proposal over the last two months have emphasized the Fund's prospective role in helping "insure a constructive economic transition during the initial period of majority rule and thus help maintain peace and progress in Southern Africa"—in short, to keep the lid on in Rhodesia while the blacks assume power. Administration spokesmen have emphasized that the Fund will seek a delicate balance between "rapid restructuring of the economy and government services to provide more training, education and economic opportunities for blacks and the maintenance of the confidence of whites in the future economic prospects of the country." Such balanced development, in the Administration's view, will not only promote political stability

during a chaotic period of transition but even "encourage blacks and whites to work together for the future development of Zimbabwe and thus demonstrate that multiracialism is a viable option in Southern Africa."

The Administration's proposed Fund offers something for everybody:

For the black poor:

More and better farmland;

Aid in improving farm practices and technologies, transport and marketing facilities;

Infrastructure projects for new roads, villages, health, education and other social services.

For the black middle class who will run the country:

Training to assume skilled and managerial posts;

Better vocational and university training;

Social and economic infrastructure projects;

Home mortgage assistance to buy housing in "European" areas;

Balance of payments relief for the new government.

For the whites who choose to remain:

Continued Western interest in their welfare;

Security and minimum, or at least cushioned, disruption of lifestyle and economic livelihood;

Continuation of "job security and benefit programs";

Orderly compensation for land transferred to blacks;

Continued growth of the "modern" sector—mining, modern commerce and modern services industry.

For the United States and Britain:

Stability in Southern Africa and, consequently, dis-incentives to Russian and Cuban adventurism;

Continued access to raw materials and markets;

A sense of continuity with comfortable economic patterns in the area.

It sounds too good to be true—and it is. The Carter Administration, in trying to please everybody, has put itself on the horns of an unworkable dilemma. The creation of that dilemma stems back to the original Anglo-American peace plan for Rhodesia conceived by the two governments in mid-1976 and accepted by Ian Smith on September 24 (but rejected by the "front-line Presidents" of the five neighboring states two days later).

As part of the price for acceptance of the peace plan, Smith, in September, 1976, exacted from the Americans and British promises of "financial guranatees" for the white Rhodesian population. The guarantees reportedly covered property, land purchases and pensions. Administration spokesmen then and now flatly deny that there were any financial incentives in the plan to ease the departure of recalcitrant whites. In any event, the guarantees were said in news reports to amount to $1.5–2.0 billion—or $5500–$8,000 per white Rhodesian. A separate fund was to provide transitional aid to the new black government.

In presenting the economic package to the Congress, Secretary of State Kissinger combined the proposal of guarantees for whites with transitional aid for blacks. The resultant Kissinger "summary of ideas"—the parent of the Zimbabwe Development Fund—was meant "to ease the economic shocks of the transition to majority rule." State Department testimony of September 30, 1976, described the purposes of Kissinger's "ideas" more fully:

"The objective of this effort would be to maintain confidence in the future of Rhodesia. This proposal would be intended to give an incentive to those who have a positive contribution to make to stay in Rhodesia and work for the future of the country. Its overall aim would be to expand industrial and mineral production in Rhodesia; to enhance agricultural potential; and to provide the funds for necessary training and skills. Its broader purposes would be to equip black Rhodesians to take advantage of the opportunities which will be opened to them in a majority-ruled Rhodesia; to expand investment in the country; and to allow the economy to adjust to the removal of sanctions. . . . It is not a plan to buy out the holdings of the white Rhodesians. No one would be paid to leave."

The Kissinger plan, in plain talk, was still the same carrot created in mid-1976 to bring Ian Smith to heel. It was a thinly disguised bribe to the Rhodesian whites to (1) relinquish power; and (2) remain in an independent Zimbabwe to underpin the economy during the crucial transition years.

In the first months of 1977, the Carter Administration, uncomfortable with a plan which still blatantly favored Rhodesian whites, wrenched Kissinger's "summary of ideas" into its own plan for "balanced development" benefitting both blacks and whites. Therein lies the dilemma.

To coax peaceful white acquiescence to black rule and continuing white participation in the economy, the Carter proposal has maintained the Kissinger emphasis on preserving the socio-economic status quo in Rhodesia. For to speak of a strong and expanding modern sector with continued white participation, as this Administration still does, and virtually ignore black demands for substantial income redistribution and wage increases is, in fact, an argument to keep things as they are.

The problem is that a change in the socio-economic structure is precisely what black Zimbabweans are demanding and, with po-

litical primacy and overwhelming numbers, will get one way or the other. For proof, look to the quick rejection last September by the "front-line Presidents" of an Anglo-American peace plan, which, while granting political independence, was still based on preservation of the socio-economic status quo. Such a plan, said the Presidents, "would be tantamount to legalizing the colonial and racist structures of power in Rhodesia."

It is blind to equate, as the American and British executives still appear to do, maintenance of the socio-economic status quo with any meaningful definition of political stability in Rhodesia. If anything, the reverse may be true.

That section of the latest Administration proposals aimed at directly benefitting blacks is a welcome advance over the Kissinger proposals but it still falls well short of meeting basic black expectations. No solution for Zimbabwe will remain stable for long unless it involves changes in the socio-economic stucture more significant than those now proposed.

The Administration is correct in its plans to try to keep the "modern" sector of an independent Zimbabwe viable and to encourage whites to help in that endeavor. But if the cost of maintaining that viability is a continuation of gross wage differentials, of white possession of the best land, of white swimming pools and maids, then the effort simply will not work. Black frustration will be too great and, with political power in their hands, it will be vented.

In short, the Administration's concept of "balanced" development is a chimera. Zimbabwe will be an overwhelmingly black African nation, with black African aspirations and black African resentment over years of colonial rule. Any American policy which ignores these facts is simply unrealistic.

The ideal solution in Rhodesia ought to guarantee to whites who choose to remain security of self and home, full political and civil rights, reasonable compensation for expropriated property, a fair share of the land, and a fair remuneration for their expertise and labor. But we should be under no illusion that our economic aid can buy these things for the whites. And we are foolish to try.

The most effective strategy for our aid in terms of building genuine long-term stability in an independent Zimbabwe would be to carry the Administration's current strategy several steps further down the path it has already travelled from the Kissinger proposals. Concentration should explicity be on the economic and social development of black Zimbabweans. They are the ones in need of development assistance; they will be the ones in power.

Specifically, the Zimbabwe Development Fund should:

(1) provide professional cross-cultural

analytical assistance to Zimbabwean leaders during the transition to develop a coherent structure for a future Zimbabwean economy, including planning for:

Region-by-region land redistribution, resettlement, and the creation of social and economic services;

The role of foreign capital, investment and trade;

Wage structure and income redistribution that is both fair and economically realistic;

(2) focus development projects on the black community, primarily on:

Agriculture: Land tenure, training and other extension services, credit and marketing mechanisms for the small farmer;

Education: A massive push in primary education and vocational training; additional assistance in modern management, public administration, technical and professional training;

Health and Social Services, particularly in rural areas and black urban and mining communities.

(3) provide financial and balance-of-payments relief to compensate for the inevitable drop in productivity and revenue during the transition.

If the grassroots social and economic transition in Rhodesia can be managed peacefully, and if black, especially poor black, needs can be met, then the "modern" sector will survive well enough without bribes or carrots. Smith will head for the bargaining table with or without windfall guarantees for white economic privilege. It is in fact irresponsible for this country to promise Rhodesian whites a continuation of anything like the privilege they now enjoy. For those who remain, the transition will be tough, and it is naive to pretend otherwise. The best thing we can do for the Rhodesian whites is to help build long-term stability in Zimbabwe by ameliorating the social and economic roots of instability in the black community. For if the Fund does not meet deeply-rooted black aspirations, there is no way that it can meet ours.

U.S. bars 2 Rhodesian blacks. The U.S. State Department had refused visas to two black representatives of the Rhodesian government, according to a report Sept. 25 in the Washington Post. Chiefs Jeremiah Chirau and Edgar Musikavanhu, both members of the Rhodesian Senate, were part of a group of six Rhodesians who had been scheduled to address various private organizations in the U.S. Washington granted waivers for visas for the four other members of the group.

The State Department explained that the visas for the two senators were denied in accordance with international policy barring entry of all Rhodesian government representatives to any country.

Other 1977 Events

Smith sets race reforms. In Parliament Feb. 23, Smith announced a series of measures intended to eliminate most of the racial barriers in Rhodesian society. The reforms, some of which would require parliamentary approval and some of which could be implemented by the government, involved:

■ Opening white-owned farmland to purchase by blacks, on condition large tracts of land would not be broken up into smaller plots (a major revision of the Land Tenure Act, which had been approved by a caucus of the ruling Rhodesia Front party Jan. 14);

■ Opening industrial and commercial land in business districts to all races while keeping trade in black and white residential areas separate;

■ Establishing certain areas for multiracial living while retaining residential segregation elsewhere;

■ Integrating all hotels and bars, but allowing owners to exclude anyone at their discretion;

■ Permitting integration of private schools and hospitals, but retaining segregation in state institutions, and

■ Commissioning black army officers and recruiting blacks as magistrates and prison officers.

Smith said the program "indicates clearly not only the government's desire to remove racial discrimination but also its desire to work with our black people in order to produce the correct political solution for our future."

Jeremiah S. Chirau, a tribal chief who headed the conservative Zimbabwe United People's Organization, indicated qualified approval of the program, saying Smith "must not slow down now that he has started towards the removal of racial discrimination." (Smith was hoping to negotiate a political settlement with Chirau and other moderate black leaders.)

In its Jan. 14 caucus, the Rhodesia Front party had voted its approval of Smith's proposal to repeal the Land Tenure Act, which divided Rhodesia's land area equally between the country's six million blacks and 270,000 whites. Further action on the repeal plan was delayed by Desmond Frost, party chairman, who Jan. 17 accused Smith of "breaking faith" with the party "by disregarding one of the basic principles of the party." It was believed that Smith wanted to repeal the act to draw support from moderate nationalist leaders for separate negotiations.

Land race reform passed. Smith's proposal for ending racial discrimination in land ownership became law in March 1977.

The change in Rhodesia's Land Tenure Act was approved March 4 by the House of Assembly. The amendment to the act that divided Rhodesia's land racially between blacks and whites allowed blacks to purchase land in agricultural and urban areas formerly limited to whites. The measure was approved 44 to 12 with 10 abstentions, and was approved unanimously March 10 by the 19 members voting in the 23-member Senate.

Passage of the measure appeared uncertain until the last minute, as the ruling Rhodesia Front party, which held all 50 white seats in the Assembly, faced a split over the amendment upon its introduction in Parliament March 1. Nine party members walked out of a caucus meeting the next day, denouncing the bill as an appeasement of black nationalists. Three other party members who were not present at the meeting also had expressed opposition to the bill. In addition, 13 of the 16 black members of the 66-member

Assembly had announced they would abstain on the bill because it did not go far enough to end racial segregation. (Although less than 500,000 acres, or 1%, of Rhodesian land remained limited to whites by the amendment, blacks still were excluded from voting or holding office on rural councils in the "European areas" which were open to black purchase.) At the last minute, three of the black oppositionists switched their votes to give Smith the two-thirds majority he needed.

In a televised speech March 15, Smith challenged his 12 rebel party members to resign their seats and test public opinion in by-elections. If their constituents voiced approval of their stand by reelecting them, Smith said, he would call a general election to test nation-wide support for his move. The next day, the 108-member Rhodesia Front National Executive voted in favor of a motion of confidence in Smith. The vote was 56 in favor, 18 opposed, with 34 abstentions.

Rhodesian black buys white's land— George Tawengwa had become the first black to buy a white-owned farm under the country's newly eased racial laws, the London Times reported May 22.

*Other racial events—*The Salisbury city council was reported July 29 to have ordered the eviction of a Colored (mixed-race) family from a Salisbury suburb.

The Adams family had been ordered out of the house in which they had lived since 1975 because the suburb was reserved for whites. Florrie Adams July 24 said she, her husband and her four children had decided to defy the order, and their case had been supported by a number of moderate whites.

Two black soldiers June 9 became the first black lieutenants in the Rhodesian army. The next day, 11 more blacks were made lieutenants.

Rhodesian Front expels dissidents. At a meeting of the standing committee of the ruling Rhodesian Front Party April 29, 13 members of the right-wing opposition were expelled. The members, 12 parlia-

mentary representatives and the party's
deputy chairman, had opposed Prime
Minister Ian Smith's plans to achieve a
settlement for black majority rule and for
easing racial restrictions.

The expulsion left the Rhodesian Front
with 38 members in Parliament. The 12
expelled members retained their seats and
were expected to form a new right-wing
party.

Frost quits party—Desmond Frost,
chairman of the Rhodesian Front, resigned his party membership July 2, criticizing Ian Smith as "tired and negative." Frost said Smith "has shown
increasing evidence of a total lack of
leadership, planning and direction" in
seeking a political settlement with the
country's black majority. Frost, a leading
party member during the Front's 14 years
in power, had opposed Smith's attempts at
racial reform.

Smith July 3 said his party was "well
rid" of Frost, whom he described as "completely two-faced." Smith added that
there were a number of other Rhodesian
Front members he would like to see leave
the party. Wickus de Kock, a member of
Parliament and a former Cabinet
minister, July 1 had resigned his seat and
announced his intention to emigrate to
South Africa.

The two resignations left the Rhodesian
Front with 36 seats in Parliament.

Political realignments follow ousters—
The 12 parliamentary representatives
who had been ousted from the Rhodesian
Front earlier in the year organized a new
conservative party called the Rhodesian
Action Party July 4. Outlining the party's
platform the next day, interim chairman
Ian Sandeman said the party approved of
a multiracial government in the future but
rejected black majority rule.

Meanwhile, moderate whites had
combined their parties into the National
Unifying Force, the Washington Post
reported July 5. Their platform called for
"a smooth transition to black majority
rule." (None of the opposition parties held
seats in Parliament.)

Salisbury bus strike. Limited bus service had been restored in Salisbury Jan. 4,
1977 after the dismissal of 800 black
drivers for staging a Christmas Eve strike.
Black commuters were boycotting buses
to protest the dismissal and detention of
the men, who were released from custody
Dec. 29, 1976.

The black boycott of Salisbury buses
was diminishing, it was reported Jan. 7, as
more black commuters started to use
public transportation.

ZANU members switch leaders.
Members of the Zimbabwe African National Union (ZANU) living in London
Jan. 14 announced their decision to switch
their loyalties from Robert Mugabe, the
ZANU leader, to his rival, Rev. Ndabaningi Sithole. A spokesman for the London
group accused Mugabe of being paid by
the U.S. Central Intelligence Agency.

Muzorewa loses supporters. Bishop Abel
Muzorewa, a contender for leadership of
Rhodesia's six million blacks, had lost four
senior officials of his United African National Council (UANC) since the beginning of August. Chakamyuka Chikesi,
secretary for external affairs, quit the organization Aug. 8 following the resignation
of Moton Malianga, UANC national
chairman. W.K. Nduka, educational
secretary, resigned Aug. 10, and Elliott
Gabellah, UANC vice president, left Aug.
21. The men appeared to have been
dissatisfied with Muzorewa's opposition to
forging a united party with the Rev. Ndabaningi Sithole and his African National
Council. Both Muzorewa and Sithole were
considered moderate nationalists who favored reaching a compromise with Rhodesian Prime Minister Ian Smith on black
majority rule.

**Rhodesia shows '76 GNP drop, trade sur-
plus.** Rhodesia's gross national product
(GNP), the measure of total output of

goods and services, fell 3.4% in real terms during 1976, the government reported May 6. GNP had increased by 5.8%, but with inflation taken into account, the GNP had dropped sharply compared with a decline of 1% in real terms in 1975.

In spite of the decline, Rhodesia was left with a 1976 trade surplus of more than $70 million compared with a deficit of $26 million in 1975, the government statistics showed. The surplus was attributed to a drop in imports (27% in volume; 18% in value) coupled with a 6% rise in exports (6% in volume; 10% in value).

The Jan. 27 London Times quoted an executive from Rhodesia's largest steel distributor, who said there had been a 34% drop in steel tonnage shipped since April 1976, compared with 1974. Companies, uncertain over the country's futu e, were cutting back on capital expenditures; mineral mines near the borders had been closed and most new exploration had been halted, the Times reported.

Rhodesia taxes raised. David Smith, Rhodesia finance minister, Feb. 24 announced a sales-tax increase to 15% from 10% to help meet the cost of fighting the guerrilla war. Speaking in Parliament, Smith said income-tax deductions from wages would be increased 10% and yearly wage increases would be frozen at 5% until June 1978.

He said the moves would bring in an extra $19.3 million to help narrow a projected budget deficit of $107 million for the fiscal year ending June 1977 and would yield additional $128 million for the fiscal year ending June 1978. Smith blamed the deficit on a fall in foreign earnings, inflation and higher fuel and transportation costs, as well as the increased military demands.

Bias & dangers denied. Rep. Richard H. Ichord (D, Mo.) in the U.S. House of Representatives March 7, denied some charges of racial bias in Rhodesia and U.S.

State Department assertions of danger to civilians in travel there. He said:

"For example, the State Department warned us that it would be unsafe to take our wives to war-wracked Rhodesia. To our surprise we found it to be more safe in the wee hours of the morning on any street in Salisbury than it is in broad daylight only two blocks from where I stand at the present time.

"I receved the impression from the State Department briefings that Ian Smith and his supporters practiced apartheid or something worse. To my great surprise, Mr. Speaker, I met black millionaires in Salisbury and was advised by a black professor on the grounds of the University of Salisbury that enrollment in the university was about 50 percent white and 50 percent black.

"To my utter amazement, Mr. Speaker, I saw black crane operators in a Rhodesian ferrochrome mill being trained to replace white operators at the same salary.

"I learned also to my astonishment, Mr. Speaker, that the black men in Rhodesia had the highest wage throughout all Africa, even including the nation of Egypt.

"Mr. Speaker, I loathe racism in any form, whether black or white. It is not my purpose to defend the status quo in Rhodesia, as I personally feel it is indefensible, but I am constrained to state that the situation existing in Rhodesia today is far superior to what existed in many sections of this country just a few years ago. This is especially true in view of the recent steps taken by the Smith government to minimize governmental-sanctioned segregation.

"The racial problems of Rhodesia are indeed complicated when we realize that Rhodesia also has the problem generated by the merger of primitive African tribal culture and western European culture.

"I loathe racism, Mr. Speaker; but I was also reared to loathe hyprocrisy, and the issues surrounding the U.N. sanctions as the alleged means of compelling Rhodesia to alter or change its internal policy are replete with hypocrisy.

"Why do I say so? I say so, Mr. Speaker. because while I was in Rhodesia the streets of Salisbury were lined with new Toyotas, new Volkswagens, new Fiats, and new Volvos. I even saw articles of trade from Rhodesia's colonizing, but now lowly esteemed, mother country, **Great Britain.**

"The truth is, every major country in the world is trading with Rhodesia, including Russia, despite the U.N. sanctions. The United States of America is practically the only country, excluding chrome and one or two other strategic materials, which is not trading with Rhodesia.

"How hypocritical have international politics become? Yet we choose to be governed by such hypocrisy and deny ourselves the advantage of lucrative trade with Rhodesia to satisfy the whims and the piques of Great Britain and the hypocritical positions of the U.N., which equate Zionism with racism.

"Continuing, Mr. Speaker, as irrefutable proof of the hypocrisy of the United Nations, in 1976 Rhodesia produced about 250,000 tons of ferrochrome. The United States bought only 47,000 tons. Who bought the other 203,000 tons? Do not tell me, Mr. Speaker, that nonmember nations of the U.N. bought the 203,000 tons.

"In 1976, Mr. Speaker, Rhodesia produced 30 million pounds of nickel. The United States bought 5 million pounds. Are we to suppose that Rhodesia dumped the other 25 million pounds in the Indian Ocean?

"Rhodesia is the second or third largest producer in the world of platinum. It is the second largest producer of tobacco. Who buys all this tobacco. Who buys all this platinum?

"Is there any wonder that we saw the streets of Salisbury lined with Toyotas, Fiats, Volvos, and Volkswagens."

Parliament opens. The new Rhodesian Parliament was opened Sept. 20 with a short speech by President John James Wrathall. Wrathall said the Rhodesian government would continue efforts to achieve a settlement of the guerrilla war that would guarantee rights and security for all Rhodesians. He placed special emphasis on the maintenance of law and order and denounced the Western nations for "selective morality" concerning guerrilla activities.

The next day, Finance Minister David Smith presented a new Rhodesian budget. The document was essentially the same as the one presented to the previous Parliament except for a rise in defense costs of $24 million to about $250 million.

War-related events. Among other developments related to the civil war in Rhodesia:

A Rhodesian judge in Bulawayo March 22 refused to hear a case against two Botswanans who had been abducted into Rhodesia by security forces and charged with illegal arms possession. The judge called the abduction "illegal" and said the court had no jurisdiction to hear the case since the accused were Botswanan nationals.

The Rhodesian government April 6 announced it had begun an operation to move 250,000 blacks from rural villages into "protected villages," guarded areas meant to keep guerrillas from getting supplies and protection from villagers. Black leader Bishop Abel Muzorewa denounced the compounds as "concentration camps."

The number of guerrillas fighting the white government was estimated at between 16,000 and 17,000, according to a report appearing in the New York Times April 24. The government's armed forces reportedly totaled 18,000, half of them black, with 40,000 more in the police and paramilitary units.

A bomb exploded in Salisbury Aug. 13 300 yards from the office of Prime Minister Ian Smith. Extensive damage was done to a shopping area nearby but there were no injuries.

Black guerrillas Aug. 20 killed 16 African men, women and children on a white-owned farm 17 miles north of Umtali, near the Mozambique border. Rhodesian security officials said the rebels had attacked the compound where the black workers lived as part of a campaign to drive blacks away from white-owned farms.

There were clashes involving all three

bordering black African nations during September.

The most intensive fighting was reported along the Mozambique border, where Rhodesian military authorities reported Sept. 3 that two white airmen had been killed in a crash along the eastern edge of the frontier. Rhodesia and Mozambique Sept. 25 traded accusations of border attacks in the southeast, with Mozambique charging that Rhodesian troops had crossed the border near Mapai. A Rhodesian spokesman denied the charge, saying Mozambique had shelled Vila Salazar, a Rhodesian border town. Mozambique authorities said Oct. 4 that heavy fighting was in progress in Mozambique's northern Tete district.

Zambian President Kenneth Kaunda Sept. 11 had charged that three Zambian soldiers had been killed and five persons wounded, including two civilians, in a Rhodesian raid Aug. 31. He said Rhodesian planes had bombed Zambian territory in the east and had used napalm.

Citing "the war situation existing in this part of Africa," the Zambian government Sept. 3 imposed a nine-hour curfew on Lusaka and three other towns near the Rhodesian border. The curfew initially was meant to last four days but was extended Sept. 7. It was finally lifted Sept. 20.

Botswana Sept. 6 accused Rhodesia of launching an attack on a village over the weekend of Sept. 3–4. No casualties were reported.

The Rhodesian government Oct. 9 protested to Botswana over an assault on a Rhodesian family traveling through Botswana by train the day before. The government said a couple had been roughed up by men who had forced their way into their train compartment and had threatened their child. Rhodesia added that Botswanan police had refused to aid the family.

In news of fighting inside Rhodesia, military authorities Sept. 30 released fatality figures for the five-year-old guerrilla war. Totals were: guerrillas, 3,396; security forces, 418; black civilians, 1,820, and white civilians, 109. The figures for September alone included a white infant

reportedly murdered by guerrillas Sept. 30 and 12 people reported killed Sept. 16 during a gunfight between police and guerrillas who had hijacked a bus. In addition, guerrillas were reported Sept. 6 to have kidnapped 45 black workers from a ranch near the Botswana border.

Amnesty International September 21 published a report alleging torture by Rhodesian security forces of blacks in detention as suspected terrorists. The London-based human rights organization said it had received reports smuggled out of the country that security forces used electric shocks and beatings during questionings. The Rhodesian government Sept. 22 denied the charges.

The Justice and Peace Commission Sept. 29 said Prime Minister Ian Smith had approved an independent inquiry into the allegations.

Rhodesia expands black forces. The Rhodesian government had taken steps to expand its black anti-guerrilla forces. A review was held Oct. 21 of the first contingent of 360 men who had completed basic training. The men were part of a new battalion of 800 black soldiers, the third all-black battalion in the Rhodesian army. Blacks comprised about 80% of the regular Rhodesian army, which was estimated at 15,000–20,000 troops. According to military estimates, there were at least 3,500 nationalist guerrillas operating inside Rhodesian territory and an estimated 12,500 more in training in neighboring black African countries.

Rhodesian emigration continues. Figures released by the Rhodesian government Sept. 26 showed that a total of 11,685 whites had left the country between January and August, while 3,972 had arrived. During the eight-month period, Rhodesia had lost a net total of 7,713 whites, 655 more than it had lost during all of 1976. The emigration in August of 1,604 whites was the highest monthly total since May.

There had been a net loss of 7,058 whites in 1976, the first year since 1967 in which Rhodesian emigration had produced a net loss of whites.

The white emigration forced the closure of four state primary schools for whites. According to a report Oct. 5 in the Financial Times of London, the four schools used to serve 2,000 pupils but only 600 were enrolled. The Education Ministry Sept. 30 had reported that 378 African primary and 14 African secondary schools had been closed in 1976 and would not be reopened. It was believed that many African students were either kidnapped or recruited by nationalist guerrillas.

Argentina had been reported to be preparing land for an estimated 1,000 white families expected to emigrate from Rhodesia, according to the Jan. 17 London Times. The report cited the Argentine monthly economic review La Prensa Economica which said thousands of acres in the northwest, which had a climate and topography similar to Rhodesia's, were being readied for settlers.

Rhodesia bans deportation news. The Rhodesian government Oct. 7 barred newspapers from reporting the deportations of persons deemed harmful to the security of the state. Minister of Law and Order Hilary Squires said the press had published "emotional and quite unbalanced pictures" about the deportations "calculated to play on the emotions of the readers and arouse unwarranted sympathy for the deportee."

The action was believed to have been taken as a result of the outcry over the expulsion of Sister Janice McLaughlin, a Roman Catholic nun from the U.S. She had been deported Sept. 22 after having been arrested Aug. 30 on a charge of compiling documents deemed likely to demoralize the Rhodesian population. U.S. diplomats in South Africa had interceded with the Rhodesian government on her behalf.

The documents that had led to her arrest were included in a report by the Roman Catholic Commission for Peace and Justice in Rhodesia, of which McLaughlin was an executive member. The report, published Sept. 21 in London, denounced the government's program of confining the rural black population to so-called protected villages to prevent their coming into contact with guerrillas. The report said the protected villages were unsanitary and the inhabitants lacked sufficient food and water and had not been compensated for the property they had lost when the army had forced them to move. The report also charged the Rhodesian army with beating and torturing black civilians and with committing atrocities on civilians and blaming the atrocities on the guerrilla forces.

(Three other commission members arrested with Sister McLaughlin were released on bail Sept. 4. John Deary, commission chairman, Brother Arthur Dupuis, press secretary, and Father Dieter Scholz were released on $1,600 bail each. Scholz later was reimprisoned but was freed Sept. 23.)

Dollar devalued. Finance Minister David Smith Oct. 13 announced a devaluation of the Rhodesian dollar by 3% against the South African rand and by 6% against other currencies. He told Parliament that the devaluation was necessary because Rhodesia's terms of trade were the most unfavorable since 1965, when Rhodesia unilaterally declared its independence from Great Britain. Smith cited the general decline in world commodity prices and the "prolonged international recession" as factors contributing to Rhodesia's unfavorable trade position.

In a report published the same day, the Standard Bank of Rhodesia warned that "there is a clear limit to the economy's ability to withstand the pressures to which it is now being subjected. . . . The economic picture is a bleak one. Given the sluggish international economy, continued economic deterioration in Rhodesia must be anticipated unless or until there is a reasonable political settlement."

(Before the devaluation, one Rhodesian dollar was worth 1.33 South African rands and US $1.60.)

U. S. Sanctions Hearings

Byrd Amendment Under Attack

> *The "Byrd Amendment" of 1971 had authorized the U.S. importation of Rhodesian chrome despite the United Nations sanctions against trade with Rhodesia. This Byrd Amendment was opposed by every U.S. Administration since it was proposed and was finally repealed by Congress in March 1977. Hearings on the issue had been held Feb. 9–10, 1977 by the African Affairs Subcommittee of the Senate Committee on Foreign Relations. Sen. Dick Clark (D, Iowa), the subcommittee chairman, presented the main objections to the Byrd Amendment Feb. 9 in the opening statement of the hearings. Among his remarks:*

. . . The so-called Byrd Amendment . . . has allowed American companies to violate international sanctions against Rhodesia for five years in order to import chrome and ferrochrome.

Repeal of the Byrd Amendment at this time, we believe, would add significantly to international pressures for a negotiated settlement of the Rhodesian conflict. Rhodesian Prime Minister Ian Smith may still hope that in the end the United States will come to the aid of his rebel regime. Through the years this hope has been bolstered by

American violations of sanctions. Misleading arguments about the strategic and economic need for Rhodesian chrome and ferrochrome have placed America on the side of racial domination in Rhodesia, and against peaceful international pressure for change. Despite clear statements by this administration that the Rhodesian regime cannot expect support from the United States, the economic, diplomatic, and psychological support that sanctions violations have provided continues. In our judgment only congressional action to end this support once and for all will convince the Smith regime that the United States is on the side of racial equality and majority rule.

All hopes for a negotiated settlement of the escalating conflict in Rhodesia lie with the British initiative. As the colonial power, only Britain can bring about a peaceful, orderly transition to majority rule.

The United States should support the British efforts in every way possible. Economic sanctions against Rhodesia were adopted at Britain's initiative in 1966 as the international pressure necessary to achieve a settlement and avoid a seriously destabilizing conflict. Our violation of sanctions has undercut a series of British efforts to resolve the Rhodesian problems through negotiations. Our support for sanctions at this time is the most significant aid we could provide.

American violation of sanctions has left this country open to charges of hypocrisy in its policy toward southern Africa. The stated policy has always been one of support for "peaceful transition to majority rule in southern Africa," opposing both racial domination and violence. Yet America has seriously weakened efforts at peaceful international pressure for change in Rhodesia by its violation of sanctions, leaving violence the only feasible alternative for those wanting racial equality.

The United States has endangered its future relations with the government of a majority-ruled Zimbabwe by its violation of sanctions. The nationalist leaders have looked to the United States for understanding and support in their struggle for freedom and racial equality. Instead, the United States has refused to make even a minor economic sacrifice for these principles.

Bishop Abel Muzorewa, a popular nationalist leader who has no army, has called the Byrd Amendment "the worst blow we have suffered from any quarter" and has reminded us, "After independence, when we go to sell our chrome, we will remember who our friends were when we needed them."

At this time I believe there is no strategic or economic need for the Byrd Amendment.

American violation of sanctions has not reduced our reliance on the Soviet Union for chrome ore. In 1971, before American companies started violating sanctions to import chrome ore, 41% of all chrome ore imports were from the Soviet Union. In 1972, the first year of sanction violations, the percentage of imports from the Soviet Union had jumped to 58%. In 1975, 49% of American chrome ore imports came from the Soviet Union, and only 11% from Rhodesia. In 1976, last year, our imports from the U.S.S.R. were 44%, and from Rhodesia, only 5%. Sanctions violations have not made a dent on American dependence on Soviet chrome ore. Interestingly enough, by 1976, high carbon ferrochrome from Rhodesia accounted for only 15% of the U.S. consumption.

America's strategic stockpiles of chrome ore and ferrochrome are in excess of its needs. There is a four years' supply of metallurgical-grade chrome ore in the stockpiles, or more than 20 years' supply for defense needs only.

Rhodesia has become an extremely unreliable source of ferrochrome and chrome ore. The closing of the Mozambique border slowed exports from Rhodesia. They were slowed again by South Africa's reluctance to take the extra burden of Rhodesian export traffic. The two rail lines that now connect Rhodesia to the outside world through South Africa are increasingly vulnerable to guerrilla attacks and South Africa's own export priorities.

Numerous other suppliers could easily replace Rhodesian exports of chrome and ferrochrome to the United States. Turkey, South Africa, Brazil, the Philippines, Madagascar, Sudan, Pakistan, New Caledonia, and Iran are all chrome exporters. Brazil, Finland, Germany, Japan, Norway, South Africa, Sweden, and Yugoslavia all supply ferrochrome to the United States. Of course, the most important source of ferrochrome is our domestic producers. With the recession, world demand for chrome and ferrochrome is low. There is excess production capacity for ferrochrome in the United States and throughout the world. The shift from Rhodesia to other sources could be easily made at this time.

It is in the long run, I think, that the United States will need access to Rhodesia's chrome. Rhodesia has 30% of the world's known reserves and South Africa has 60%. If the United States insists on short-run support for the minority racist regime in these countries, it runs the risk of permanently alienating the black majorities who are bound to prevail in those countries eventually. Our economic and strategic interests, as well as our political and moral interests, lie with supporting racial equality and majority rule in Rhodesia and throughout southern Africa. . . .

Secretary of State Cyrus R. Vance testified Feb. 10 in support of the legislation that, in effect, repealed the Byrd Amendment. Among his remarks:

The administration fully supports this bill. We urge the Congress pass it into law as rapidly as possible. To do so would, I firmly believe, strengthen the hand of the United States and others who are working to find a peaceful solution to the Rhodesian problem. Moreover, it would return the United States to conformity with its obligations under the U.N. Charter. American industry is not dependent on Rhodesian chrome, and repeal will not harm our economy.

President Carter has on many occasions stated clearly and forcefully his commitment to human rights. That commitment, which I know you share, and which is expressed in the provisions of the U.N. Charter, will be a major factor as this administration formulates its foreign, as well as its domestic, policies. We are guided by this commitment in our approach to all the problems of southern Africa. It requires our firm and clear opposition to racial injustice wherever it exists.

The world faces an explosive situation in southern Africa. Negotiations for a Rhodesian settlement have faltered, though our efforts to nurture them continue. Violence is intensifying. The Namibian dispute is not moving toward solution; indeed it adds to the danger that violence in southern Africa will spread. And in South Africa itself a system of institutionalized racial discrimination, which this administration strongly opposes, feeds black unrest.

The Rhodesian situation is of great urgency, however, for there the extent of armed conflict is broadest and the threat of escalation most immediate. We view with deep concern the dangerous situation in Rhodesia that has arisen out of the attempt of the illegal, minority government to maintain itself in power. If the Rhodesian authorities, who represent less than 4 percent of the population, persist in this course, the inevitable outcome will be a bitter legacy for the future of all the inhabitants of that territory.

Intensified conflict in Rhodesia also entails serious adverse economic effects on countries in the region. Furthermore, the possibility of non-African forces interfering cannot be discounted.

We must continue to try to help head off a disaster in Rhodesia. We believe that change there is necessary. It is certainly inevitable. Our challenge is that it be both rapid, peaceful and orderly. This can only come through a negotiated settlement which leads quickly to a system of majority rule and respect for the rights and dignity of all, regardless of their race. In our effort to help achieve this goal we shall continue to confer with the British Government, African leaders, and the South African Government.

I have said recently that the Rhodesian authorities should understand clearly that under no circumstance can they count on any form of American assistance in their effort to prevent majority rule in Rhodesia or to enter into negotiations which exclude leaders of the nationalist movements.

I underscore that statement again today. But the key to peace lies in Mr. Ian Smith's hands, and repeal of the Byrd amendment would do far more to persuade him to use it. It is essential that the Congress and the executive branch work together in this respect to present a unified American position.

Throughout the world community, people are watching to see what the United States decides to do. African and other leaders place considerable importance on the action Congress will take with regard to repeal of the Byrd amendment—and, I might add, they want to know how deeply the administration is committed to its repeal. Let no one be in doubt about the depth of our commitment.

In his talk with Ambassador Young last weekend, President Nyerere of Tanzania laid stress on repeal of the Byrd amendment as part of an active role by the United States in tightening United Nations economic sanctions against Rhodesia. Other African leaders have recently expressed the same sentiment to us.

Passage of the Byrd amendment in 1971 put the United States in violation of its international obligations. The economic sanctions imposed by the U.N. Security Council in 1966 and 1968 were based on the Council's right to determine that a threat to the peace existed in the Rhodesian situation and to invoke enforcement measures, as it did, under chapter VII of the U.N. Charter. A legal obligation for all member states was thus created. As a permanent Member of the Security Council the United States could have vetoed the sanctions resolutions. It did not, but in fact supported and voted for the sanctions. As a matter of international law, we are committed, under article 25 of the charter, to abide by them.

With the passage of the Byrd amendment, the United States, whose record in enforcing sanctions had been as good as or better than that of any nation, became one of a handful of nations which, as a matter of official policy, violates the sanctions. We thereby put ourselves at odds with the will of the international community in the only effort ever made by the United Nations to use mandatory economic sanctions. We have acted in violation of our own often-proclaimed devotion to international law.

By repealing the Byrd amendment we would remove this symbol of ambivalence in American policy toward Rhodesia and toward international law. We would return to adherence to our obligations under the U.N. Charter.

When the Byrd amendment was passed, it was argued that, for strategic and economic reasons, the United States needed continued access to Rhodesian chrome. However, it should now be clear that access to Rhodesian chrome and other minerals is not an important element in U.S. security or overall economic policy....

Another witness Feb. 10 was Julius L. Katz, assistant Secretary of State for economic and business affairs. He said:

Enactment of the Byrd amendment in 1971 was opposed by the Nixon administration and in subsequent years the previous administration supported efforts to bring about its repeal.

It has been and remains our view that Rhodesia cannot be considered a reliable supplier. Transportation routes for export of raw materials from Rhodesia have been cut off one by one until the only remaining possibility is the South African route. Insurgent actions pose a growing threat to operation of the mines which if forced to shut down for even a temporary period could require months to get back into service due to flooding and cave-ins.

Repeal of the Byrd amendment and the consequent cutting-off of imports of Rhodesian chrome will require some degree of readjustment of the United States and is likely to have some affect on prices. However, our analysis indicates that dislocations should be relatively short-term and can be largely overcome over a period of time.

The first consequence of stopping the inflow of chrome from Rhodesia will mean materials will need to be found elsewhere. The prospects for finding other sources of material are good. While most of our chromium will continue to come from our regular major suppliers, including South Africa, the U.S.S.R. and the Philippines, there are other smaller suppliers who could help fill the gap. These include: India, Finland, Brazil, Turkey and Albania. In addition, imports of greater quantities of lower grade ores are now useable due to the increasing use of the AOD process for production of steel. Finally, private stocks of chrome materials are large.

The Bureau of Mines estimates 400,000 short tons are held in private stocks at the present time. This amount approximates 6 to 9 months consumption.

In addition, the strategic and critical material stockpile contains the equivalent of 3.82 million tons of metallurgical chromite ores in the form of ores and ferro alloys. Of this, 3.59 million tons are reserved to meet the needs of national security. A release of any portion of these strategic reserves during peacetime is permitted under existing legislation when the President determines that the release "is required for the purposes of common defense." The 0.23 million tons in excess of strategic needs could be made available to U.S. industry, if the necessary legislation were enacted by Congress....

I have stressed a number of economic reasons in support of U.S. backing of the UN economic sanctions against Rhodesia and repeal of the Byrd Amendment. The basic economic reason, however, is that such a move is a rational economic step looking forward to a time when majority African rule in Rhodesia will come about. A rapid and peaceful transition in Rhodesia is in our long-term economic interests. Our current commerce with Rhodesia is perceived as an impediment to that transition.

Finally, our economic interests do not stop in Rhodesia. The U.S. carries on a thriving and growing economic relationship with the other nations of Black Africa both in trade and investment. By failing to repeal the Byrd Amendment we jeopardize this relationship. African countries are also an important source of supply for us for a whole range of strategic goods including petroleum, uranium, manganese, copper, cobalt and diamonds as well as the whole range of tropical products like coffee and cocoa. Our disregard of the UN sanctions have indeed placed American business at a disadvantage in its relationship with African countries in such areas as resource development, investment, and export opportunities.

Index